Germany 19…

Mar…
and Philip Pedley

Series Editors
Martin Collier
Erica Lewis
Rosemary Rees

Heinemann

HEINEMANN ADVANCED HISTORY

Heinemann Educational Publishers
Halley Court, Jordan Hill, Oxford OX2 8EJ
Part of Harcourt Education Limited

Heinemann is the registered trademark of
Harcourt Education Limited

First published 2000

ISBN 0 435 32721 6

08 07 06 05 04 03
14 13 12 11 10 9 8 7 6 5

Typeset by Wyvern 21 Ltd

Printed and bound in the UK by The Bath Press Ltd

Picture research by Ginny Stroud-Lewis

Photographic acknowledgements
The authors and publisher would like to thank the following for permission to reproduce photographs: Bilderdienst Suddeutscher Verlag: 7, 136; AKG: 13, 25, 29, 35, 65, 66, 67, 68 (top and bottom), 69, 108, 111, 114, 120, 126, 130, 131, 139, 196; AKG London: 55, 112; Hulton Getty: 44, 49; Imperial War Museum: 64, 87; Keystone/Hulton Getty Picture Collection: 133.

Diagram on page 19: Alan White, *The Weimar Republic*, Collins Educational, 1997

Cover photograph: AKG London

To the memory of Elizabeth and Cuthbert Pedley

CONTENTS

A2 SECTION: ANALYSIS AND INTERPRETATION

Weimar and Nazi Germany

HOW TO USE THIS BOOK

This book is divided into distinct sections. The AS sections on Weimar Germany and Nazi Germany are similar in style. Both attempt to explain what happened in Germany in the period in question. The text of this descriptive analysis gives the student in-depth information and some analysis. The questions at the end of each chapter will challenge the student to use the information in the chapter to analyse, prioritise and explain the important aspects of the subject. In that way they will acquire a clear understanding of the key features of each topic.

The A2 part on Nazi Germany is more analytical in style. Students who are intending to use an A2 section should read the relevant chapter in the AS part of the book. For example, those studying women in Nazi Germany should read the sections on pages (51) and pages (113–120). It is hoped that the A2 part is written in such a way that it is useful for AS students who wish to extend their understanding of the subject.

At the end of each of the AS and A2 sections there are Assessment Sections. These have been based on the requirements of the new AS and A2 specifications provided by the three Awarding Bodies, Edexcel, AQA and OCR. There are exam-style source and essay questions for each specification. There then follows detailed guidance on how students might answer the questions, together with sample answers.

AS SECTION: WEIMAR GERMANY, 1919–29

Introduction

From 1914 to 1918 Germany and its main ally Austria-Hungary fought an exhausting war against Britain, France, Russia (until 1917) and the United States of America. By 1918 Germany was weary, the economy was fully stretched and food was becoming increasingly scarce. The entry of the United States into the war in 1917 meant that the Allies had a new source of manpower and materials at their disposal. The initial success of the German offensives of March and April 1918 opened up the possibility of a German victory. However, the German advance was checked by American and French forces as German supplies ran low. By September 1918 it seemed that military defeat was inevitable.

In November 1918, the German Kaiser Wilhelm II was forced to abdicate (give up his throne). Two months later the National Assembly met and set up the Weimar Republic. The new Republic (which was named after the town in which the National Assembly first met) was based on a constitution which made it different from the more authoritarian style of government in Germany before 1914. Despite its many problems the Weimar Republic survived until 1933. However, from its birth in 1919 until the start of the economic depression in 1929, the Weimar Republic was to face many challenges.

- **Opposition to the Republic.** There were many Germans who opposed the new Republic. On the left of German politics, communists, such as the Spartacists in 1919, attempted to overthrow the government in a revolution. On the other extreme, monarchists, such as Wolfgang Kapp in 1920, or extreme nationalists such as Adolf Hitler in 1923, attempted to destroy democracy in

Germany. However, the most serious threat to the Republic came from those within the German establishment. Many leaders of the army, civil service and legal system disliked the new constitution. Their actions from time to time were greatly to weaken the Republic. The most significant threat came from the President of the Republic from 1925, Field Marshal Paul von Hindenburg.

- **The Treaty of Versailles and reparations.** The fact that the Weimar Republic was born out of defeat was to weaken it considerably. The Treaty of Versailles which formally ended the war was imposed on Germany by the Allies. It made Germany responsible for the war and imposed reparations (financial payments). Although the treaty did not treat Germany as harshly as it might have done, reparations did contribute to financial problems in 1922–3. The most important impact of the treaty was that it associated the Weimar Republic with defeat and humiliation. The German politician Gustav Stresemann attempted to improve the terms of the treaty for Germany in the 1920s and restored Germany's diplomatic position. However, he did not manage to persuade the Allies to halt reparations altogether.

- **The Weimar Constitution.** The new constitution in 1919 promised social reforms and freedoms not seen before in Germany. However, it also attempted to reflect the nature of German politics by creating a strong President and a parliament (the Reichstag) elected by proportional representation. This system worked effectively as long as the politicians were prepared to support the constitution. However, the President was given powers under Article 48 which could, in times of 'national emergency', be used to undermine the democratic constitution. Also the new constitution meant that the political parties had to work together in coalition governments with a proportional representation voting system. This did not work because of the negative attitude of many of the politicians to coalition government.

The years 1919–29 in Germany should not automatically be judged as years of failure. The new political system overcame the economic and political threats in the immediate post-war years of 1919–23. Thereafter the economy grew, the new welfare state developed and Germany experienced a period of cultural freedom not seen before. However, the political system remained weak and the problem of Versailles still remained.

CHAPTER 1

Defeat, unrest and the creation of the Weimar Republic, 1918–20

DEFEAT AND UNREST

Defeat and mutiny. As allied troops approached Germany's borders in October 1918, it was clear to many of Germany's leading generals that it had lost the war. In September, General Ludendorff advised the government to seek peace terms with the Allies: France, Britain and the United States of America. A new government led by Prince Max of Baden opened negotiations with the Allies. As news of defeat spread it created unrest in the armed forces. German sailors based at the ports of Wilhelmshaven and Kiel refused orders to go to sea to fight the British. In Berlin there were calls in the **Reichstag** for the **Kaiser**, Wilhelm II, to abdicate. On 4 and 5 November 1918, the mutiny spread to other ports. Councils of workers and soldiers (soviets) were set up in Rostock, Bremen and other towns. In Munich, a revolt led by socialist Kurt Eisner resulted in the proclamation of a republic in Bavaria.

KEY TERMS

Reichstag is the German Parliament.

Kaiser was the German Emperor.

KEY THEME

Division in the socialist movement The **SPD** Socialist Democratic Party was the main socialist political party in Germany. It was moderate in its politics and had supported the war effort. Its leaders in 1918 were Friedrich Ebert and Philipp Scheidemann. In March 1919 its membership was around 1 million.

The **USPD** was an anti-war group which broke away from the SPD in 1917. It was more left wing than the SPD. Many of its members hoped for some form of revolution in Germany. By January 1919 it had 750,00 members.

The **SPD**, who were partners in the coalition led by Prince Max, threatened to withdraw their support from the government unless the Kaiser Wilhelm II abdicated (gave up his throne). On 9 November, Prince Max announced Wilhelm's abdication after persuading the Kaiser that it was the only way to prevent civil war in Germany. The Kaiser fled immediately to Holland.

The most powerful political group in Germany was now the SPD led by Friedrich Ebert and Philipp Scheidemann. Immediately after the abdication they withdrew from Prince Max's government, thereby causing it to fall, and replaced it with one of their own. These events had made it impossible for Germany to resist the armistice terms offered by the Allies. On 11 November German delegates

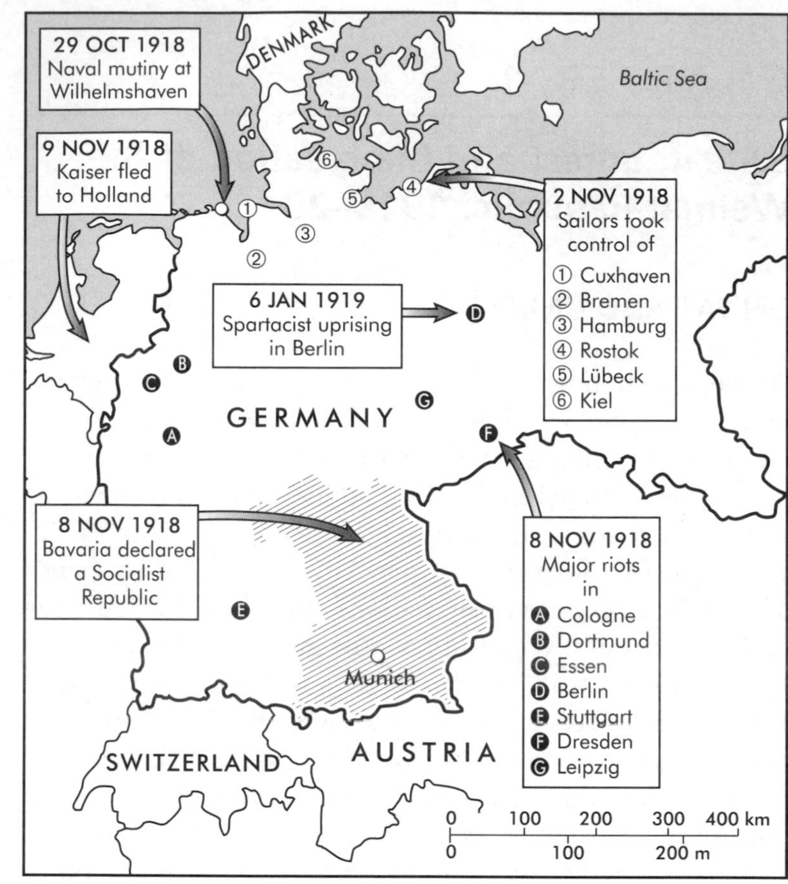

Points of unrest in 1918–9.

met with representatives of the Allies at Compiègne and signed the agreement that ended four years of war.

THE SPARTACIST REVOLUTION

The new Chancellor Ebert faced an even more pressing problem at home. On 25 November 1918 a conference of representatives from the different states (in German known as *Länder*) which make up Germany met in Berlin and agreed to set up a national assembly. However, extreme left-wing groups in Germany rejected any form of democratic parliament and pressed for a revolution. At the end of 1918 the greatest threat came from a group led by revolutionaries **Karl Liebknecht** and **Rosa Luxemburg**. Originally part of the **USPD**, they broke away from that party in December 1918 and formed the Spartacist Union.

KEY PEOPLE

Karl Liebknecht was a barrister before being elected to the Reichstag in 1912 as a member of the SPD. He opposed the war in 1914 and was expelled from the Reichstag in 1916 because of his anti-war views. Liebknecht rejected the post-war democracy as proposed by Ebert.

Rosa Luxemburg had worked with Liebknecht to set up a revolutionary wing of the SPD as early as 1905. Imprisoned between 1915 and 1918 for her anti-war views, she still managed to smuggle out letters calling for a revolutionary end to the war. Luxemburg believed that revolution needed to take place across Germany rather than simply in Berlin for it to be successful. Therefore, she opposed the Berlin uprising of early January 1919 as being too soon.

The Spartacists threaten. The Spartacists were not strong in number and did not represent the working people as a whole. In December 1918 the First Congress of Workers' and Soldiers' Councils in Berlin refused to allow

The aims of the Spartacists

- They hoped for a revolution on similar lines to that in Russia in 1917 followed by an alliance with Lenin's Soviet Russia.
- The Spartacists wanted to see the cancellation of the National Assembly and all power transferred to soldier and worker councils as happened in Soviet Russia in January 1918.
- They claimed that they would seize all large and medium farms as well as large industrial companies. The coal, iron and steel industries would be run by the state.
- The police and army would be disarmed and workers' militias created.

Supporters of Karl Liebknecht and Rosa Luxemburg. Notice the date on the banners is 14.1.19.

Liebknecht and Luxemburg to address its meeting. Of the 500 delegates to the congress only around ten were Spartacists. Without popular support the Spartacists took to the streets in demonstrations in an attempt to whip up support for their cause. Their policies and tactics frightened the SPD-led government, who looked to the army to keep order. (On 9 November, Chancellor **Ebert** had a conversation with a leading figure in the army (*Reichswehr*), General **Gröner**, who promised army support against revolution and loyalty to the new government. In return Ebert promised to support and supply the army against the militias of the left. This was to be an important alliance in the coming months.)

The Spartacist revolt. On 1 January 1919, members of the Spartacist Union held their first congress in Berlin. With the support of other extreme left-wing groups they formed the German Communist Party (KPD). This was followed by a revolt in Berlin that began on 5 January. Newspaper offices were taken over and a revolutionary committee formed. However, the uprising was poorly organised and crushed by the government using the ***Freikorps*** troops led by General Walther von Lüttwitz. On 15 January 1919, members of the Horse Guards Division of the army murdered Karl Liebknecht and Rosa Luxemburg.

The consequences of government reaction. The use of the *Freikorps* in crushing the Spactacists was to have important consequences for the Republic. A significant threat to the Weimar Republic was the opposition to it of many within the Wilhelmine establishment – the pre-1918 military, judiciary and civil service. In 1918 their influence in the new Republic was by no means guaranteed. They resumed that influence as a result of the actions of Ebert and his colleagues in late 1918. Ebert turned to the establishment as the means by which forces of moderate socialism could defeat a more radical left of the USPD and then the KPD and Spartacists. By the Ebert-Gröner agreement of November 1918, Ebert, as one of the leaders of the Weimar Republic, came to an agreement with General Gröner about the need to protect Germany from communism. General Gröner was an important figure in the army having taken over from Ludendorff as senior

KEY TERM

'Freikorps' The *Freikorps* were anti-communist volunteer groups formed by demobilised servicemen. They attracted to their ranks the recently demobilised, the unemployed and those made bitter by Germany's defeat. Industrialists who feared the rise of communism often financed the *Freikorps*.

KEY THEME

Ebert and the army
Increasingly Ebert used the *Reichswehr* against his enemies on the left. This was a mistake as many of the army's officers and soldiers were anti-democratic and against the Republic.

The army refused to be reformed by the state because of its supposedly strong 'non-political' nature. The leader of the army from 1920 to 1926, **General Hans von Seeckt**, developed the idea of the army working as a 'state within a state' i.e. the interests of the army were more important than those of the state.

The army was unreliable as a law enforcer. It did little to stop the work of murder squads and the political violence which resulted in the murder of KPD leaders Liebknecht and Luxemburg in 1919, or of Weimar politicians Rathenau, Erzberger and over 200 others.

quartermaster general in the army. By the agreement, Ebert promised that the government would ensure that the army would receive proper supplies, and that the government would not support the revolutionary armies that were appearing all over Germany. For his part, Gröner promised that the army would support the new Republic. This agreement represented a huge political mistake by Ebert and his SPD colleagues in believing that the threat to the Republic came primarily from the left. Because of this misjudgement, they used anti-democratic forces such as the *Freikorps* to restore 'order', both in January 1919 in Berlin and in the spring of 1919 when they were used extensively to end strikes and to shut down the so-called 'Republics of Councils' created in cities such as Munich. This helped to make worse the political violence that was to threaten the Republic itself. Throughout the period, one of the gravest problems for the state was that the means it used to end violence were often the organisations that started the violence.

THE FIRST NATIONAL ASSEMBLY, 1919

The election to the National Assembly took place on 19 January 1919.

The new National Assembly and continuing unrest. On 6 February the new National Assembly met at the town of Weimar, well away from the revolutionary atmosphere of Berlin. It chose Friedrich Ebert to be the new President of the German Republic. As a result of the election no party had a clear majority. The main pro-Republic parties, the SPD, Centre and DDP, formed the first 'Weimar coalition'. Philipp Scheidemann of the SPD led the first

The results of the election to the first National Assembly, 1919.

Party	Percentage of vote	Number of seats
SPD	38	165
Centre	19.7	91
DDP	18.5	75
DNVP	10.3	44
USPD	7.6	22
DVP	4.4	19

Party name	Leaders	Political standpoint
DDP	Walther Rathenau	Pro-Weimar, left-wing liberal
DNVP	Karl Helfferich Alfred Hugenberg	Conservative, monarchist, anti-Weimar, racist
DVP	Gustav Stresemann	Became pro-Weimar under Stresemann, right-wing liberal
KPD	Ernst Thälmann	Communist party, founded 1919, anti-Weimar
NSDAP	Adolf Hitler	Extreme right-wing, racist, anti-Weimar
SPD	Friedrich Ebert, Philipp Scheidemann, Hermann Müller	Largest socialist party, pro-Weimar
Centre Party	Matthias Erzberger, Heinrich Brüning	Catholic, pro-Weimar party. BVP split from main party in 1920

The parties and their political standpoints.

Chancellor	Date	Partners
Friedrich Ebert (SPD)	November 1918 – February 1919	Coalition of socialists
Philipp Scheidemann (SPD)	February 1919 – June 1919	SPD, Centre, DDP
Gustav Bauer (SPD)	June 1919 – March 1920	SPD, Centre, DDP (from October)
Hermann Müller (SPD)	March 1920 – June 1920	SPD, Centre, DDP
Konstantin Fehrenbach (Centre)	June 1920 – May 1921	DDP, Centre, DVP
Joseph Wirth (Centre)	May 1921 – October 1921	SPD, DDP, Centre
Joseph Wirth (Centre)	October 1921 – November 1922	SPD, DDP, Centre
Wilhelm Cuno (non-aligned)	November 1922 – August 1923	DDP, Centre, DVP

Chancellors/coalition partners of the Weimar Republic, 1919–23.

government which immediately faced significant challenges. Although the Spartacists had been defeated, there were many uprisings in the first months of 1919.

In February and March forces directed by Defence Minister Gustav Noske crushed uprisings in Berlin and Munich. A more serious challenge to the state came from the establishment of a soviet republic in Bavaria in April 1919. The army and the *Freikorps* also crushed this rebellion. The threat from the left in 1919 was real. Discontent in the army and unrest on the left threatened the new Republic. However it survived because few in the army were prepared to support open revolt against a government which stood against the communists.

SUMMARY QUESTIONS

1 What were the main threats to the Weimar Republic in 1919?

2 Explain the events of the Spartacist Revolution.

CHAPTER 2

The Treaty of Versailles

BACKGROUND TO THE TREATY

One of the most important issues facing the new state was the peace treaty drawn up by the victorious powers at Versailles. The leaders of the victorious powers had different ideas about the shape of the treaty.

- The priority of **President Wilson** of the United States was the creation of the League of Nations. To Wilson the League would be the means by which peace could be maintained by compromise. Wilson was concerned with the idea of national self-determination as a means of building a more peaceful Europe. His manifesto for a lasting peace was set out in his Fourteen Points.
- The French led by **Georges Clemenceau** were guided by security considerations. Their aim was to limit the power of Germany by proposing the confiscation of territory and restriction on German military strength. The French also encouraged the strengthening of Poland at the expense of Germany. At the back of the minds of the leading politicians at Versailles was the unpredictable nature of the new Bolshevik state in Russia. A strong Poland could therefore act as an important barrier against Soviet expansion.
- The British Prime Minister, **David Lloyd George**, was concerned that French power in Europe would be overly strengthened at the expense of Germany. As a result, Lloyd George and Wilson argued against the French being given the Saar, rich in coal, or the Rhineland, which was instead to be demilitarised (all military forces and organisation removed). However, Lloyd George came under significant political pressure from home to support the French idea of imposing damaging reparations on Germany. To establish Germany's liability for reparations, Article 231 was included making Germany responsible for the outbreak of war.

The German delegation at Versailles.

THE VERSAILLES SETTLEMENT

The German delegation that went to Versailles was not permitted to take part in the negotiations. In May 1919 the terms of the treaty were presented to a horrified German delegation. There was considerable resentment at the 'war guilt' clause and the fact that the treaty was harsher than Wilson's Fourteen Points had originally suggested. The Foreign Minister Ulrich von Brockdorff-Rantzau suggested open refusal of the treaty. Rather than accept the treaty, Scheidemann's cabinet resigned, to be replaced by one led by Gustav Bauer of the SPD. The new government included as Vice-Chancellor Matthias

Erzberger of the Centre Party, who supported conditional acceptance of Versailles. This was partly because Germany did not have the military force to prevent an allied attack. On 28 June the Foreign Minister Hermann Müller and Minister of Communications Johannes Bell signed the Treaty of Versailles. Its terms were as follows.

Territorial provision

- Germany lost territory of economic importance (up to 20 per cent of coal production and 15 per cent of agricultural resources), as well as territory of symbolic importance, such as West Prussia. Some areas were to be lost without a plebiscite (a vote). These were Alsace-Lorraine (to France), Memel (to Lithuania), Eupen and Malmedy (to Belgium), Danzig (to be a free port under League of Nations control) and West Prussia and Posen (to Poland). It was the loss of land to Poland that perhaps caused the greatest upset in Germany as most people in West Prussia and Posen were German speakers. This therefore contradicted Wilson's policy of self-determination.
- After plebiscites, all of North Schleswig (in 1920) was lost to Denmark and parts of Upper Silesia (in 1922) were lost to Poland.
- The Rhineland was to become a demilitarised zone to act as a buffer between France and Germany. It was to be occupied by the Allies for fifteen years.
- The Saar was placed under League of Nations control and its rich coalfields were to be controlled by France.
- The Kiel Canal was opened to warships and merchant ships from all nations.
- *Anschluss* or union with Austria was forbidden by Article 80 of the Treaty.

Military terms

- Germany's military capability was destroyed – the army being limited to 100,000 men and the navy to six battleships, six cruisers and twelve destroyers, but no submarines.
- Germany was to have no military aircraft.

Colonial losses

- All German colonies were to be handed over to the Allies and then organised by the League of Nations as mandates (other powers were allowed to administer them). Most noticeably, German East Africa became a British mandate and German South-West Africa became a South African mandate.

War guilt and reparations

- One of the most unpopular aspects of the treaty in Germany was Article 231 in which Germany was made fully responsible for the outbreak of the war. The thought behind this article was to establish the principle of German liability that could lead to reparations (compensation) being paid to the Allies. However, such a judgement became quickly widened into a moral question of the extent of Germany's supposed 'war guilt'.
- Reparations were not set until 1921. However, in the meantime Germany was to hand over all merchant ships of more than 1,600 tons, half of those between 800 and 1,600 tons, and a quarter of its fishing fleet. It was to build 200,000 tons of shipping a year for the Allies for the next five years.
- Germany was to bear the cost of the army of occupation. It was forced to agree to the sale of German property in Allied countries.

The politicians of the Republic who were faced with the 'war guilt' clause attempted to have it dropped from the final treaty. The Allies, however, were in no mood to compromise, and on 28 June 1919 the treaty was signed without change.

RESULTS OF THE TREATY OF VERSAILLES

- **Germany still strong diplomatically**. Versailles left Germany humiliated and scarred but it was also left potentially strong. There was disillusion in Germany that it had been excluded from the League of Nations – but the treaty left Germany as a united nation state with the potential to regain its status as an important

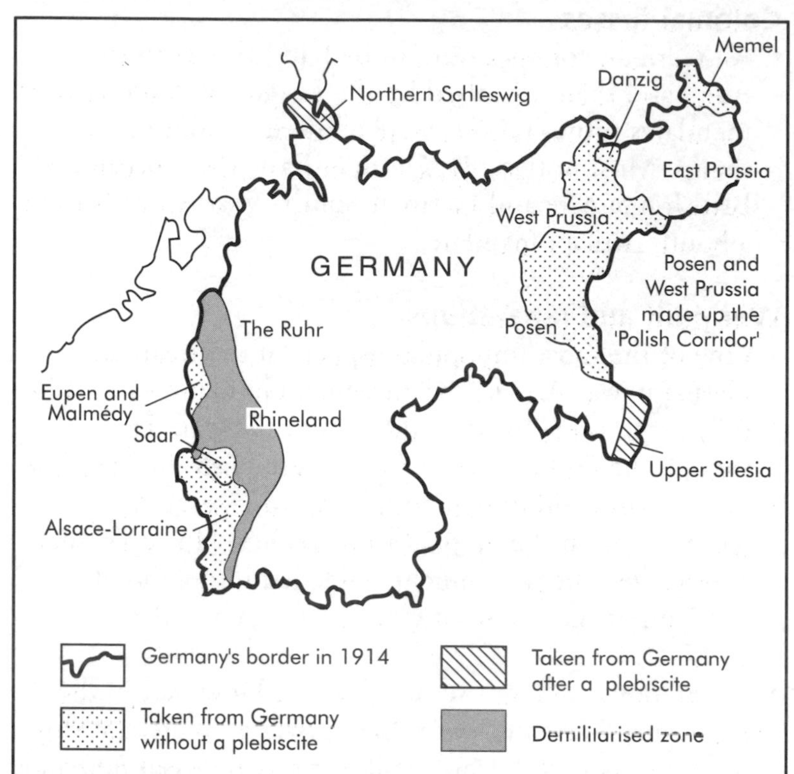

Germany's losses under the Treaty of Versailles.

diplomatic power, even in the short term. This was proved by the **Treaty of Rapallo** in 1922 between Germany and the Soviet Union. Equally important was the fact that Versailles left Germany as the power most likely to dominate Eastern Europe. These are important points because they place German opposition to the Treaty into context. Germany was not weakened as much as many people who opposed the Treaty suggested.

- **Psychological damage**. The extent of the damage the treaty inflicted on Germany as a great power was not as great as the psychological damage it inflicted on the national consciousness. In the short term, Germany was humiliated. The politicians of the Republic had no choice but to sign the treaty and there was little public support for further conflict. The alternative to signing would have been further allied military action.
- **Hindenburg and the myth of the 'stab in the back'**. As part of the discussions on the treaty in Germany the leading generals, including Hindenburg, advised that the German army was in no state to resist the Allies

KEY TERM

Treaty of Rapallo, 1922
By the Treaty of Rapallo, Germany and the Soviet Union cancelled any reparations between the two countries.

militarily. In November 1919, Hindenburg gave evidence to the Investigation Committee of the National Assembly (a committee of the German Parliament studying Versailles). His testimony backed up the suggestions of the right-wing parties and press that Versailles was a humiliating and shameful peace (*Schmachfrieden*) which should not have been signed. According to Hindenburg and his political allies, the treaty was signed because of the anti-patriotic sentiments of the group of left-wing politicians, the so-called 'November criminals', who had founded the Republic – Friedrich Ebert, Hermann Müller and Matthias Erzberger. They were also blamed for the 'stab in the back' of the armed forces that led to military collapse in 1918. Such theories were extremely useful to the anti-republican right. They absolved the military from responsibility for their own failings in 1918 and they played on popular resentment of the treaty. This resulted in increased support for anti-Versailles parties, such as the nationalist DNVP whose percentage of the vote increased from 10.3 in January 1919 to 14.9 in June 1920.

KEY TERM

'Stab in the back'. Unrest in Germany in 1918 was the result of military failure. However the 'stab in the back' theory turned that reality on its head. In right-wing circles it became an extremely popular, if entirely inaccurate explanation for Germany's defeat. The theme had been promoted by leading army officers including General Ludendorff, who was to become the symbolic leader of the nationalist right. To ex-soldiers such as Adolf Hitler, the 'stab in the back' became a central part of their political philosophy.

Such accusations as the 'stab in the back' became widely accepted. This was because they were simple and they gave many Germans an acceptable framework by which they could explain defeat. They acted to reduce support for the Republic and the parties who were involved in its creation. Such accusations of treachery gave the anti-Republican right a misplaced belief in the morality of their illegal actions. It was these myths, which were developed as a result of the Treaty of Versailles, which were to cause one of the greatest threats to the Republic's legitimacy.

SUMMARY QUESTIONS

1 What aspects of the Treaty of Versailles undermined the Weimar Republic?

2 Describe the reasons for opposition to the Treaty of Versailles in Germany.

CHAPTER 3

The Weimar constitution

MAIN FEATURES OF THE CONSTITUTION

Legal expert, scholar and liberal, Hugo Preuss, wrote the first draft of the constitution. He attempted to build on the traditions of German politics as well as balance power between the different institutions of the state. After much debate, the constitution was adopted on 31 July 1919.

- The new constitution created the Reich (state) as a **parliamentary democracy** with the Chancellor and cabinet needing majority support in the Reichstag.
- The **Reich** was to be a federation of eighteen states (*Länder*).
- The constitution provided for a strong executive in the form of a **President** elected on a seven-year cycle and with strong counterbalancing powers against the legislature (the Reichstag). The President could dissolve the Reichstag and could block new laws by calling a referendum. Most importantly, by Article 48 the President could suspend the Reichstag and rule by decree in the case of 'national emergency'.
- The **Reich Chancellor** led the German government, accountable to the Reichstag.
- The new Parliament was to be made up of two houses: The **Reichsrat** which had the power to delay laws. Its members were chosen by the parliaments of the *Länder*. The **Reichstag** for which elections were to be held every four years. The constitution introduced **proportional representational** voting for the Reichstag that had a strong influence on the nature of politics in the years ahead. All men and women over the age of 20 could vote.
- The **Bill of Rights** guaranteed individual rights such as freedom of speech and the right to belong to a union.

KEY TERM

Proportional representation is when seats are given in proportion to the votes cast, i.e., if a party wins 50 per cent of the votes cast, it receives 50 per cent of the seats.

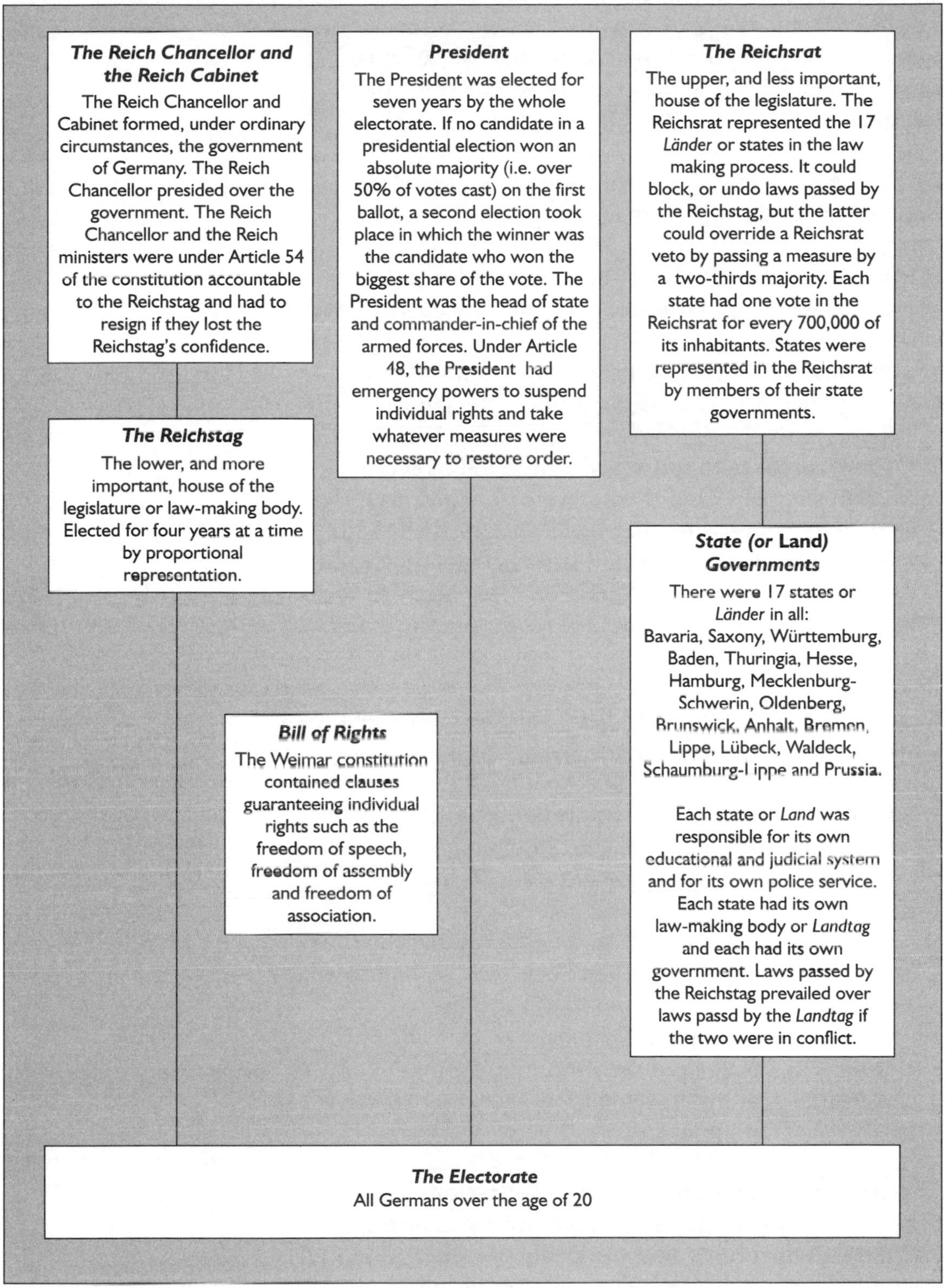

The Reich Chancellor and the Reich Cabinet
The Reich Chancellor and Cabinet formed, under ordinary circumstances, the government of Germany. The Reich Chancellor presided over the government. The Reich Chancellor and the Reich ministers were under Article 54 of the constitution accountable to the Reichstag and had to resign if they lost the Reichstag's confidence.

President
The President was elected for seven years by the whole electorate. If no candidate in a presidential election won an absolute majority (i.e. over 50% of votes cast) on the first ballot, a second election took place in which the winner was the candidate who won the biggest share of the vote. The President was the head of state and commander-in-chief of the armed forces. Under Article 48, the President had emergency powers to suspend individual rights and take whatever measures were necessary to restore order.

The Reichsrat
The upper, and less important, house of the legislature. The Reichsrat represented the 17 *Länder* or states in the law making process. It could block, or undo laws passed by the Reichstag, but the latter could override a Reichsrat veto by passing a measure by a two-thirds majority. Each state had one vote in the Reichsrat for every 700,000 of its inhabitants. States were represented in the Reichsrat by members of their state governments.

The Reichstag
The lower, and more important, house of the legislature or law-making body. Elected for four years at a time by proportional representation.

State (or Land) Governments
There were 17 states or *Länder* in all:
Bavaria, Saxony, Württemburg, Baden, Thuringia, Hesse, Hamburg, Mecklenburg-Schwerin, Oldenberg, Brunswick, Anhalt, Bremen, Lippe, Lübeck, Waldeck, Schaumburg-Lippe and Prussia.

Each state or *Land* was responsible for its own educational and judicial system and for its own police service. Each state had its own law-making body or *Landtag* and each had its own government. Laws passed by the Reichstag prevailed over laws passd by the *Landtag* if the two were in conflict.

Bill of Rights
The Weimar constitution contained clauses guaranteeing individual rights such as the freedom of speech, freedom of assembly and freedom of association.

The Electorate
All Germans over the age of 20

The Weimar constitution.

Did the constitution weaken the Republic?

For historians looking for structural reasons as to why the Republic collapsed, it is easy to argue that the Weimar constitution of 1919 was a source of weakness for the Republic.

For. The argument that the constitution weakened the Republic takes the following line:

- Many of its main features were not accepted, e.g., proportional representation, parliamentary government or civil liberties.
- The constitution was the product of a compromise between the most successful parties in the January 1919 election to the National Assembly, i.e., the Social Democrats (SPD), Centre Party and DDP. Yet at no election after 1919 did these three parties poll even close to the number of votes they had achieved in 1919 (in 1919 they polled 23.1 million votes between them, the next highest was 14.3 million in 1928). Therefore, it can be argued that the constitution's base was narrow and unrepresentative.

Against. On the other hand, there is a strong argument to make that the Weimar constitution was not so disastrous:

- The Weimar constitution, compromise as it was, reflected a broad spectrum of political opinion. It even included those on the nationalist right such as the DNVP.
- It reflected successful constitutional practice at the time and had built into it checks and balances which, if used carefully, might have led to political stability.
- The most convincing point to make on this side of the argument is that the problem with the Weimar constitution was not its design, but its misuse by the new Republic's opponents.

The impact of proportional representation

One of the most controversial aspects of the constitution was the introduction of proportional representation in the elections for the Reichstag. This led to **coalition governments** that rose and fell with spectacular frequency.

KEY TERM

Coalition governments are formed when no single party has an overall majority of seats in parliament. As a result the parties have to negotiate with others to gain an overall majority, and then share the government.

KEY TERM

Minority government. One that does not have a majority in parliament but attempts to rule alone without forming a coalition.

In the period up until 1923, a series of **minority governments** failed to establish themselves, the longest in office in the period in question being that led by Joseph Wirth which lasted eighteen months. In a period of such political instability, it has been assumed that a majority system of voting might have been more effective in combating attacks from left and right, and would have been more effective in guaranteeing Weimar's stability and survival. However, such a view ignores the complexity and subtlety of the German political and party system of the time. Proportional representation was introduced because it represented continuity in party politics from before 1914.

Parties as interest groups. The main political groupings, e.g. socialists or conservatives, were represented in the same proportions in the Reichstag in 1919 as they had been in 1912. Parties in pre-1914 Germany were more representative of sectional interests which were often linked to class but not necessarily so, for example, the Centre Party gaining much of the Catholic vote. Proportional representation allowed these interests to continue to be represented – an important factor for stability in such uncertain times. It was not until the late 1920s when these sectional interests broke up that voting patterns altered. The failure of the coalition governments, as discussed later in the chapter, was not that the voting system forced them into being but that the leading political parties chose not to operate the system effectively. This was particularly so in the case of the SPD, whose leaders found it difficult to break the habit of opposition and accept the compromise offered by Weimar.

The interest groups the parties represented.

Party	Group/class represented
DNVP	Anti-Republic nationalists, business people, landowners and upper middle class
DVP	Anti-Republic nationalists, upper and middle class
Centre	Catholic
DDP	Pro-Republic business people, intellectuals and middle class
SPD	Working class and lower middle class
USPD	Radical working class and intellectuals
KPD	Revolutionary working class

The introduction of proportional representation was accepted by most across the political spectrum. It was an ideal to which the SPD was committed. For many of their political opponents, it was the means by which the socialists could be prevented from having total control over the government.

The presidential powers, Article 48 and the constitution

Much is made of the powers given in the constitution to the *Reichspresident*. In particular, the use of Article 48 by President Hindenburg from 1930 onwards has focused attention on the excessive powers granted by the constitution. However, in the period 1919–23 the checks and balances written into the constitution acted to strengthen the political system. The aim behind the authors of the constitution was clear. By insisting that the President was elected directly by the people for a period in office of seven years, with the power to disband the Reichstag and dismiss the government, they created a counterbalance to any potential 'elected parliamentary dictatorship'.

The positive side to Article 48. There had been no tradition in Germany before 1914 of parliamentary sovereignty – that the Reichstag was the most powerful institution in government. The creation of strong executive powers was a further attempt at creating political continuity. Ebert used Article 48 as an instrument for the preservation of the Republic, the best example occurring in November 1923 when he used it to give power to the army to put down the Munich Putsch (see pages 70–71). Although the constitution allowed Hindenburg and others legally to undermine Weimar democracy later in the decade, it also allowed government sufficient flexibility to overcome the main problems facing the Republic between 1919 and 1923.

A delicate system of checks and balances. By building in checks and balances, and a long list of civil rights, the constitution authors were attempting to prevent any one group or region dominating the Republic. The relationship between the central government and that of the regions (the *Länder*) was complex. In recognising an element of regional authority, e.g., over police, and regional influence, such as the representation of the *Länder* in the national second chamber (the Reichsrat), the constitution again reflected pre-1914 practice. For the political system to succeed, it was essential that it was recognised as legitimate by the majority of the population. That this was the case is unquestionable, the 1924 election showing a large majority for the parties that supported the Republic.

SUMMARY QUESTIONS

1 In your notes draw a chart with two columns similar to this:

Positive points of the constitution	Negative points of the constitution

Try to list at least three points in each column.

2 Do you agree with the view that 'the Weimar Constitution was flawed from the start'?

CHAPTER 4

Unrest and financial collapse, 1920–3

UNREST, REPARATIONS AND INSTABILITY, 1920–2

The Kapp Putsch, 1920

There were many on the political right in Germany who wished to see the new Republic overthrown by force. The issue of the supposed 'stab in the back' simply strengthened their resolve. Amongst those most violently opposed to the Weimar Republic were **General Ludendorff** and **Wolfgang Kapp**, who formed the National Association in October 1919 to raise support for their cause. Kapp in particular wished to see the restoration of a monarchy. General von Lüttwitz, who was a leading organiser of the *Freikorps*, joined them in their conspiracy.

As the terms of the Treaty of Versailles demanded a reduction in the numbers in the army to 100,000, so the state started to disband various units. It was against this background that the conspirators were able to find support for an uprising. In March 1920, the government ordered the disbanding of the Ehrhardt Marine Brigade who were stationed in Berlin. The leader of the brigade was Hermann Ehrhardt, who was a leader in the *Freikorps*. Lüttwitz rejected the disbandment and, on 13 March, used 5,000 troops from the brigade to seize government buildings in Berlin. Only the Commander-in-Chief of the army, General Reinhardt, was prepared to use force against the uprising, but all other commanders were unwilling to release troops. The government fled to Stuttgart. However, the putsch collapsed because the trade unions called a general strike and the cautious civil service refused to accept Kapp's orders. The unions' strike was so effective because it included workers from the key industries of electricity, water and gas.

The aftermath of the Kapp Putsch. However, the government did not move against its opponents in the

KEY PEOPLE

General Ludendorff was an important figure from the First World War. In particular he was famous for successes against the Russians on the Eastern Front in 1914. He was the architect of the Brest-Litovsk Treaty with Russia in 1917. After the war he attacked the new Republic bitterly.

Wolfgang Kapp (1858–1922) was by profession a journalist. He formed a right-wing party, the *Vaterlandspartei* (Fatherland Party), during the war. After 1918, Kapp was a member of the Reichstag.

The Kapp Putsch, 1920.

army. This was because of the Ebert-Gröner Agreement made in 1918 and its reliance on the establishment. Indeed, the new head of the Army Command was **Hans von Seeckt**, despite his refusal to allow his troops to be used to put down the uprising. The main reason why the government didn't act was because the Kapp Putsch had set off a wave of strikes and communist inspired uprisings across the country. On 19 March a huge Spartacist revolt took place in the mining region of the Ruhr. A new cabinet was formed by Hermann Müller in late March 1920 and they used Seeckt's army to put down the Ruhr uprising in April. In Bavaria, the Kapp Putsch worked. The SPD government of Bavaria was forced to resign, to be replaced by one of the right. The significance of the Kapp Putsch is that it worsened the division between the right-wing groups and the Republic.

Elections of 1920. Elections for the Reichstag were held in the aftermath of the Kapp Putsch. The main 'Weimar Coalition' parties of the SPD, Centre and DDP suffered heavy losses. Before, the coalition commanded 78 per cent of the seats in the National Assembly. Now it dominated only 45 per cent of the Reichstag.

The result of the failure of the mainstream parties to gain a majority was that the parties who supported the Republic were weakened. Government was also weakened as it became dominated by a series of coalitions opposed by parties such as the DNVP, USPD and KPD. The new coalition government led by Konstantin Fehrenbach (Centre) was given support from the DVP but excluded the socialists. Virtually straightaway it faced the problem of reparations.

KEY PERSON

Hans von Seeckt was put in charge of the army three months after the Kapp Putsch. His allegiance to the new Republic was put to the test during the Munich Putsch in 1923. When asked by President Ebert: 'Whom does the Army obey – the government or the mutineers?', Seeckt replied 'Herr Reich President, the army obeys me'.

In 1926 Seeckt was dismissed from his post for allowing duelling betweeen officers.

Party	Percentage of vote	Number of seats
SPD	22	102
Centre	13.6	64
DDP	8.3	39
DNVP	15.1	71
USPD	19.7	84
DVP	13.9	65

The results of the election in 1920.

Reparations and Versailles

The pressure continued on the new Republic to keep to the terms of the Versailles Treaty. The treaty had been based on Article 231, by which Germany was made responsible for the war and therefore liable to pay reparations to the Allies. On 1 May 1921 the victorious powers finally set reparations at 20,000 billion gold marks. This agreement was known as the **London Payments Plan** and instructed a payment of 2,000 million gold marks a year plus 26 per cent of the value of Germany's exports.

This plan was accepted by the Weimar government as they feared further occupations. There had been allied occupations of Duisburg, Dusseldorf and Ruhrort in March 1921 in response to a German rejection of earlier terms. On 4 May the Fehrenbach government resigned rather than accept these demands, to be replaced by a government led by Joseph Wirth who was also from the Centre Party. The Allies had little sympathy with German claims of economic problems, and by the London Ultimatum of 5 May they threatened to invade the Ruhr (see page 16) unless the Germans agreed to their demands. For many in France who were still upset that they had not been given this region under the Treaty of Versailles, there was also little sympathy with Germany's problems. On 11 May, but against bitter opposition from nationalists, Wirth agreed to accept the demands for reparations under the policy of **fulfilment**.

KEY TERM

Fulfilment By seeking to fulfil the treaty obligations on the payment of reparations, which would have crippled the German economy, Chancellor Wirth and Minister of Reconstruction Walther Rathenau (Foreign Minister from January 1922) sought to demonstrate that the terms were impossible. They hoped this would lead to some kind of revision of the allied demands.

Genoa and Rapallo

Germany's diplomatic weakness at this stage is still clear. At the Genoa Conference in April 1922, 28 states met to discuss the world's general economic problems and the situation of the Soviet Union in particular. The German delegation, led by Foreign Minister Walther Rathenau, was undecided over whether to attempt to build a better understanding with the Allies or with the Soviets. Their decision was made for them by French leader Poincaré's insistence that Germany pay its reparations in full. The German delegation opened negotiations with the Soviets and the signing of the **Treaty of Rapallo** a few months later in April 1922 marked a break from international isolation. By the treaty the two countries agreed to drop claims for war compensation and set up full diplomatic and favoured trading status.

Continuing political violence and instability, 1921–2

Although the policy of fulfilment was undertaken to give Germany time in dealing with the Allies, and France in particular, it was followed against the backdrop of continuing political violence in Germany. In March 1921 the army and police crushed KPD uprisings in Hamburg and central Germany. Although the *Freikorps* had been disbanded, right-wing groups sustained a programme of political violence. In June 1921 the USPD leader Karl Gareis was shot, as was Matthias Erzberger two months later. In June 1922 right-wing extremists shot the Foreign Minister, **Walther Rathenau**. The outrage amongst supporters of the Republic at such acts of terrorism led to the passing of the Law for the Protection of the Republic. This imposed severe penalties on acts of political violence. The act was intended to end such violence but was to prove weak because many judges who opposed the Republic refused to implement it in practice. Although political violence was not confined to the actions of the right, 354 out of the 376 political murders were attributed to them rather than their political opponents.

KEY EVENT

The murder of Walther Rathenau provoked widespread condemnation. In Berlin over 700,000 demonstrated in frustration at his murder. Rathenau had been Minister for Reconstruction before taking on the post of Foreign Minister. His policy of fulfilment had won widespread support.

FINANCIAL COLLAPSE AND THE RUHR CRISIS, 1922–3

Growing financial crisis

By the middle of 1922 the main problem for the German state was that its currency was unstable because of the effects of the war. In 1919 the national debt was 144,000 million marks. There is an argument to suggest that this was because of government policy and rearmament before the war. However, if this was the case, then the problems increased during the war. Reparations simply made matters worse. In July 1922 the government asked for permission to suspend reparation payments but the Allies refused. Germany also declared that it would be unable to make reparation payments in 1923 and 1924. By December 1922 the national debt had reached 469,000 million marks. A new centre–right government led by Wilhelm Cuno had taken office in November 1922 but it was faced with a disastrous financial situation. There is a suggestion, that was made by the Allies at the time, that Germany deliberately engineered the crisis in order to end reparations. At the end of the year, the Reparations Commission declared that Germany had failed to deliver promised coal and timber to the Allies.

The response of the French was to occupy the Ruhr with Belgian support. On 11 January 1923 French engineers were sent into the Ruhr to secure production of coal. They were backed up by 60,000 French and Belgian soldiers. The whole of Germany was outraged by the occupation. Cuno's government encouraged the workers and population of the Ruhr to offer **passive resistance.** Cuno ordered the immediate suspension of reparations payments. The French and Belgian authorities responded by arresting mine owners and by taking over the mines and railways.

KEY TERMS

Passive resistance was the refusal to work or collaborate with the French and Belgian forces of occupation

Hyperinflation happens when the amount of money in an economy increases, pulling prices up, and the spiral of printing money and price rises goes out of control.

The policy of passive resistance worked in that the amount of coal delivered to France and Belgium was considerably reduced. However, the cost to Germany was great.

- The government had to pay out millions of marks to those who had lost revenue as a result of passive resistance.
- The denial of vital revenue from this area and all the other financial pressures resulted in the government issuing more banknotes.
- By August 1923 there were 663 billion marks in circulation leading to **hyperinflation**.
- In December 1922 the exchange rate stood at 8,000 marks to the dollar; by November 1923 it had reached 4.2 billion.

Bread prices in Germany (in marks)
1918
0.63
January 1923
250
September 1923
1,500,000,000
November 1923
201,000,000,000

As the currency collapsed so did the policy of passive resistance. The currency collapse had a hugely damaging effect on many groups of society, making savings, pensions,

Selling worthless paper currency in Germany in 1923.

government loans, mortgages and many salaries worthless. The middle and working classes suffered terribly. By the end of 1923 only 29.3 per cent of trade union members worked full time. The currency had collapsed and with it all confidence in the financial system.

Stabilisation of the currency. In August 1923, a new government led by Gustav Stresemann was formed. It began to take measures to stabilise the situation.

- In September 1923 payments of reparations were resumed and the French agreed to set up a commission to study the problem of the German economy.
- In November 1923 the *Rentenmark* was established by the Finance Minister Hans Luther to replace the old mark. Mortgage bonds on industrial and agricultural assets covered this new currency and the printing of it was strictly limited.
- Luther took further measures to balance the budget including the sacking of 700,000 state employees.
- In November a *Rentenbank* (shortly to become the Reichsbank) was opened and **Hjalmar Schacht** was appointed special currency commissioner. It was Schacht's task to replace the worthless currency with the *Rentenmark* (which became the Reichsmark in 1924).

Continuing unrest, 1923

There was still unrest on the fringes of politics. In October 1923 a KPD planned uprising, the 'German October', in Saxony and Thuringia was crushed before it started. In Hamburg the planned uprising took place but was easily defeated. The use of the army to crush the uprising offended the socialist SPD to the extent that it left the government. The following month an attempted **NSDAP** putsch in Munich led by a certain Adolf Hitler was contained by the police (see pages 70–71).

KEY PERSON

Hjalmar Schacht was one of the most significant figures in the world of German finance during the Weimar and Nazi years. During the First World War Schacht worked in the economic section of the German occupation in Belgium. In 1916 he became director of the National Bank of Germany. Despite his conservatism and his support for the return of a monarchy, Schacht helped found the pro-Weimar DDP in 1918. As special currency commissioner in the Finance Ministry in 1923, he played a vital role in the creation of the *Rentenmark*. As a result he was made President of the Reichsbank in late 1923.

KEY TERM

NSDAP *Nationalsozialistische Deutsche Arbeiter Partei* – The National Socialist German Workers' Party is the full title of the Nazi Party.

SUMMARY QUESTIONS

1 Outline the main threats to the survival of the new moderate democratic government in the period 1918–23.

2 List the reasons for hyperinflation in 1923.

CHAPTER 5

Weimar politics and economic problems, 1924–9

WEIMAR POLITICS

Stresemann's government collapsed in late November 1923 to be replaced by one led by Wilhelm Marx of the Centre Party. However Stresemann continued to serve as Foreign Minister until 1929. The Republic was in a state of emergency that was only lifted in early 1924. In the Reichstag elections of May of that year the nationalist and communist parties made significant gains at the expense of the more moderate parties of the centre. This was caused by the uncertainty created by the economic crisis.

Elections to the Reichstag, 1924-8

The table shows the results of the elections in May and December 1924 and May 1928. The figures shown in each column represent the number of votes cast (in millions), the percentage of votes cast and the number of seats gained in the Reichstag.

The results of the elections to the Reichstag, 1924 and 1928.

Party	May 1924			December 1924			May 1928		
DNVP	5.6	19.5%	95	6.2	20.5%	103	4.4	14.2%	73
DVP	2.7	9.2%	45	3.0	10.1%	51	2.7	8.7%	45
Centre	3.9	13.4%	65	4.1	13.6%	69	3.7	12.1%	62
BVP	0.9	3.2%	16	1.1	3.7%	19	0.9	3.1%	16
DDP	1.7	5.7%	28	1.9	6.3%	32	1.5	4.9%	25
SPD	6.0	20.5%	100	7.9	26.0%	131	9.2	29.8%	153
KPD	3.6	12.6%	62	2.7	9.0%	45	3.2	10.6%	54
NSDAP	1.9	6.5%	32	0.9	3.0%	14	0.8	2.6%	12
Others		9.8%			7.8%			14.1%	

The Dawes Plan

Stresemann and Dawes. Stresemann believed that fulfilment was Germany's best course of action in dealing with the Allies. In his view, Germany's greatest need was

Chancellor	Date	Partners
Gustav Stresemann (DVP)	August 1923 – October 1923	SPD, DDP, Centre, DVP
Gustav Stresemann (DVP)	October 1923 – November 1923	DDP, Centre, DVP
Wilhelm Marx (Centre)	November 1923 – June 1924	DDP, Centre, BVP, DVP
Wilhelm Marx (Centre)	June 1924 – January 1925	DDP, Centre, DVP
Hans Luther (Non-party)	January 1925 – December 1925	DVP, DNVP, BVP
Hans Luther (Non-party)	January 1926 – May 1926	DDP, DVP, BVP
Wilhelm Marx (Centre)	May 1926 – December 1926	DDP, Centre, DVP, BVP
Wilhelm Marx (Centre)	January 1927 – June 1928	DVP, DNVP, BVP
Hermann Müller (SPD)	June 1928 – March 1930	SPD, DDP, Centre, BVP, DVP

Chancellors/coalition partners of the Weimar Republic, 1923–30.

raw materials, new markets for its goods and new sources of capital. In short Germany needed to be strengthened and made secure economically. According to Stresemann, this was even more so the case because Versailles had removed Germany's military strength. Most importantly Germany needed to restore confidence in its economy. To this end he encouraged the creation of the Dawes Plan. The Dawes Plan was put together by a committee of economists and other experts chaired by the American banker **Charles Dawes**. Their aim was to find a solution to the reparations problem under the slogan 'Business not Politics'. In April 1924 the committee produced its report.

- The plan suggested that the French leave the Ruhr and that further sanctions be harder to apply.
- Reparations would be paid over a longer period and credit would be advanced to help rebuild the German economy. In the first years, an international loan of 800 million marks would be granted to cover four-fifths of

the reparation payments. The higher level of 2,500 million marks a year set by the London Payments Plan would be paid after 1929.

- The Reichsbank would be reorganised under Allied supervision. Reparation payments were to be paid in such a way as not to threaten the stability of the German currency.

Difficulties in passing the Dawes Plan. There were many aspects of the Dawes Plan that were disliked by many parties within the Reichstag, in particular the acceptance of the continuation of reparation payments. The SPD vote in the May 1924 election had collapsed, down from 171 to 100. Their ideological divisions over whether they should take part in 'bourgeois coalitions' made the task of pushing

Key points about Stresemann

- The so-called 'Stresemann Years' (1924–9) were named after the politician Gustav Stresemann who was Reich Chancellor in 1923 and Foreign Minister from 1924 to 1929. In this time there was a failure to rectify the structural political defects of the Weimar state (as discussed on page 20). The weaknesses that were to contribute to a breakdown of democracy at the end of the decade can be traced to the middle years of the 1920s. They should be seen in themselves as years of political instability.
- Similarly, this period saw the beginnings of economic depression and social discord that were to worsen after1929.
- It was only in diplomacy, in which Stresemann excelled, that the nation's situation was improved.
- The view that stability was reflected in the cultural flowering of the Weimar period is also misleading. The opposite is true; the modernism of 'Weimar culture' stood in stark contrast to the conservatism of large sections of a disapproving society. It could be argued that these years were ones of cultural division that was to be reflected in the events of the early 1930s and beyond.

the agreement through the Reichstag on the required two-thirds majority even harder. The Plan was approved in the Reichstag on 29 August 1924 with the necessary support coming from some members of the **DNVP**. The DNVP was the largest party of the right throughout this period. As a large party it was broadly based, including former members of groups as diverse as the pre-1914 Conservative Party, the National Liberals and Christian Social groups. Although many within the party opposed both Versailles, the democratic Republic and the Dawes Plan, there were others who were prepared to work within the system as this vote shows. Industrialists and members of the business community who saw it as in their interest lobbied many DNVP members to vote in favour of the Dawes Plan.

KEY THEME

DNVP supporters were, in the main, landowners, the upper middle classes and large industrialists.

The failure of coalition politics

The collapse of Luther's coalition. In December 1924, a new election brought a revival in the fortunes of the SPD, who gained 31 seats (mainly at the expense of the KPD who lost 17 seats). The new coalition of January 1925 led by Hans Luther excluded the socialists but included members of the nationalist DNVP for the first time. This was to prove the undoing of this government as the DNVP objected to the terms of the Locarno treaties (see page 42) negotiated by Stresemann and only passed with support from the SPD in November 1925.

The problems caused by the SPD. A new coalition was sought but the SPD still objected to joining a coalition with 'bourgeois parties' (i.e., the DDP, Centre or DVP). The problems for the Republic's political system of coalition governments were made worse by the behaviour of the SPD. However, as already discussed, the fact that they acted as an interest group was common to all the leading parties. Between 1924 and June 1928 the SPD resisted becoming involved in forming workable coalition governments despite its position as the Reichstag's largest party. The main reason for this course of action was a belief that coalition with the 'bourgeois' parties would lead to a compromise of the party's ideals. This belief was strengthened by the adoption of a Marxist based series of policies by the Heidelberg programme of 1925. The consequence of such action was to reduce the influence of

President Paul von Hindenburg.

the socialists in the Reichstag, although their tacit support for governments, such as that of Marx in 1926, was often the key to that government's survival. However, such rejection of political responsibility also weakened the whole process of democracy as it contradicted the concept of representation and accountability. So the actions of the SPD played into the hands of the opponents of the Republic. They also weakened its political legitimacy.

The election of President Hindenburg. On 26 April 1925 General Hindenburg was elected President of the Weimar Republic. Hindenburg's election was to have serious consequences for the survival of the Republic, particularly in the light of the powers invested in the presidency by the constitution. As the victor of the Battle of Tannenberg in 1914 he was much respected. He won the election because of the split in the anti-right-wing vote. Hindenburg won 14.6 million votes in comparison with 13.7 million votes for Wilhelm Marx of the Centre Party and 1.9 million for Ernst Thälmann of the KPD. From the start of his presidency, Hindenburg made it clear that he would not accept SPD participation in coalition government. This was to have serious consequences for government stability.

Government instability, January 1926–February 1928. In January 1926, **Hans Luther** formed a minority coalition involving the Centre Party, DVP and DNP. This cabinet was not to last long, foundering on the instructions it gave to the country's diplomatic corps to use the old imperial flag (a black, red and white tricolour). The Reichstag passed a vote of no confidence in May 1926.

Wilhelm Marx replaced Luther as Chancellor. On 20 June 1926 a referendum took place on the confiscation of royal property, the vote failing to reach the required majority. The Marx cabinet relied on the support of the same parties as its predecessor and had the tacit support of the SPD. That support was removed in late 1926 and the cabinet fell. In January 1927, **Marx** reformed the government. This time it included the nationalist DNVP. There was always a strain on the cabinet, the interests of the DVP, the ***Bayerische Volkspartei*** (BVP) and DNVP parties often being different. Nevertheless, some important social

KEY TERM

The **'Bayerische Volkspartei' (BVP)** was a Catholic party based in Bavaria. In the 1928 election it gained 3.1 per cent of the vote.

legislation was passed, including a comprehensive reform of unemployment insurance in July 1927. The coalition collapsed in February 1928 over the issue of religion in education.

The Reichstag election of May 1928

The election of May 1928 was an important turning point for the Weimar Republic. The left made important gains, the SPD increasing its share of seats by 22 to 152 and the KPD showing a rise of 9 seats to 54. More significantly, as the parties of the centre and right saw their share of the vote drop, so there was a rise in the vote of splinter parties such as the *Bauernbund* (23 seats and 4.5 per cent of the vote) which represented farmers' interests.

The shift to extremes: changes in the DNVP. The sharp fall in the DNVP vote (down from 20.5 per cent of the vote in 1924 to 14.2 per cent in 1928) was to lead to demands for change within the party. The publishing of what became known as the **Lambach Article** in 1928 was the trigger for a shift in the party's policy. Written by Walter Lambach, the piece urged DNVP members to renounce their nostalgic desire for the return of the monarchy and become reconciled to the permanence of the Republic. Such was the backlash amongst party members that **Alfred Hugenberg** was elected leader of the DNVP in October 1928 on an anti-democratic platform and promptly brought the party into closer contact with the NSDAP.

The significance of the election of May 1928. The election of Hugenberg to the leadership of the DNVP in October 1928 clearly showed the anti-democratic feelings of a majority of the DNVP membership. The results of the 1928 election also highlight a subtle but real shift away from the established parties to those on the fringes of political life. Protest interest parties such as the *Bauernbund* or the *Deutsches Landvolk* gained ten seats. It is true that the vote for the NSDAP in this election fell to 2.6 per cent, but the KPD vote rose to 10.6 per cent. What this election shows is that the drift away from the centre ground parties began before the 1929 crash and that growing popular disillusion with the Republic was increasingly shown at elections.

KEY PERSON

Alfred Hugenberg was a leading nationalist and industrialist of the Weimar period. By the late 1920s he was considered the most influential newspaper and film company owner in the country. He used his extensive media interests to attack the Weimar Republic and constitution.

ECONOMIC PROBLEMS

Background

The most important reason for growing disillusion with the Weimar Republic was the deteriorating economy. The view generally accepted by most historians is that of the German economist **Kurt Borchardt** (1982). He argued that 1924–9 were years of slow growth and 'relative stagnation' in the economy. Borchardt suggests that the main reason for this was that trade union power kept wages high and therefore squeezed profits and middle-class income. Borchardt believes the Weimar economy was structurally weak before 1929. Historians such as C-L Holtfrerich (1984) have challenged such a view that high wages were the main cause of the Republic's economic problem. However, there is widespread agreement that Germany's economy was generally unstable before 1929.

Monetary stability

Foreign investment. Between 1924 and 1929 there was monetary stability which was particularly important to those classes that had suffered because of the hyperinflation of 1923. This was due to the establishment of the *Rentenmark* and the effects of the Dawes Plan. As a result of the Dawes Plan, there was a significant influx of foreign capital, around 25.5 billion marks between 1924 and 1930. The vast majority of this capital came from the United States and it enabled the reconstruction of German industry to take place. However, such a policy had its dangers – a downturn in the world economy, and, in particular, the US economy, could lead to the rapid withdrawal of such investment.

Delay of reparation payments. The growth in available capital in Germany was also due to the delaying of reparation payments at the highest rate, as suggested by the Dawes Plan, allowing investment in the German economy. (The Dawes Plan allowed the Germans to pay at the rate of only 1 million marks a year until 1929 when the rate would be increased to 2.5 million marks.) As a result, national income was 12 per cent higher in 1928 than in 1913 and industry experienced spectacular growth rates.

Labour unrest

The period 1924–9 was one of economic growth, but the term 'stability' is an inappropriate one to apply, particularly with industrial relations in mind. There is also little evidence in the voting figures of a return of confidence in the mainstream parties of the Republic; quite the opposite is true. Whilst the vote of the Centre Party held up from 1920 to 1929, it and the DDP saw a considerable drop from the election of 1919. Similarly, the number of votes won by the DVP fell from 3.9 million in 1920 to 2.7 million in 1928.

Unemployment. Unemployment figures support the view that many of the economic problems may have had their roots in the supposed years of stability. For example, in late 1928 the figure of those without work stood at 3 million or 14.5 per cent of the workforce. The collapse in food prices from 1922 led to widespread rural poverty.

Industrial unrest. Thc main problem for many Germans was to adjust to a period of relative normality in comparison with the recent years of turbulence. Yet that turbulence left a legacy which made industrial peace virtually impossible. The main issue for employers from 1923 to 1929 was to claw back the initiative that they felt they had lost to labour from 1918 to 1923. Although all sides had temporarily accepted the spirit of cooperation expressed in the constitution of 1919, the mid 1920s saw an increasingly organised attack by employers on the rights of labour. In 1923, the legislation of 1918 that enforced an eight-hour day was altered to allow employers to institute a ten-hour day in some circumstances. Employers resisted union demands for higher wages in this period to the extent that between 1924 and 1932 around 76,000 cases were brought to **arbitration**. There is little doubt that employers increasingly resented having to use such a procedure. In late 1928 over 210,000 workers in the Ruhr were locked out because the ironworks' owners would not accept the findings of arbitration. The DVP took up the fight on behalf of industrialists who opposed increasing unemployment insurance contributions in 1929–30. This reflected growing economic and political divisions shown by the refusal of the DVP to collaborate constructively with the

KEY TERM

Arbitration is when two sides come together to settle a dispute with the help of a third party.

Year	Strikes and lockouts	Working days lost
1924	1973	36198
1925	1708	2936
1926	351	1222
1927	844	6144
1928	739	20339
1929	429	4251

Industrial disputes, 1924–9

SPD from the mid 1920s. In fact the growing antagonism between the parties, which made constructive coalition government nearly impossible, had its roots in increasing conflict between those groups the parties represented.

Müller's Grand Coalition, 1928–30

The Young Plan. In June 1928 a ministry dominated by socialists was formed led by Hermann Müller of the SPD. However, this new coalition was broad enough to include members of the SPD, DDP, DVP, Centre and BVP. The main task of this so-called 'Grand Coalition' was to steer the Young Plan through the Reichstag in 1929. This plan dealt with the issue of reparations that re-emerged in 1929 because, under the Dawes Plan, Germany was due to start paying the higher rate of reparations. In September 1928, Germany asked France for a speedy evacuation of the Rhineland. The French, however, insisted that the issue of the Rhineland be linked to that of reparations. The Young Plan made the following points:

- For the first time, the timescale for reparation repayment was set; Germany was to make payments for the next 59 years until 1988. It was to pay 2,000 million marks a year instead of the 2,500 million marks as laid down by the Dawes Plan.
- Responsibility for paying reparations was to be given to Germany. Transfer of payments from German marks into foreign currency was to be handled by a new institution, the Bank for International Settlements, in Basle, Switzerland.
- Payments were to increase gradually and from 1929–32 Germany was to pay 1,700 million RM less than it would have paid under the Dawes Plan.

- If Germany agreed to the Plan, the French promised to evacuate the Rhineland by June 1930, five years ahead of schedule. This was an important victory for Stresemann.

Opposition to the Young Plan. Opponents of the Republic, however, were not impressed by the Young Plan and aimed to use the fact that Germany had still to pay reparations to discredit the Republic. Under Article 73 of the constitution, a referendum could be petitioned for. Hugenberg formed the Reich Committee for a Referendum to oppose the Young Plan, and the ***Stahlhelm*** leader, Franz Seldte, managed to raise some 4 million signatures for their petition. The campaign was particularly important because it included, on the invitation of Hugenberg, Adolf Hitler. In being associated with respectable figures, such as the industrialist **Fritz Thyssen** or the leader of the Pan-German League, Heinrich Class, Hitler's stature amongst those of the right grew considerably. The Reich Committee based their campaign around the 'Freedom Law' (see page 73) which demanded a repudiation of Article 231 of the Treaty of Versailles and an immediate evacuation of areas occupied by allied powers. The number of signatures on the petition was enough to demand a referendum on the issue. This was duly held on 22 December 1929 and resulted in a defeat for the right. Only 13.9 per cent of those who voted supported the Freedom Law. This was despite the support for their campaign from the President of the Reichsbank, Schacht. The Reichstag eventually passed the relevant Young Plan legislation in March 1930. By the following June, the French had evacuated the Rhineland.

KEY TERM

The **'Stahlhelm'** was a right-wing organisation founded by Franz Seldte and Theodor Duesterberg. It was strongly monarchist and nationalist. Its main aim was to counter the spread of communism. Its membership consisted mainly of ex-First World War soldiers.

KEY PERSON

Fritz Thyssen was a nationalist and anti-democrat. In the early 1920s he gave considerable amounts of money to the Nazis, having access to the huge Thyssen fortune which was made in the steel industry. Having helped the Nazis to power in the 1930s, he began to regret his actions and denounced the Nazis in 1938.

The Wall Street Crash, 1929

However, events were becoming increasingly overshadowed by the collapse of the New York stock exchange in October 1929. Much of the economic recovery of the mid-1920s had relied on short-term loans from abroad. As the depression deepened, those who had lent money now demanded repayment. The most obvious problem was the growth in unemployment. By February 1929, 17.7 per cent of the population was unemployed. The growing crisis was to stretch and then break the 'Grand Coalition'. The issue which was at the heart of the coalition's collapse was unemployment insurance. As discussed on pages 38–9, the late 1920s saw greater conflict between industrialists, who were mainly represented by the DVP, and workers, whose interests were supported by the SPD. Many industrialists believed that the Weimar state was too generous in its social benefits. In 1927 the law on unemployment insurance had been changed. From then onwards, the Reich Institution in charge of unemployment benefits was to pay a fixed benefit to all those out of work who were insured. This arrangement worked with unemployment at around 1.3 million as it was in 1927; however, as unemployment began to rise, so the Reich Institution had to borrow from the government to pay out benefits. By late 1929, it had borrowed 342 million RM and put a strain on the government's budget. The coalition partners had different ideas on how to address the problem.

- The SPD believed that contributions to the fund to help the unemployed should be increased. It argued that central and local governments, employers and those on fixed wages should pay 4 per cent more to help the unemployed.
- The DVP disagreed and argued that contributions should *not* be increased. Instead they believed that benefits should be cut.
- The Centre Party negotiated a deal whereby a decision on the issue would be put off until the autumn of 1930.

In March 1930 SPD deputies rejected this compromise and therefore brought down the socialist-led Müller government. Such action was close to political suicide. The SPD had given up power and this led to the forming of the first Brüning cabinet without any SPD ministers.

SUMMARY QUESTIONS

1 What evidence is there to support the claim that 'between 1924 and 1929 Germany was politically unstable'?

2 Write a summary of the state of the economy in Germany between 1924 and 1929. In it try to balance the positive factors against the weaknesses.

CHAPTER 6

Foreign policy and the role of Gustav Stresemann

BETTER RELATIONS WITH THE ALLIES, 1924–5

From 1919 to 1924 relations between the Allies and Germany continued to be poor. The Treaty of Versailles, Germany's agreement with the Soviet Union at Rapallo in 1922, the Ruhr crisis and other problems, all contributed to a continuing mistrust. After the antagonism in relations between Germany and the allied powers, 1924 saw a significant change in attitudes on all sides. The election of a Labour government under Ramsay MacDonald in Britain in January 1924 produced a more friendly line to Germany and subsequent governments maintained this. For the German Foreign Minister **Gustav Stresemann** this created opportunities to achieve some revision of reparations and Versailles through constructive diplomacy. **Stresemann's aims** in foreign policy were revisionist in that he desired to see an alteration to the terms of Versailles. He differed from many of his contemporaries in his methods of working towards that end.

Locarno

Background to Locarno. Stresemann's diplomatic strategy was further strengthened by a change in French attitudes in the wake of the Ruhr occupation of 1923. Then the French under Poincaré were extremely belligerent towards Germany and hoped for a withdrawal of the German frontier to the Rhine. Although the primary aim of the French in 1923 was to maintain security, the international backlash against their aggression resulted in a more sympathetic policy towards Germany, in particular in the wake of a victory for the left in the French elections of May 1924. The change in emphasis could be seen in the diplomatic events of 1925. There was a very real possibility at the end of 1924 that an Anglo-French agreement would be achieved to address the issue of French security.

KEY PERSON

Gustav Stresemann was a very important figure in the Weimar era. His most important achievement as Foreign Minister was to restore Germany's diplomatic status. Stresemann was a nationalist who wanted to see Germany recover from the depths of defeat in 1918. Although a monarchist, he accepted the Weimar Republic as the best chance for political stability. His death in 1929 robbed Germany of an important politician. However, it is impossible to judge what his impact on German politics would have been if he had lived.

KEY THEME

Stresemann's aims
Stresemann wished to see better relations with France, a resolution of border issues and a revision of Versailles.

Stresemann saw this possibly leading to the prolonging of the occupation of the Rhineland and therefore proposed a settling of the security issue. This was made more urgent by the statement issued by the Allies in January 1925 that they would not vacate Cologne by the due date of the 10th of that month. In April 1925 Aristide Briand became French Foreign Minister. Briand accepted the British suggestion that some kind of pact be signed securing France's eastern borders. Months of negotiations followed which ended in the meetings at Locarno in October 1925.

The Locarno Treaties, 1925. The Locarno treaties that were the outcome were signed on 1 December.

- A treaty of mutual guarantee of the Franco-German and Belgian-German borders was signed with Britain and Italy guaranteeing the agreement.
- All parties agreed not to use force to alter these frontiers.
- A series of arbitration treaties were signed at Locarno between Germany and France, Poland, Czechoslovakia and Belgium.

Stresemann held out against a Locarno style settlement for Germany's eastern borders, hoping for revision of them at a later date. Not only was he successful, but he managed to secure guarantees from France that it would not attack Germany in the event of a war with Poland in which Germany was not the aggressor. Soon after the treaties, the first evacuation from the Rhineland took place in 1925. However, despite further talks on the subject between Stresemann and the French Foreign Minister Artiste Briand in September 1926, there was no more movement on the issue until 1929.

KEY THEME

Membership of the League of Nations
Germany was initially excluded from the League of Nations when it was first created in 1919. This led to resentment in Germany because it meant that it was unable to work within the League for a revision of the Treaty of Versailles.

Diplomatic improvements, 1925–6

The post-Locarno period up to 1929 saw an improvement in Germany's diplomatic situation.

- As part of the Locarno agreements, Germany was admitted to the **League of Nations** on 8 September 1926. It was agreed at the talks that although Germany was granted a permanent seat on the Council, it was free from the military obligations laid out in Article 16. This

was part of the process of calming the doubts expressed by the Soviet Union over Germany's admittance.
- In April 1926, the Treaty of Berlin was signed between the Soviet Union and Germany, reaffirming the Treaty of Rapallo of 1922 and stressing each country's neutrality in the event of attack by a third power.
- Despite these overtures to the Soviet Union, or perhaps because of them, relations between Germany and the Western Powers continued to improve. In late 1926, the allied occupation forces in Germany were cut by a further 60,000. In January 1927 the Allies finally withdrew the Inter-Allied Military Commission (IMCC) which had been set up to oversee German disarmament as demanded by the Treaty of Versailles.
- There were also economic side effects to the improvement in diplomatic relations, for example, a commercial treaty was signed between France and Germany in August 1927. However, some tensions did remain with France which were heightened by Hindenburg's speech on 18 September of the same year in which he denied Germany's war guilt and rejected Article 231.

GUSTAV STRESEMANN – SUCCESS OR FAILURE?

Introduction. The naming of the period 1924–9 the 'Stresemann Years' indicates that it was in the sphere of foreign relations that the Weimar Republic appeared to succeed most. There is little debate amongst historians as to the aims of Gustav Stresemann's foreign policy – to restore Germany to 'great power' status. The more controversial debate has revolved around the question of the extent of its success. Historians such as W. Walsdorf (1971) claimed that Stresemann failed in his main foreign policy objective of revising Versailles. Those such as E. Kolb (1988), who point to Stresemann's considerable success given the difficult international situation in which he was operating, have countered this.

Gustav Stresemann.

The arguments for success.

- **Fulfilment.** Significant progress was made towards the revision of some of the articles of the Treaty of Versailles that so dominated the foreign policy of the period. Stresemann did this through the policy of 'fulfilment', i.e. by fulfilling the terms of the treaty, Germany could show how unjust and unworkable they were.

- **The Soviet Union.** Simultaneously, Germany worked towards agreement with the Soviet Union as shown by the Treaty of Berlin of 1926, which prompted the Western Powers into a more sympathetic approach to Germany.
- **Locarno.** The achievements of German diplomacy in the Stresemann era are considerable, in particular the greater understanding with France as reflected in the Locarno treaties of 1925. Stresemann tried to avoid Locarno becoming a precedent for the settlement of Germany's eastern borders, aiming for their revision at a later date. Not only was he successful, he also managed to secure guarantees from France that in the event of a war with Poland in which Germany was not the aggressor France would not attack Germany.

KEY THEME

French attitude to Versailles There were many in France who had wished to see Germany treated more harshly at Versailles. In particular, many French people had hoped that France would be given the area on the left bank of the Rhine. Although the attitude of some in France softened towards Germany, many were still very hostile.

- **Revision of Versailles.** Soon after the Locarno treaties, the first evacuation from the Rhineland took place in 1925. This contrasts with the **attitude of the French government** to the German suspension of loan repayments in 1923 and the subsequent invasion of the Ruhr. Yet the extent of the French change in attitude towards Germany must not be exaggerated. The meeting between Stresemann and Briand at Thiory in September 1926 failed to find a solution of the contentious issue in Germany of France's continued occupation of the Rhineland. There was not enough political willpower in France to bring about withdrawal. However, a solution to the problem of the Rhineland was linked to reparations repayments by the Young Plan in 1929–30. This was testimony to both the desire of all parties to find a collective solution to the problems facing them and the success of Stresemann's tactics to effect a revision of Versailles.
- **Growing diplomatic influence.** Stresemann's policies resulted in Germany regaining diplomatic influence and the ability to influence the Allies. The absence of a Locarno style settlement of Germany's eastern borders in 1925 is a case in point. Germany's acceptance into the League of Nations in 1926 with a permanent seat on the

Council is another. Perhaps the most important aspects of the revision of Versailles were the two plans to reorganise reparations, Dawes and Young, which gave Germany some breathing space to develop its economy. The removal of the IMCC in 1927 and the French withdrawal from the Ruhr both point to the success of the policy of fulfilment in achieving positive outcomes for German interests.

- **Dawes Plan.** The Dawes Plan was fundamental in strengthening the German industrial base and better relations with the USA in particular, improving trade.
- **The Young Plan.** The Young Plan of 1929 was Stresemann's last major diplomatic achievement. Most importantly, it linked the evacuation of the Rhineland to the successful revision of the reparations programme. There were considerable other benefits to Germany, including a rescheduling of the debt to 2,000 million marks to be paid yearly until 1988. Stresemann did not see the treaty ratified, his death coming in October 1929.

The argument for failure. The success Stresemann enjoyed was not recognised universally in Germany where there was no consensus on the best tactics for achieving a revision of Versailles. In this sense, therefore, it is impossible to conclude that Stresemann's diplomacy resulted in domestic political stability.

- **Versailles.** The main issues of Versailles, Article 231, reparations and the 'stab in the back', continued to undermine the Weimar Republic. Whilst 'fulfilment' brought some relief, the policy did not alter the humiliation felt in large sections of German society. There are numerous examples of this, not least the referendum of December 1929 on the Freedom Law that opposed the signing of the Young Plan. The fact that 5.8 million Germans were prepared to vote for a law which **rejected Stresemann's policy** and labelled him a traitor shows that the perception of the success of the 'fulfilment' policy was limited. The issue of Versailles plagued politics and was the main cause of disagreements between the DNVP and the DVP/DDP, e.g., the collapse of their coalition in 1925 over Locarno.

KEY THEME

Oppostion to Stresemann
Many on the far right, including Adolf Hitler and the Nazis, attacked Stresemann's diplomatic policy. Their attacks were also personal: Stresemann was married to the daughter of a Jewish industrialist.

- **Not much room for manoeuvre.** There is little doubting Stresemann's achievements, in particular with regard to Locarno. Through the lack of military means at his disposal, there were few options available other than to follow the peaceful policy he did. Although his policy did lead to greater economic stability, the gradual approach to the restoration of German power meant that those who proposed more radical action to end Versailles were still able to act as a destabilising influence on German politics. It was not the policy of Stresemann that was responsible for this but the existence of the Versailles Treaty.

SUMMARY QUESTION

1 German foreign policy in the period 1924–9 – success or failure?

CHAPTER 7

Weimar culture and society

THE DEVELOPMENT OF A MODERN 'WEIMAR CULTURE'

The years 1924–9 saw the development of a style which was unique to the Weimar Republic, that of *Neue Sachlichkeit*. *Neue Sachlichkeit*, with its matter-of-fact style, was used to expose the weaknesses and injustices of Weimar society as it had developed by the mid 1920s.

KEY TERMS

'Neue Sachlichkeit' means matter-of-factness or objectivity.

'Bauhaus' was the cultural and artistic movement most commonly associated with the Weimar Republic. It was a movement with modern ideas and expression.

'Neue Sachlichkeit'

- Architecture and consequently many other art forms were dominated by the ***Bauhaus*** movement associated with Walter Gropius. He stressed the relationship between art and technology, the functionality of design and the freedom from the past. The influence of the *Bauhaus* should not be underestimated as it provided the inspiration for creativity as diverse as the painting of Kandinsky to the architects and urban planners who built the new houses and towns in the mid 1920s and in particular Weissenhof near Stuttgart in 1927.
- The departure from tradition was mirrored in the music of Schonberg and the ironic literature of the *Neue Sachlichkeit* writers, such as Thomas Döblin or the satirist Kurt Tucholsky.
- A seriousness also permeated much of literature. In particular this period saw the publication of numerous works based on the First World War, one of note being the pacifist *All Quiet on the Western Front* by Erich Maria Remarque published in 1928.
- Alienation from the Weimar Republic was a common feature of writing on the left and right but it was also prevalent amongst an artistic community that attacked its failure to construct a viable new political culture. This is best represented in Ernst Toller's *Hoppla wir leben* (1928) in which a revolutionary is released from an

asylum after many years of incarceration, only to find that society and politics have stagnated in decline.

- In the theatre, the works of writers such as Freidrich Wolf and Peter Lampel became the dominant force of the mid 1920s, concentrating on a range of social issues. An excellent example was Lampel's *Revolte in Erziehungshaus*, performed first in 1928, that led to a prolongued debate on education reform.
- That the movement summed up the public mood is a debatable issue for, as will be seen, the public mood was very much divided. What it did reveal was a disenchantment with Weimar and a scepticism about its ability to reform. This is very clear in the writing of authors such as Alfred Döblin, who in the 1929 novel *Berlin Alexanderplatz* castigated the decline of the Weimar years.

The conservative side to Weimar culture

What is popularly described as 'Weimar culture' was only one manifestation of cultural expression in the mid 1920s.

The exterior of the 'Bauhaus' factory at Dessau designed by the architect Walter Gropius.

The objectivity of the *Neue Sachlichkeit* contrasted with the nostalgia, romanticism and escapism of popular literature, the modernity of *Bauhaus* with the traditional taste of the majority of the population.

- **Literature**. Many writers on the political right, such as Arthur Möller and Oswald Spengler, contributed to an anti-democratic German 'destiny' literature which glorified the experiences of the First World War trenches. This became highly popular through the work of authors such as Ernst Jünger and Werner Beumemelberg. This was countered by the anti-war offerings of Remarque and Ludwig Renn. It was not only in its treatment of war that literature was divided. Whilst the *Neue Sachlichkeit* author described social issues, so in the cinema films such as *Die freudlose Gasse* (1925) by G.W. Pabst, discussed topical issues in a matter-of-fact way. Yet there was a parallel culture at this time which very much rejected the objectivity of *Neue Sachlichkeit* and found refuge in escapism. This was reflected in the increased sales of authors such as Hans Grimm or Lons Flex.
- **Cinema**. In the cinema escapism found its expression in the films of Charlie Chaplin. The significance of their popularity was that their works of comedy, fantasy, nostalgia and mythology were in direct contrast to the modernity of *Neue Sachlichkeit*.

Conclusion – a clash of cultures

There is little doubt that cultural divisions ran deep, reflecting the political and social polarisation of the period. Therefore, the cultural developments of the period did little to help stabilise the Republic but became part of the process by which it was undermined.

As shown with the Treaty of Versailles, the legacy of the First World War was to create division within Germany and this was reflected in culture. But the important point is that neither of these two poles of cultural expression gave support to the regime or the values which underpinned it. They stood as opposites yet both hostile to the Republic. So whilst the Weimar Republic became identified with cultural change and liberation, these forces did not act as a foundation for stability. In reality quite the opposite is true. Those who felt left behind or alienated by the changes blamed the new democracy for such 'decadence' and in particular for the freer attitude towards women and morals. What Weimar culture and such movements as the *Bauhaus* represent is the opposite of stability.

WEIMAR SOCIETY

Women

The role of women and the debate about their status was an important feature of Weimar society. The proportion of women who worked outside the home during the Weimar years remained roughly the same as before 1914, as the table below shows. It also shows that the type of work women did remained roughly the same.

Women in employment in Germany, a comparison between 1907 and 1925 (figures are the percentage of the workforce which was female).

Type of employment	1907	1925
Domestic servants	16	11.4
Farm workers	14.5	9.2
Industrial workers	18.3	23
White collar and public employment	6.5	12.6
Percentage of women in employment	31.2	35.6

The most obvious change is the growing number of women in new areas of employment, most noticeably in public employment (e.g., civil service, teaching or social work), in shops or on the assembly line. This raised the issue of the type of woman who was suitable for such work. Despite the large numbers of women who worked during the war in so-called 'men's work', e.g., heavy industry, after the war these better-paid jobs were taken back by men. Social attitudes were still conservative and married women were not expected to work outside the home. Those who did, the ***Doppelverdiener***, became the source of considerable debate. Condemnation of working women increased after 1924 when rationalisation of companies often saw the better-paid man laid off first. Criticism became sharper with the post-1929 depression. In 1932 the Law Governing the Legal Status of Female

KEY TERM

'Doppelverdiener' was a second wage earner. For many, this was a term of abuse to be aimed at married women who worked.

Civil Servants and Public Officials was passed which made possible the dismissal from the civil service of women who were second wage-earners. There was opposition to this measure from some sections of society, not least from the 20,000 or so women who were university students in 1932. However, the reaction against such a measure must not be exaggerated. The vast majority of Germans, both male and female, accepted the traditional view of women's role in society.

The Welfare State

The Welfare State promised in the constitution. The foundations of a German welfare state were laid at the end of the nineteenth century. What made the period of the Weimar Republic different was the fact that the concept of the welfare state was enshrined in the constitution. What was also new was the idea that welfare was a basic right for all German citizens. The constitution was bold in its welfare plans. The reality was often that many of the plans were not realised because of opposition or economic crisis. These are some of the points in the constitution:

- The family was at the centre of Weimar society (Article 119) and it was the responsibility of adults to protect and nurture young people (Articles 120–122).
- Religious freedom was guaranteed (Articles 135–141).
- Economic life was commented on in a series of articles (151–65). These included the respect for private property, a commitment to build new housing (Article 155) and to employee protection (Article 157).

Although many of the hopes of those who framed the constitution were not realised, there was important social reform in the period.

Public welfare. The aim of the welfare reform of the period was to free those claiming benefits from any stigma. Before the war, claimants had lost the right to vote as a result of their destitution. The First World War created a new class of claimants from orphans and war widows to disabled soldiers. The Reich Relief Law and Serious Disability Laws in 1920 created the framework of support. In 1924 the system for claiming relief and assessing the needs of the claimants was codified. However, despite attempts to improve the levels of support, many claimants still received benefits at a subsistence level. In 1927 the Labour Exchanges and Unemployment Insurance Law introduced unemployment insurance. This was to become an important political issue.

Housing and public health. Before the First World War the state had built public housing. Public spending on housing grew rapidly throughout the 1920s. By 1929 the state was spending 33 times more on housing than it had been in 1913. Indeed, between 1927 and 1930, 300,000 houses were either built or renovated. The effect of this was to considerably improve the quality of homes on offer to many Germans. Better health insurance also meant that there was better medical provision. This can be seen by studying a number of statistics, such as those shown in the table.

Before 1914	After 1914
Deaths from tuberculosis in 1913, 143 in every 10,000	Deaths from tuberculosis in 1928, 87 in every 10,000
Deaths from pneumonia in 1913, 119 in every 10,000	Deaths from pneumonia in 1928, 93 in every 10,000
4.8 doctors per 10,000 Germans in 1909	7.4 doctors per 10,000 Germans in 1930
63.1 hospital beds per 10,000 Germans in 1910	90.9 hospital beds per 10,000 Germans in 1930

Public health statistics, 1909–30.

Youth. The Weimar state intervened to attempt to improve the upbringing of the nation's children. The Reich Youth Welfare Law of 1922 claimed the right of all children to a good upbringing. The practical measures it proposed to help ensure this included a new youth welfare system. The problem was that many of the aims of the system were not realised. The issue of juvenile crime and rehabilitation of young people was covered by the Reich Youth Welfare Law, 1922 and the Reich Juvenile Court Law, 1923.

Financing the welfare state. The cost of the welfare state was partly met by an increase in taxation. In 1919 the Finance Minister Matthais Erzberger created a new framework of taxation which would pay for the proposed extension of welfare. As a result the proportion of the national income which came from taxation rose from 9 per cent in 1913 to 17 per cent in 1925.

SUMMARY QUESTIONS

1 Explain the ways in which the Weimar Republic was 'politically stable and economically prosperous' between 1924 and 1928.

2 Describe the main provisions of the Welfare State in Weimar Germany.

AS ASSESSMENT – WEIMAR GERMANY

Sources exercise in the style of AQA.

Study the sources below and then answer the questions.

Source A

By 1 January 1919, the new government had almost collapsed. Chancellor Ebert was isolated, with no armed force to protect his government. A communist putch was expected any day. General Gröner suggested that Gustav Noske, the man who had dealt with the Kiel Mutiny, should be brought to Berlin; Ebert agreed at once. The job of defence minister would be nasty, dangerous, perhaps impossible. It had almost been given to Colonel Reinhart, a career army officer, but Reinhart refused. Noske was exasperated and demanded a decision be made. Someone asked him if he would take the post. 'Of course!', Noske replied. 'Someone must become the police dog. I won't shirk the responsibility'.

An extract from *The Kings Depart* by R. M. Watt.

Source B

A cartoon by the left-wing artist George Grosz. The cartoon was published in 1919 in *Die Pleite.*

Source C

There were many Germans after 1918 who found it impossible to accept the political results of the war, and felt that 'under the Kaiser, everything was better'. The normal state of the Weimar Republic was in crisis. After the shock of defeat and the humiliation of Versailles, followed the awful experience of the inflation. Millions of Germans who had passively accepted the transition from Empire to Republic suffered deprivations that shattered their faith in the democratic process and left them cynical and alienated. Their feelings were reflected in a series of new political threats to the Republic.

Taken from *Germany 1866–1945*, by G. A. Craig.

Questions

Reading. Before answering this question you should have read Chapters 1–4 (pages 1–30) of this book.

1 Study Source A. Explain the meaning of 'communist putsch' in the context of what happened in Germany in January 1919. Use your own knowledge to answer this question.

How to answer the question. Please note that this is typical of a low mark question so do not spend too much time on it in an examination. To reach full marks you should do the following:

- Show that you are aware that the Spartacist uprising took place at this time and that the far left saw revolution as the way to destroy Ebert's temporary government. The question also asks you to show an understanding of 'the context' of January 1919. In your answer, therefore, you should explain how Ebert's government was threatened from left and right, how it feared a left wing take over and how Ebert was pushed into asking the army for support.
- A further point to might make might be to explain the fear amongst all moderate socialists and others who wanted democracy in Germany of a revolution like the one that had taken place in Russia in 1917.

2 Study Sources A and B. Explain how the cartoonist who drew Source B challenges the interpretation of events of January 1919 given in Source A. Refer to your own knowledge when answering this question.

How to answer this question. In answering this question you should try and compare the information from both sources. You should use this information and your own knowledge about the role of the army in crushing revolution to draw conclusions.

- **Style.** Firstly you should look at the different styles of the sources. The cartoonist challenges Source A because it is a polemical attack. Source A on the other hand attempts to be an objective account. Therefore Source B challenges Source A by using satire.

- **Content**. You should go through the different ways Source B challenges Source A. However do not just list the differences, try and come to a conclusion that backs up what you know about the authors and shows your own knowledge.

3 Study Sources A, B and C. In what ways was the new German government weakened as a result of the steps it took to survive the dangers facing it in 1918–23? You should use your own knowledge to answer this question.

How to answer this question. This question wants you to make links between the sources and your own knowledge to explain what happened.

Plan. Before you write an answer to this question it is important that you write a plan. Your plan should include the main points of argument or analysis which you are going to use to answer the question. Examples of your main points in writing this essay are:

- The German government was weakened by its reliance on the army to defend the new Republic despite the fact that many within the army were against the Republic.
- The government was also weakened by divisions on the left, mistakes in economic policy and the burden of Versailles.

Structure of your answer. These two points give you plenty to explain. To reach the highest level you need to do the following:

Introduction. In your introduction you should briefly explain your main points. There is no need to go into detail in the introduction.
Prioritise. You should try and explain which 'ways' are more important than others. You first main paragraph(s) should explain the key 'way' using appropriate evidence.
Conclusion. Your conclusion should be brief and sum up your line of argument.

Information to use. The question has asked you to use your own knowledge and the sources. In explaining the ways in which the German government was weakened you need to make sure that you use both.

Sources. The following information can be used from the sources:

- Source A shows the potentially dangerous link to the army. It shows that Noske was prepared to do the job. The comment about the 'police dog' is useful.
- Source B shows how the left was most bitter and how Ebert's government was seen as betraying the revolution.

- Source C makes the link to Versailles and hints at hyperinflation.

Own knowledge. You can use your own knowledge from reading Chapters 1–4 of the book. These are the main themes:

- The army's involvement in politics from an early stage was most important in weakening the new German government. However the army and the *Freikorps* were not only tolerated in its actions but encouraged by Ebert and successive Chancellors who wanted to see the extreme left crushed. There are many examples to illustrate this point; the murder of Karl Liebknecht and Rosa Luxemburg, the Ebert -Gröner pact and the crushing of Kurt Eisner's revolt in Bavaria. The steps the government took divided the left which proved to be a long running weakness for successive coalition governments.
- The steps the government took in signing Versailles, the issue of reparations and policy during the Ruhr crisis all added to the weakening of the Republic's position.
- You might include information about the constitution and how it was drawn up in such a way to reflect the German political culture but some aspects had the potential for weakening the Republic, in particular proportional representation.

Style. Here is an example of a direct style using evidence.

The most important way in which the actions of German governments weakened themselves was by tolerating and encouraging the use of the army and Freikorps *to crush opposition on the left. This was despite the fact that most within the ranks of army and Freikorps opposed the Republic. These moves by Ebert are clearly shown in Source A and the Ebert-Gröner pact signed in 1918. However they weakened the Republic because successive governments thereafter did not recognise the significance of the threat from the right. The bitterness of the left against Ebert and the moderate socialists in the SPD can been seen in Grosz's cartoon (Source B). This was made worse by events such as the crushing of the Bavarian Revolution in 1920. The divisions on the left were to weaken Parliamentary government throughout the 1920s.*

Essay questions

Reading. Before answering this question you should read Chapter 3 (pages 18–23) in this book.

1 Describe how the Weimar government and constitution were set up in Germany after the defeat in November 1918.

How to answer this question. The question is asking you to describe the most important features of the German government as set up at the end of the First World

War. The years you will be targeting are 1918–1919 when the government and constitution were created.

Plan. Before you start writing your answer you must plan it clearly. In your plan you need to identify the main features about the government and constitution you are going to explain. If you organise your work well, you stand a much better chance of reaching the highest level. You need to be comprehensive in your use of evidence, thereby covering the following areas:

- An explanation of the abdication of the Kaiser and the debate about a new form of government. The rationale for the new constitution and a description of how it was drawn up should be included.
- You should then include a detailed description of the new form of government as laid out in the constitution. This would include a description of the relationship between and functions of the President, Reichstag and Länder.
- The answer should also highlight some of the other areas of the constitution; its electoral system and the clauses relating to society.

When writing there are a few points that you should follow:

- You must make sure that your answer is direct to the question.
- There is no need to describe other events of the time, stick to the main features of the government and the constitution.
- You must make sure that your answer contains factual detail.
- Write in short paragraphs. Don't forget to include a very brief introduction and conclusion.

Style. Below is an example of how you might write a section on the main features of the constitution.

The new constitution was drafted by legal expert, scholar and liberal Hugo Preuss. He attempted to build on the traditions of German politics and well as balance power between the different institutions of the state. The new constitution created the Reich (state) as a parliamentary democracy with the Chancellor and cabinet needing majority support in the Reichstag. However, the new state was to be a federal state, the Reich comprising of 18 states (Länder). While the central state was granted powers such as that of taxation, the new Länder were represented by the Reichsrat which had the power to delay laws. Its members were chosen by the parliaments of the Länder. However the Reichstrat has less power than its predecessor the Bundesrat.

2 Explain why Germany was so unstable politically between 1918 and 1923.

Reading. Before answering this question you should read the relevant sections in pages 1–31 of this book.

How to answer this question. The question is asking you to explain the causes of political unrest in Germany between 1918 and 1923. You need to focus on the causes of instability, create an argument that you can sustain throughout the question and use well selected and accurate information.

Plan. Because this is a question that asks you to analyse you need to identify your main arguments. You also need to make up in your mind what you think are the most important factors to explain instability in this period. These are examples of what might be the main points of your plan:

- The new political structure faced considerable obstacles that included dealing with defeat and humiliation at Versailles as well as a weak democratic tradition.
- These obstacles were made worse by periodic attacks on the democracy from left and right that increased instability.
- The new constitution and the demands of coalition government acted as a further factor in creating an atmosphere of instability.

Style. These points need to be explained in clear paragraphs that will follow a brief introduction. Below is an example of the style you might chose to use to answer a question such as this one.

The instability of the Weimar Republic was made considerably greater by the demands of the Treaty of Versailles. Successive governments had no choice but to accept the demands of the Allies despite considerable opposition in Germany. In May 1919 the government led by Scheidemann resigned rather than accept the Treaty and, in particular, the hated War Guilt clause. The most important significance of Versailles is that it gave opponents of democracy in Germany a weapon with which to attack and destabilise the Republic. Hindenberg's testimony to the Investigation Committee of the National Assembly backed up the suggestions of the right wing parties and press that Versailles was a humiliating and shameful peace (Schmachfrieden) which should not have been signed. That the Treaty was signed, according to Hindenberg and his political allies, was because of the anti patriotic sentiments of the group of left wing politicians, the so called 'November criminals' who had founded the Republic e.g. Freidrich Ebert, Hermann Müller, Matthias Erzberger. They were also blamed for the 'stab in the back' of the armed forces that led to military collapse in 1918.

Such theories were mighty useful to the anti-Republican right. They absolved the military from responsibility for their own failings in 1918 and they played on popular resentment of the Treaty. This resulted in increased support for anti Versailles parties such as the nationalist DNVP whose percentage of the vote increased from 10.3% in January 1919 to 14.9% in June 1920. Indeed these accusations as the 'stab in the back' became widely accepted because they were simple and they gave many Germans an acceptable framework by which they could explain defeat. They acted to reduce support for the Republic and thereby politically destabilise it. The myths which were developed as a result of the Versailles Treaty which were to cause one of the greatest threats to the Republic's stability.

3 Why did Germany suffer hyperinflation in 1923?

Reading. Before answering this question you should read pages 26–9 in this book.

How to answer this question. The question is asking you to explain the causes of the hyperinflation in 1923. You need to focus on the causes of hyperinflation. It is important that you do not focus on one cause but that you explain a variety of causes.

Plan. Because this is a question that asks you to analyse you need to identify your main arguments. You also need to make up in your mind what you think are the most important factors to explain why hyperinflation took place.

- Hyperinflation was the result of a complexity of factors which included problems caused by reparations and the policy of 'passive resistance' during the Ruhr crisis.
- However there was inflation before 1923 that was the result of the stabilisation of the German economy. In particular the new political system could not deal with the social consequences of a strict financial policy aimed at keeping inflation low but which might have included the loss of thousands of government jobs.
- The war and the increase in the national debt played a considerable role in creating inflation in Germany.

Style. For an example of the style of writing you should use in this question, see the example given for Question 2.

4 How were successive German governments able to maintain stability in the period 1924–29?

Reading. To answer this question you should read pages 31–47 in this book.

How to answer this question. The question is asking you to describe the reasons for stability in Germany between 1924 and 1929. You need to identify the reason for stability. However you might also challenge the idea that Germany was as stable in this period as it seemed.

Plan. In your plan you need to identify the main causes for greater stability.

- Economic stabilisation, the Dawes Plan and foreign investment all contributed to a more stable economy and political system. The challenge from the extremes of left and right was considerably reduced.
- Stresemann's foreign policy restored Germany diplomatically and took the pressure off the political system.

However you should also include a point in your plan that qualifies the level of stability you have described, e.g.:

- Despite improvements there was still political instability, economic unrest and the burden of Versailles had not been removed.

Style. You need to ensure that you link the description of each relevant factor to stability. You should also try and link various factors explicitly. Below is an example of how you can do this:

Between 1924 and 1929 there was monetary stability which was particularly important to those classes that had suffered because of the hyperinflation of 1923. This was due to the establishment of the Rentenmark and the effects of the Dawes Plan. As a result of the Dawes Plan, there was a significant influx of foreign capital, around 25.5 billion marks between 1924 and 1930. The vast majority of this capital came from the USA and it enabled the reconstruction of German industry to take place. This monetary stability helped to give the political system greater stability. In particular there was a reduction in support for the parties on the extreme wings of German politics, for example, in the election in May 1928 the NSDAP polled only 2.6 per cent of the vote.

AS SECTION: THE RISE OF THE NAZI PARTY

Introduction

The Nazi Party was founded in 1919. For much of the 1920s it was an insignificant party on the fringe of German politics. Led by Adolf Hitler, it preached an extreme message of anti-Semitism, the destruction of the Treaty of Versailles, living space for Germany in the east (*Lebensraum*), a social revolution and the end of the Weimar Republic. In 1923, Hitler and his followers failed to take power by force in the Munich Putsch. Imprisoned in Lansbach Castle, Hitler wrote *Mein Kampf* (*My Struggle*) setting out his ideas. In the 1928 election the Nazis performed very poorly, polling only 2.6 per cent of the vote. However, five years later Hitler was offered the position of Chancellor of Germany. The reasons for this are as follows:

- **Economic collapse**. The Nazis increased in popularity as the German economy collapsed in the wake of the Wall Street Crash in 1929. The desperation of many Germans led them to turn to the political extremes. As a result, the Nazis became one of the largest political parties.
- **Nazi organisation and tactics**. Reform of the Nazi Party in the 1920s meant that it was ideally placed to take advantage of the increasing dissatisfaction of many Germans with the main political parties and the Weimar Republic. Another important factor was Hitler's realisation after 1923 that the party would only achieve power through legal means rather than just violence.
- **Role of the establishment**. To many in the German establishment, the Nazi movement offered the only realistic alternative to communism on the left. Therefore, from the early 1930s, Hitler and his party became courted by bankers, businessmen and politicians who hoped that they could use the Nazi movement to undermine the Weimar Republic and protect their interests. It was on their advice that President Paul von Hindenburg appointed Hitler as Chancellor in 1933.

CHAPTER 8

The rise of the Nazi Party to power in 1933

THE NAZI LEADERSHIP

Adolf Hitler

Leader of the Nazi movement from 1919 to his death in 1945, Hitler was the central figure in the Nazi state from 1933 onwards. Much of the following pages concentrate on his political philosophy and the consequences of his decisions and actions.

Hitler in war crowd in 1914.

Hitler was born in Braunau in Austria on 20 April 1889. As a young man before the First World war he lived as a social outcast in Vienna. A second-rate painter, he earned a living by selling cheap sketches. Hitler was in Munich in 1914 when war broke out and received the news with enthusiasm. He enlisted in the Bavarian Infantry and served throughout the war. Twice wounded, he was decorated with the Iron Cross (First Class) in 1918, an honour rare for a Lance-Corporal. Embittered by Germany's defeat, Hitler entered politics in Munich in 1919.

Throughout his political career, which is explained in detail on the following pages, Hitler's views remained constant. These views became the bedrock of Nazi ideology.

- **Anti-Semitism and racial supremacy.** Hitler believed in the idea of Aryan racial supremacy, that humanity could be divided into different racial groups and that the Nordic Aryan group was the superior. He also believed that the roots of all evil and Germany's problems were the Jews of Germany and the wider world. These racist ideas were at the heart of his personal political philosophy. Related to this was Hitler's hatred of communism, which he saw as a Jewish ideology.
- ***Lebensraum* and Versailles.** Hitler believed that it was the destiny of the Aryan people to expand to the east of Germany, in what is known as *Lebensraum* or living space. This had partly been thwarted by the removal and redistribution of land at the Treaty of Versailles, which Hitler promised to destroy.
- **Anti-democracy.** Hitler hated democracy and saw the leaders of the Weimar Republic and the system of parliamentary government as responsible for the weakening of Germany. He therefore promised to destroy the Republic.
- ***Führerprinzip*.** From the start of his political career, Hitler insisted that the Nazi Party and Germany be dominated by one powerful leader, the Führer.

Hermann Göring

Göring

A First World War fighter pilot hero, Hermann Göring became a close ally of Hitler in 1922. He played an important part in the Munich Putsch in 1923 and became popular with Nazi activists. His marriage to a Swedish aristocrat, Carin von Kantow, helped to win respectable conservative support for the Nazi movement. In 1928 Göring was elected to the Reichstag and in 1932 he became its President. His status and political contacts helped him to play a key part in the deal to appoint Hitler Chancellor in January 1933. As Prussian Minister of the Interior, Göring organised the infiltration of the state police by members of the SA and SS. It is widely accepted that it was Göring who organised the Reichstag fire in February 1933 in order to discredit the communists. He drew up the death list for the Night of the Long Knives in August 1934 and relished giving news of the purge of Röhm to the world's press.

Although he lost control of the police system to Himmler, Göring's power was increased when he took control of the

Luftwaffe (air force) and the Four Year Plan office in 1936. As part of the drive for self-sufficiency, he established the *Reichswerke Hermann Göring* which employed 700,000 workers and absorbed 400 million RM of investment. Göring was also to become responsible for removing Jews from German economic life and for the exploitation of conquered territories.

KEY TERM

Blitzkrieg This term, meaning 'lightning war', describes the tactics used by the German military in this period. They integrated air strikes and tank attacks to ensure rapid progress.

Göring warned Hitler of a war with Britain and France and helped to organise the Munich Conference in September 1938. Although he was appointed a Reichmarshall as a result of the Luftwaffe success during the **blitzkrieg** of 1939–40, his reputation was undermined by defeat in the Battle of Britain and the failure to prevent British bombing of Germany. Despite this, Göring was appointed official deputy to Hitler in June 1941 and in July he ordered Reinhard Heydrich to prepare a 'general solution of the Jewish question'.

After 1942, Göring's position declined rapidly. He was blamed for the failure to prepare the economy for total war and was sidelined by the appointment of Speer as Armaments Minister in 1942. Increasingly disabled by pain from a wound suffered in the Munich Putsch and by his addiction to morphine, Göring withdrew from politics and spent much of his time decorating his hunting lodge at Karinhall with art treasures looted from occupied lands. In his absence he was easily undermined by his rivals Speer, Göbbels and, especially, Martin Bormann. In April 1945 he was accused of treachery by Bormann and Hitler expelled him from all offices. He was arrested by the Americans and after defending himself at the Nuremberg trials, he committed suicide.

Joseph Göbbels

Göbbels joined the Nazi Party in 1925 as a supporter of the radical ideas of Gregor Strasser. He soon became the party's expert on propaganda and was appointed *Gauleiter* (party leader) of Berlin in 1926. Göbbels invented the 'Hitler Myth', publishing pamphlets and organising demonstrations and election campaigns. In January 1933 he was appointed Minister of Propaganda and Popular Enlightenment. He immediately took control of newspapers, films, radio and the arts. Göbbels was a master of publicity, carefully exploiting the Reichstag fire in February 1933, the burning of books in May 1933 and the Berlin Olympics in 1936.

Göbbels

Göbbels was violently anti-Semitic (anti-Jewish). He was the author of the Nuremberg Laws of 1935 and the organiser of the *Kristallnacht* attack on the Jews in November 1938. He also organised the 'Eternal Jew' exhibition in Berlin and produced the anti-Semitic film *Jud Suss* in 1937. His affair with the Czech actress Lida Baarova, and his opposition to war in 1939, led to him temporarily losing favour with Hitler. However, his successful war propaganda and anti-Semitism saw him restored to favour by 1942. Following the defeat at Stalingrad, Göbbels argued for a policy of 'total war' in a speech at the Berlin Sportsplatz in February 1943.

Göbbels played a vital part in repressing the July Bomb Plot in 1944 and was awarded with the title Reich Plenipotentiary for Total War Mobilisation. At the end of the war he proposed a policy of scorched earth and all-out resistance in the face of allied advances. He attempted to make several deals with the British and Americans. Together with his wife Magda and their six children, Göbbels remained with Hitler in his bunker to the end. He witnessed Hitler's testament and committed suicide with his wife after first killing all their children.

Heinrich Himmler

Himmler

Himmler joined the Nazi Party in 1922 and took part in the Munich Putsch in 1923. In 1929 he was appointed head of Hitler's personal bodyguard, the SS, and in 1930 he was elected to the Reichstag. His thirst for power and organisational ability enabled him to increase the strength of the SS from 200 in 1929 to 52,000 by 1933. In September 1933, Himmler took control of all political police units and became head of the Prussian police and Gestapo in April 1934. His main role was to secure Hitler's dictatorship through state terror. He set up the first concentration camp in Dachau in 1933 and masterminded the Night of the Long Knives which smashed the power of the SA and led to the dominance of the SS.

Himmler believe that Aryan racial superiority could only be achieved with the elimination of inferior social and racial groups. He tried to make the SS a racial elite. He was a leading supporter of the Final Solution in 1941 and urged SS officers to fulfil their task of exterminating Europe's Jews at a speech at Poznan in 1943. Himmler controlled the political administration in the occupied territories and in August 1943 he was made Minister of the Interior. After the July Bomb Plot in 1944, he became Commander-in-Chief of the reserve army. Convinced that Germany was on the verge of collapse by February 1945, he tried to make peace with the Allies and he offered himself as leader of a new German state. Hitler immediately stripped him of all his offices. He was arrested by British troops in May 1945. On 23 May he committed suicide.

Rudolf Hess

Rudolf Hess was inspired to join the Nazi Party in 1920 when he heard Hitler speak. He took part in the Munich Putsch in 1923 and helped Hitler write *Mein Kampf*. As a reward for his absolute loyalty and work in the Nazi Party organisation, Hitler appointed him Deputy Leader and Reich Minister without Portfolio in 1933. He joined the secret Cabinet Council in 1938 and the Ministerial Council for the Reich Defence in 1939. On the outbreak of war, he was the third most important Nazi after Hitler and Göring.

Hess

Hess had always been a strong supporter of the idea of *Lebensraum* in the East and he feared that war with Britain and Russia would end in German defeat. On 10 May 1941, he sensationally flew to Scotland in an unofficial attempt to secure peace with Britain. He was imprisoned and Hitler declared him insane. He was sentenced to life imprisonment at the Nuremberg Trials in 1946. He died in Spandau prison in Berlin in 1987.

Martin Bormann

By the end of the Second World War, Martin Bormann was the second most powerful Nazi after Hitler. He joined the Nazi Party in 1927 and, because of his dedication and efficiency, he was appointed to the staff of Rudolf Hess in 1934. After helping to establish party control over the civil service, he became Hitler's Private Secretary in 1935. This position gave Bormann considerable power. It also allowed him to promote his racist and atheistic policies.

Bormann

Bormann's influence grew after the flight of Hess to Scotland in 1941 and again as Hitler withdrew from public life after the defeat at Stalingrad in 1943. In the bunker, Bormann controlled all access to Hitler and was able to undermine his rivals. In 1943 he attempted to use the *Gauleiters* to oppose Speer and in 1945 he engineered the expulsion of both Göring and Himmler from the party. Bormann witnessed Hitler's marriage to Eva Braun and his last 'political testament' and supervised the handover of power to Admiral Dönitz. He attempted to escape from the bunker on 1 May, but was almost certainly killed in Berlin soon after.

Albert Speer

Albert Speer joined the Nazi Party in 1931 and became Hitler's favourite architect on the death of Paul Troost in 1934. He developed the Nazi style of politics, i.e., parades and rallies, and was commissioned by Hitler to design the new Reich Chancellery in Berlin and the Party Palace in Nuremberg. In 1937 Speer was made responsible for the rebuilding of Berlin and other German cities in a neo-classical monumental style. He was also in charge of the 'Beauty of Labour' Department of the German Labour Front and was elected to the Reichstag in 1941. He joined the Central Planning Office in 1942 and succeeded Fritz Todt as Minister of Armaments and War Production.

Speer

Speer transformed the German war economy. Under his direction it became much more productive and efficient. At his trial Speer denied all knowledge of the Final Solution but accepted that the Nazi regime was morally guilty. He was sentenced to 20 years in Spandau prison. During his imprisonment he wrote *Inside the Third Reich*, which was a detailed account of his years as part of the Nazi regime. He died in London on 1 September 1981.

THE NAZI PARTY, 1919–29

KEY PERSON

Anton Drexler was a Munich locksmith. He founded the German Workers' Party as a nationalist and anti-Semitic organisation.

The Nazi Party was born of humble origins. It was founded by **Anton Drexler** in January 1919 as the German Workers' Party. It developed against a background of political turmoil as the new Weimar Republic struggled to establish itself. It assumed its new name, the National Socialist German Workers' Party (NSDAP) and a 25-point programme at the Hofbrauhaus meeting in Munich in Bavaria in February 1920. Included in this manifesto, written by Drexler and Hitler, were themes that remained constant throughout the 1920s and beyond:

- The revision of the Treaty of Versailles and the ending of reparations. By revision of the treaty the Nazis meant the scrapping of Article 231 by which Germany accepted guilt for the war.
- Citizenship of the German state to be given to those of German blood. To the Nazis, this automatically excluded the Jews.
- *Lebensraum* (living space) for the German people.
- The creation of a strong government.
- War profiteering (making money from war) to be made a criminal offence.
- Large department stores to be divided up and leased to small traders.

The early years

Because of the work of Hitler and other members, including **Ernst Röhm, Alfred Rosenberg** and **Dietrich Eckhart**, the new party became one of the more noticeable amongst the many splinter groups of the right. This was partly because of Hitler's talent as a public speaker. In December 1920, the party increased its membership and was able to buy a local newspaper which it named the *Volkischer Beobachter* (*People's Observer*). In the following three years, Hitler consolidated his leadership of and influence on the party, becoming chairman in July 1921. This was followed by the creation of the **SA** that was to become the paramilitary wing of the party. As Germany was in political turmoil, so the SA was involved in widespread political violence and thuggery. On 4 November 1921 it engaged in a running battle with socialists at a political meeting in Munich and in street violence also against the socialists in Coburg in October 1922.

The Munich Putsch. By mid 1923 the party had some 55,000 members, many of whom were attracted by the Nazi's 'catch-all' manifesto and the radical nationalism of the movement. Throughout the **Ruhr crisis** of 1923,

KEY PEOPLE

Ernst Röhm Influential amongst the *Freikorps* – group of nationalist soldiers – Röhm helped to ease Hitler's introduction into politics and created the Nazi storm troopers, the SA. Although estranged from Hitler from 1925 to 1930, he returned to run the SA until he was killed on Hitler's orders in the 'Night of the Long Knives' purge in 1934.

Alfred Rosenberg and Dietrich Eckhart Both Rosenberg and Eckhart helped to shape the Nazi *Weltanschauung* (worldview) throughout the 1920s and 1930s. Eckhart published the first Nazi paper, the *Volkischer Beobachter*, until his death in 1923. Rosenberg continued to be the leading Nazi thinker, helping to create the destructive pseudo-scientific philosophy with which much of the party's anti-Semitism was justified. He was tried at Nuremberg in 1946 and hanged by the Allies.

KEY TERMS

SA stands for *Sturmabteilung* or storm troopers.

Ruhr crisis The Ruhr crisis of 1923 was prompted by the French invasion of the Ruhr, Germany's rich industrial area. The French took over mines and industry in retaliation for Germany's non-payment of reparations.

KEY TERM

Munich Putsch The attempted takeover in 1923 came about because of tension between the Reich or central government and the local government in Bavaria over the refusal of the latter to arrest nationalists. The aim of the uprising was to create a dictatorship with General Ludendorff as President.

KEY THEME

Hitler's imprisonment The judges at the Munich trial were sympathetic to Hitler's views and he was treated well in jail. Hitler was allowed to receive visitors and he lived a comfortable lifestyle in Landsberg castle. Such was the sympathy of the authorities that Hitler only served nine months of his prison sentence.

KEY TERM

The concept of **'Führerprinzip'** placed Hitler at the centre of the Nazi Party. Each party region had a local leader, a *Gauleiter*, who was responsible to Hitler alone.

Hitler and the Nazi press kept up its barrage against the Weimar Republic. After a failed attempt at direct action on 1 May, the Nazis attempted a further coup on 8/9 November. Known as the **Munich Putsch**, it was in many ways a farcical failure. On the evening of 8 November Hitler and 600 SA soldiers stormed a public meeting in Munich, Hitler declaring that 'The national revolution has broken out'. The following day Hitler, Hermann Göring, Julius Streicher and General Ludendorff led a march into the centre of Munich only to find their way barred by the police. Sixteen Nazis were killed during a brief street battle in which the Nazis were humiliated. However, Hitler turned defeat into a kind of triumph. His trial for high treason in February/March 1924 gave him and his comrades a nationwide platform for his beliefs, transforming the whole event into a propaganda coup. The sympathy of the judges ensured he received the minimum term of five years' **imprisonment**. The episode convinced Hitler that the Nazis could not come to power by using violence alone.

'Mein Kampf'. Imprisoned in Landsberg Castle in 1924, Hitler wrote *Mein Kampf* (*My Struggle*) which was to become his enduring political testament. In what is a generally incoherent and rambling text, Hitler developed his *Weltanschauung* (worldview or outlook). The main points were the elimination of Jewry from German life, the provision of *Lebensraum* (living space) in the east for the Germanic peoples and the destruction of communism.

Party reorganisation

In May 1924, the Nazis, in alliance with other parties of the right, won an impressive 1.9 million votes (6.5 per cent) in elections to the Reichstag. By the December elections of the same year, that figure had fallen to around 907,000 votes (3.0 per cent). Two months after Hitler's release from prison on 27 February 1925, the NSDAP was refounded. Throughout the year the party was reorganised into a centralised, bureaucratic entity. An index of all members was created and, at the party conference at Bamberg in February 1926, a new autocratic and centralised structure was discussed which stressed complete obedience to Hitler, the ***Führerprinzip***, and adherence to the 'Programme of 1920'. This was formally accepted at a membership meeting of the party in May 1926.

Legality and control of the SA. In the light of the failure of the Munich Putsch, Hitler insisted that all action had to be dictated by the policy of '**legality**'. This was despite the opposition of some in the party such as **Gregor Strasser.** As part of this drive, Hitler attempted to calm the SA. The staged march past by many of its members at Weimar in July 1926 was intended to show the public at large the extent of party control over its paramilitary arm. In the summer of 1926, Captain Franz von Pfeffer was appointed leader of the SA to implement guidelines on the movement's role. From now on the SA was to undertake more mundane roles such as training and the stewarding of rallies. This did not prevent SA street fighting in cities such as Berlin and Munich, a fact that was to cause considerable tension within the movement.

There were other administrative and organisational reforms undertaken in these years. In 1926 the Hitler Youth and the Nazi Students' Association were founded. At the Nuremberg Party Congress in 1927, further reorganisation took place with unsuitable ***Gauleiters*** being replaced and the central bureaucracy further reorganised. Despite such changes, the performance of the party in the election of May 1928 was dismal, registering only around 800,000 votes (2.6 per cent) and gaining only 12 seats in the new Reichstag.

Growing national exposure in 1929. Such a poor overall result masks the fact that when campaigning on specific regional issues, the Nazis were able to attract a significantly higher proportion of the vote, e.g., in 1928 in the agricultural north-west. The disappointment at the ballot box acted as a stimulus to further reorganisation and October 1928 saw the creation of the first Nazi professional body, the Association of National Socialist Jurists. This was to be followed in 1929 by similar bodies for doctors, teachers and students. Of far greater significance to the fortunes of the party was the opportunity presented by the campaign against the **Young Plan** from the summer of 1929. Formed by the leader of

KEY TERMS

Legality The policy of 'legality' was based on Hitler's insisitence that power could not be achieved through a putsch, as was attempted in 1923. Instead, legal means would be used, foremost being elections.

'Gauleiters' were Nazi regional bosses.

KEY PERSON

Gregor Strasser was a leading Nazi and rival to Hitler for the leadership of the party in the early 1920s. At this time there were many members of the party who wanted to see the destruction of the capitalist economic system in Germany. Strasser informally led this wing of the party and promoted these views at the Bamberg Party Congress. Hitler was concerned that such ideas might lose the Nazis the support of the middle classes. Hitler and Strasser argued in 1932 about Strasser's role in the party and the state. Strasser was murdered on the Night of the Long Knives in June 1934.

the DNVP, Alfred Hugenberg, the Reich Committee for a Referendum to Oppose the Young Plan included respected national political figures of the right, including Franz Seldte of the *Stahlhelm* movement. Hugenberg also invited the NSDAP to join the coalition, which Hitler accepted but only after prolonged negotiations on finance and guarantees of Nazi independence. The subsequent referendum in December 1929 on the so-called **Freedom Law** resulted in humiliation for the coalition, only 13.8 per cent voting in favour. The campaign, though, had given considerable national exposure to both Hitler and the spectacular Nazi rallies such as that of 200,000 party members and supporters at Nuremberg in August 1929. The impact at the ballot box was immediate: local council elections in November 1929 saw a significant rise in the Nazi vote and in the state election in Thuringia in December they polled 11.3 per cent.

The Wall Street Crash

The **Wall Street Crash** and the rise in unemployment had an important effect in creating further division in German politics. In March 1930, the Müller cabinet broke up after the strains of the coalition became all too apparent over the issue of unemployment insurance. A new cabinet was formed on 30 March under the leadership of the **Heinrich Brüning** of the Centre Party, but it was heavily influenced by President Hindenburg. Although commanding only minority support in the Reichstag, Hindenburg made it clear that if the government were brought down by a vote of no confidence he would use **Article 48** of the constitution to rule by decree. The rejection of the cabinet's financial bill in July led to it being reintroduced by decree. A motion was immediately passed in the Reichstag condemning this tactic and demanding the withdrawal of the decree as the Reichstag had a right to do in the constitution. The President's response was to dissolve the Reichstag and call an election for September 1930 (the finance bill finally being introduced again by decree).

KEY TERMS

The **Young Plan** set a time limit of 59 years for the repayment of reparations and cut the annual amount Germany was obliged to pay. Agreement to the plan was linked to a withdrawal of allied troops from the Rhineland five years earlier than previously planned.

The **Freedom Law** included the repudiation of the 'war guilt' Article 231 of the Treaty of Versailles, immediate withdrawal of allied troops from German soil and any politician who signed compromising treaties with foreign powers to be deemed a traitor!

The Wall Street Crash. Worldwide bankruptcies and the closure of business followed the Wall Street Crash in New York in October 1929. This hit German industry hard, in part because its growth in the 1920s had been funded to a large extent by American capital that was now withdrawn.

KEY PERSON

Heinrich Brüning was Chancellor of the Weimar Republic from 1930 to 1932. As a member of the Centre Party, he increasingly used Article 48 as the means by which he could govern. Brüning failed to deal with the worsening economic situation of the time. He did, however, end reparations in 1932.

THE COLLAPSE OF DEMOCRACY

1930 and the growth in Nazi support

This period of turmoil in national politics also saw significant changes at local level. In June 1930, the Nazis won 14.4 per cent of the vote in elections for the Saxony ***Landtag***, over 9 per cent higher than the previous year. The previous spring, Joseph Göbbels had been appointed to lead the party's propaganda unit and he organised the planning and execution of the comprehensive electioneering programme, not only in Saxony but also in the nationwide polls. The result in the September election was a triumph for the Nazis. Not only did their representation in the Reichstag increase from 12 to 107 seats, but also the vote they captured increased from 800,000 in 1928 to 6.4 million in 1930. As a result, the reformed Brüning cabinet governed with even less support and had to rely on the 'toleration' of the SPD and, ever increasingly, the use of Article 48.

Growth in the party membership. The election victory of 1930 acted as an important stimulus to Nazi Party membership. Between September and the end of the year nearly 100,000 new members joined up and the period saw spectacular growth in sectional party organisations. Of particular note was the expansion of the NS *Agrarpolitische Apparat* (AA), founded by **Walther Darré** in 1930. Created with the expressed aims of extending Nazi influence in the countryside, and infiltrating existing farmers' organisations, the AA was highly successful.

Revolt of the SA, 1931. Similar campaign tactics to those used at national level meant that the momentum of election success was maintained. Throughout 1931 the Nazis averaged around 40 per cent in local elections. However, the debate over 'legality' within the party, and in particular the SA, persisted. In March 1931 the leader of the Berlin SA, **Walther Stennes**, and some of his members rebelled against the orders of Hitler to obey the law. The revolt failed to win the support of the majority of SA troopers although it highlighted the tensions in the Nazi movement. This should also be placed in the context of the

KEY TERMS

Article 48 of the constitution allowed the President, in times of emergency, to pass laws (decrees) without the agreement of the Reichstag.

'Landtag' was a regional parliament.

KEY THEME

Who supported the Nazis? Support for the Nazis came from a number of areas: youth, the lower middle classes, industrialists (especially after the Wall Street Crash in 1929), nationalists (who wanted to overturn the terms of the Treaty of Versailles) and those people with anti-semitic or anti-communist views.

KEY PEOPLE

Walther Darré was the leading Nazi expert on agricultural affairs. He was also put in charge of the SS's Central Office for Race and Resettlement.

Walther Stennes was a good example of an SA leader who disliked Hitler's insistence on the tactics of legality. In February 1931 Hitler issued a decree ordering the SA to end street fighting. Stennes refused. After the failure of his revolt he joined forces with Gregor Strasser, the other leading Nazi dissident.

crackdown in 1931 on the SA in Prussia on the orders of the Prussian Prime Minister, Otto Brann.

1931: Economic collapse and Nazi opportunity

It was the economic collapse in the summer of 1931 which again gave the Nazis opportunity and turned attention away from their tactics and divisions. The main aim of Brüning's economic and financial policy had been to remove the burden of **reparations**. A combination of an impending freeze on payments and the possibility of an Austro-German trade agreement prompted a flight of foreign capital out of Germany. The result in July 1931 was the collapse of the Austrian Creditanstalt Bank, followed by financial panic and the closure of all German banks for a three-week period. The political confusion which followed, and the rise in unemployment (which in September stood at 4.3 million), prompted Hugenberg to attempt to re-form a 'National Opposition' of the right with the aim of bringing down Brüning's government. The so-called 'Harzberg Front' of *Stahlhelm*, DNVP and Nazis met in October 1931 but collapsed after internal arguing.

KEY THEME

Reparations The issue of reparations was taken seriously by US President Hoover who proposed a suspension of payments for a year. The international commission formed to investigate the problem further recommended the ending of payments, which was agreed at the Lausanne Conference in the summer 1932. By this time Brüning had long since left office.

1932: Political intrigue and Nazi electoral success

The presidential election of March/April 1932 saw Hindenburg returned to office, but of significance for the future was the vote registered for Hitler. Despite saturation electioneering, the Nazi leader managed to poll only 30.1 per cent on the first ballot and 36.8 per cent on the second, compared to Hindenburg's 49.6 per cent and 53 per cent. Yet the Nazis still managed to present such a defeat as a success as their vote had more than doubled from the Reichstag election.

Political intrigue. Defeat, however, resulted in the emergency decree of April 1932 which banned the SA and SS, mainly in response to the growing street violence and evidence that the Nazis had been drawing up plans to stage a coup if Hitler had won the election. Such a move was taken against the background of intrigue amongst the President's ministers and advisers. The Minister of the Interior, **General Gröner**, who had introduced the ban, was undermined by a whispering campaign led by **General von Schleicher**, but with the full backing of the Nazis.

KEY PEOPLE

General von Schleicher became an increasingly important political figure in the last years of the Weimar Republic. As a leading army officer, he had some influence with President Hindenburg. In December 1932 he was made Chancellor. Schleicher then attempted to form a government with Nazi support, but failed. The Nazis murdered him in June 1934 because Hitler was convinced that he was plotting against them.

General Gröner was the strong man of the Brüning cabinet. As Minister of Defence 1929–32 and Minister of the Interior 1931–32 he tried to protect the Republic by banning the SS and SA.

Schleicher met with Hitler on 8 May 1932; Hitler accepted a new presidential cabinet in return for the removal of Brüning and the lifting of the ban on the SA and SS.

So now Schleicher could influence the removal of Brüning and help bring about a more right-wing government. Gröner resigned from the cabinet after being shouted down by Nazi deputies in the Reichstag on 10 May. On 29 May Hindenburg demanded Brüning's resignation, which he received the next day. A new cabinet was formed with **Franz von Papen** as Chancellor and Schleicher the new Minister of Defence. The date for new elections to the Reichstag was set for the end of July and the ban on the SA lifted on 16 June. The street violence in the run-up to the election left over 100 dead. This violence was used as the perfect excuse for the removal of the SPD dominated Prussian government, which was overthrown by Papen on 20 July 1932. The SPD failed to react and the unions had been weakened by the division on the left between KPD and SPD. The elections to the Reichstag eleven days later saw the Nazis increase their vote to 37.3 per cent, which translated into 230 seats. The Nazis became the largest party in the Reichstag.

KEY PERSON

Franz von Papen was a conservative politician who played a leading role in bringing Hitler to power. Chosen by Hindenburg to replace Brüning as Chancellor in June 1932, he was dismissed in December of the same year. To get his own back on Schleicher (who had played a part in his dismissal) he persuaded Hindenburg to appoint Hitler as Chancellor in January 1933. Papen became Vice-Chancellor in Hitler's first cabinet.

1932–3: THE NAZIS ARE BROUGHT TO POWER

Despite such apparent success, the election did not give the Nazis an outright majority or automatic power, Papen refusing to hand over the chancellorship to Hitler. As a result, the newly elected Reichstag was immediately dissolved on 12 September after the government lost a vote of no confidence by 512 votes to 42. The new election in November saw a fall in the Nazi vote of some 4 per cent (34 seats) but they were still the largest party. This result simply reinforced the political stalemate. Hindenburg wished to continue presidential government, but refused to appoint Hitler as Chancellor without his having first achieved a majority in the Reichstag. However, the Nazi leader had the ability (in **coalition with the Centre Party**) to vote down a government at will. The only alternative for the establishment seemed to be to rule without the Reichstag and suppress all opposition.

KEY THEME

The Nazi coalition with the Centre Party The Catholic Centre Party was an important ally of the Nazis in 1932 and 1933. Despite the threat the Nazis posed to established religion, Hitler manage to reassure Catholics with promises of protection.

Party	September 1930			July 1932			November 1932			March 1933		
DNVP	2.6	7.0%	41	2.2	5.9%	37	3.0	8.3%	52	3.1	8.0%	52
DVP	1.6	4.5%	30	0.4	1.2%	7	0.7	1.9%	11	0.4	1.1%	2
Centre	4.1	11.8%	68	4.6	12.5%	75	4.2	11.9%	70	4.4	11.2%	74
BVP	1.0	3.0%	19	1.2	3.2%	22	1.09	3.1%	20	1.07	2.7%	18
DDP	1.3	3.8%	20	0.37	1.0%	4	0.34	1.0%	2	0.33	0.9%	5
SPD	8.6	24.5%	143	8.0	21.6%	133	7.2	20.4%	121	7.18	18.3%	120
KPD	4.6	13.1%	77	5.3	14.3%	89	5.98	16.9%	100	4.8	12.3%	81
NSDAP	6.4	18.3%	107	13.7	37.3%	230	11.7	33.1%	196	17.3	43.9%	288

Elections to the Reichstag, 1930–3. Figures are number of votes (in millions), percentage of the votes cast, number of seats gained.

In attempting to find a way out, Hindenburg sacked Papen and appointed Schleicher as Chancellor on 3 December. His first act was to attempt to draw the Nazis into a coalition by offering the vice-chancellorship to Gregor Strasser. The leading Nazi's instinct was to accept such an offer as the only way the party was going to gain power but he was forced to back down and resign after a fierce battle with Hitler. Without the Nazis, the Schleicher government lacked support, a fact which soon became apparent with the strong opposition to its economic policy presented on 15 December.

KEY THEME

Hitler's first cabinet The new cabinet in fact only included three Nazis, Hitler as Chancellor, Wilhelm Frick as Minister for the Interior and Hermann Göring as Minister without Portfolio. The Vice-Chancellor was to be Franz von Papen and other parties of the right were well represented: Hugenberg of the DNVP was put in charge of the Economics Ministry and Franz Seldte of the *Stahlhelm* was made Minister of Labour.

Hitler's first cabinet

From 4 January 1933, Papen and Hitler held talks about the composition of a future government based on a broad nationalist coalition very similar to the Harzberg Front. Support for such a coalition came from a variety of sources, including the Agrarian League and industrialist organisations. The leading banker Hjalmar Schacht supported Hitler and wrote to the President backing his cause. This support had an impact on Hindenburg who turned to Papen to form a viable government, particularly as it was clear that Schleicher could command little support in the Reichstag. As negotiations between Papen and Hitler progressed, the former conceded the role of Chancellor to the latter, but in a cabinet that would be a coalition of the right. It was this factor and the acceptability of the prospective minister of Defence, General von Blomberg, which persuaded Hindenburg to accept Schleicher's resignation on 27 January and to install Hitler as Chancellor on the 30th.

Hitler accepting the Chancellorship from Hindenburg.

SUMMARY QUESTIONS

1 Write a list of reasons why the Nazis came to power in 1933.

2 Describe the role of Hindenburg in Hitler's rise to power.

AS SECTION: NAZI GERMANY, 1933–45

Introduction

From 1933 to 1945, Nazism dominated Germany. However, such domination was not immediate. From 1933 to 1934 the Nazis **consolidated power** using a mixture of violent and legal methods. The new Nazi state revolved around the personality of the Führer, Adolf Hitler. Below Hitler the state was chaotic. Increasingly important in the running of the state was the *Schutzstaffel* better known as the SS. With its independent organisation and considerable influence the SS became a 'state within a state'.

Nazi **economic policy** was mainly aimed at rearming Germany and preparing it for war. However Hitler and his economic advisers had other important priorities. Given the high levels of unemployment in 1933, it was politically important for the regime to reduce the number of Germans out of work. It was also important for the regime not to reduce living standards in the drive for self-sufficiency (autarky) from 1936 onwards. During the war, the economy was not fully geared to war production until 1942.

Hitler attempted to transform **society** by creating a racially pure national community, a *Volksgemeinschaft*. The Nazis had very clear ideas about the role of women and the importance of youth and these were reflected in policies directed at these two groups. However, there were obstacles to the ability of the Nazis to transform society, the Protestant and Catholic Churches remaining an alternative influence throughout.

At the heart of Nazi ideology was a deep-seated **anti-Semitism**. The process of Nazi action against the Jews of Germany was clear. Firstly they were identified and separated out from the rest of society. This process was accompanied by propaganda and indoctrination of young people. The next step was a move to violence on a large scale. In 1938 an important turning point took place with the attack on Jews and their property in what became known as *Kristallnacht*. The war years saw the horror of the Holocaust and the extermination of around 6 million of Europe's Jews.

The Nazis faced little organised **opposition** to their rule. Instead opposition was isolated. The most powerful non-Nazi force was the army. However, despite isolated examples of opposition, it was not until the war was nearly lost that any significant attempt was made to remove Hitler.

Hitler's **foreign policy** was guided by his central beliefs: German nationalism, the destruction of the Treaty of Versailles, the creation of *Lebensraum* and his fierce anti-Semitism and anti-communism. Early success in the war from 1939–42 was followed by defeat on the Eastern Front in the Soviet Union and on the Western Front in France, followed by the invasion of Germany in 1945.

CHAPTER 9

The Nazi consolidation of power

THE END OF THE CONSTITUTION

The Reichstag fire and its aftermath. Those who believed that they had 'tamed' Hitler and his movement were to be proved very much mistaken. Although Hitler's 'Appeal to the German People' broadcast on 1 February was conservative in nature, the SA began to take revenge on the enemies of National Socialism. Twenty-one days later a decree in Prussia (which had fallen under the jurisdiction of Reich Commissioner Göring) resulted in the police being reinforced by 'volunteers' – the SA. On the 27th of the same month, the Reichstag in Berlin was gutted by fire. A young communist, Marinus van der Lubbe, took the blame for burning down the Reichstag. The Nazis exploited real fears of a communist-led uprising to justify a clampdown on the left (including the arrest of KPD politicians). They also managed to persuade Hindenburg to issue the decree **For the Protection of People and State** which ended civil liberties guaranteed in the Weimar constitution.

KEY THEME

The decree **For the Protection of People and State**, introduced to guard against communist acts of violence endangering the state, allowed for imprisonment without trial, the ending of press freedom and the ending of the right of assembly, amongst other restrictions. It also allowed the central government to take over local state government (the *Länder*) and introduced the death penalty for certain offences.

Election 1933. Despite a campaign of irregularity and intimidation organised by Joseph Göbbels, the Nazis failed to win an absolute majority in the March election, polling 43.9 per cent nationally. However, the Nazis achieved a majority by gaining the support of the nationalist DNVP which won 52 seats to add to the 288 seats won by the Nazis. As all communist KPD deputies were barred from the Reichstag (despite gaining 4.8 million votes), the result gave Hitler a distinct political advantage.

Hitler seeks legality. However, Hitler was not yet the dictator he wanted to be. To change the constitution he needed two-thirds of the seats in the Reichstag, which he did not have. He was keen to impress Hindenburg and the wider establishment that he could control the more **radical**

elements in the Nazi movement. On 21 March 1933, Hitler held an impressive display of his legality and respectability at the ceremonial opening of the Reichstag which was held in Potsdam, the historic seat of the Prussian monarchy and army. President Hindenburg, the son of Kaiser Wilhelm II and many leading generals witnessed Hitler's commitment to traditional German values. However, Hitler's intentions were more clearly seen in a piece of legislation introduced the same day. The Malicious Practices Law banned criticism of the regime and its policies.

The Enabling Act, 1933. The opening of business of the new Reichstag on 23 March was marked by the presentation of an **Enabling Act**. By the terms of the Act, the government gave the power to pass laws to the cabinet which allowed the government to alter the constitution as it saw fit. It granted Hitler four years of power as a dictator. It was passed by an overwhelming vote of 441 to 94. This was achieved because the communist deputies were banned and the Nazis won the support of the Centre Party. Their 74 deputies were won over to vote for the Enabling Act by a number of reasons:

- Franz von Papen, a leading member of the Centre Party, was Vice-Chancellor and his influence was reassuring.
- Hitler promised that he would not restrict Catholic influence in education.
- Many Catholic deputies were intimidated by the threats of the SA and had no wish to suffer the same fate as the communists.

Only the much harassed SPD deputies voted against the Enabling Act. After this, the government no longer had to rely on the Reichstag or emergency powers to legislate. The Weimar constitution was dead.

'GLEICHSCHALTUNG' (COORDINATION)

As part of the consolidation of Nazi power, Hitler attempted to coordinate all aspects of German political and social life under Nazi control.

KEY TERM

Radical elements There were many in the Nazi movement, and especially in the SA, who hoped that a Nazi government would introduce far-reaching economic and social changes. Some wanted the government to challenge Germany's capitalists. Nearly all Nazi radicals wanted to see the government discriminate against the Jews from the start.

Local government. The next step the Nazis took after the Enabling Act was the destruction of local state government. Every German region, such as Bavaria, had its own state government (*diet*). On 31 March 1933 these were all dissolved by the Minister of the Interior, Wilhelm Frick, with the exception of the *diet* of Prussia. They were ordered to reconvene but with a membership which reflected the recent elections from which communists had been barred. New state governors, *Reichsstadthalter*, were appointed with full powers to introduce Nazi policies. The centralisation of the state was completed in January 1934 by the abolition of the upper house of the Reichstag (the Reichsrat); the provincial governments and the local governments were made completely subordinate to the central government.

Civil service. By the Law for the Restoration of the Professional Civil Service of 7 April 1933, Jews and political opponents of the Nazis were thrown out of the civil service. To bring the running of party and state closer together, the Nazis passed the Law to Ensure the Unity of Party and State on 1 December 1933.

The German Labour Front. On 1 May 1933, the trade unions enjoyed their traditional May Day celebrations. The following day the offices of all unions were taken over and trade unions banned. A committee under Dr Robert Ley was set up 'for the protection of German Labour'. On 10 May the German Labour Front (DAF) was established under Ley's leadership. The Nazis aimed to set up an organisation which would control labour and end disputes by promoting harmony. Not only workers, but also professionals and management groups were encouraged to join the Labour Front. On 16 January 1934 a new Labour Charter was announced. This charter summed up the ideas of the Nazis on economic cooperation between labour and management. In reality, the Labour Front curbed the influence of the workers. It did have real significance, as by 1935 it represented around 20 million workers, the whole of the German workforce.

Abolition of political parties. The process of creating a dictatorship also included the disbanding of all other political parties.

- After the Reichstag fire the communist KPD had been outlawed.
- In June 1933 the SPD was banned and the DNP, DVP and DNVP disbanded themselves.
- To avoid confrontation with the Nazis, the Centre Party followed suit on 5 July.
- The actions of these parties made it easier for Hitler to abolish organised political opposition with the Law against the Formation of Parties of 14 July 1933.
- Similarly, professional groups lost their independent organisations and were forced to join Nazi bodies.

NIGHT OF THE LONG KNIVES

Tension between establishment and SA. By the spring of 1934 Hitler's dictatorship seemed secure. Germany was a one-party state in which the rule of law had been abolished in a permanent state of emergency. Left-wing opposition had been ruthlessly repressed. However, conservative forces threatened Hitler in business, the civil service and, above all, in the army. It was clear to many that the plan to trap Hitler in a conservative coalition had failed. Conservatives were alarmed at the lawlessness of the Nazi government and the actions of the SA in particular. But Hitler also felt threatened by the personal ambitions of Ernst Röhm who was leader of the two million strong SA. Röhm disliked the cautious compromises Hitler had made with the establishment. He believed that Germany needed a revolution. He also wanted the SA to amalgamate with the army to form a People's Army under his leadership. Such a viewpoint was treated with suspicion amongst the generals of the **Reichswehr**.

Pressure mounts on Hitler. In April 1934, a group of leading generals demanded that Hitler discipline the Brownshirts of the SA. A call for a return to normal decencies and an end to the violence of the SA was made by Vice-Chancellor von Papen in June 1934. Hitler was

KEY TERM

'Reichswehr' was the name of the German army from 1933 to 1935. In this period the size of the army was restricted by the Treaty of Versailles to 100,000 men. Because of its size and because of its conservative nature, the *Reichswehr* was concerned about the growing size of the SA and Röhm's ambitions.

acutely aware that such conservative groups were still politically important because they had President Hindenburg's ear. Röhm had important enemies in the Nazi movement, most noticeably Hermann Göring and Heinrich Himmler. In April 1934, Göring made Himmler acting head of the Gestapo in Prussia. The two of them pressurised Hitler to take decisive action against Röhm and the SA to prevent a second revolution which might undermine the Nazi position. They argued that Hitler must move to limit the power of the SA.

The Blood Purge. Hitler acted against the SA on 30 June 1934, the so-called 'Night of the Long Knives'. With the excuse that the SA was on the verge of uprisings in Berlin and Munich, Hitler ordered a purge of the leadership of the SA. He travelled to Bavaria in person where he ordered the arrest of Röhm who was shot two days later. In all around 180 leading Nazis were executed. These included SA leaders such as Karl Ernst and Edmund Hennes. Others were also murdered, including ex-Chancellor von Schleicher and an old rival of Hitler's, Gregor Strasser. In all about 400 political opponents were killed.

KEY TERM

Führer was a term used to denote leader. Hitler added the powers of President to those he already had as Chancellor when Hindenburg died in 1934, and adopted the title, Führer.

HITLER BECOMES FÜHRER

The Night of the Long Knives was a vital step for the Nazis on the road to the consolidation of power. On 13 July 1934, Hitler formally explained to the Reichstag his reasons for purging the SA. He made no mention of those that had not been members of the SA but had been murdered. A law was put together by Wilhelm Frick, the Minister of the Interior, which declared Hitler's actions legal. The Reichstag quickly passed this law. Despite the murder of General von Schleicher, the Night of the Long Knives resulted in a closer alliance between Nazi state and army. The SS under Himmler saw its dominance within the Nazi state established.

Upon the peaceful death of President Hindenburg on 2 August, Hitler was able to abolish the position of President, assuming all powers for himself as **Führer** (leader) of the German state. On the initiative of the

A British cartoon published after the Night of the Long Knives in 1934.

Minister of Defence, Field Marshal Werner von Blomberg, all officers of the army were called on to take a personal **oath of loyalty** to the Führer. This was of critical importance in securing the dictatorship. On 19 August 1934 a plebiscite (vote) was held. The German people were asked to show whether they approved of Hitler becoming Führer. The result was a great victory for Nazi propaganda: 43.06 million Germans voted and of this figure 89.93 per cent voted 'Yes' in favour of Hitler. This was a crucial moment for the regime which was now more secure.

KEY THEME

Oath of loyalty This was an important turning point for Hitler. Because every member of the army swore an oath of loyalty to Hitler personally, it made opposition to him far less likely.

SUMMARY QUESTIONS

1 Explain the importance of the Night of the Long Knives.

2 Give three examples of how the Nazis consolidated power using legal means and three examples of how they consolidated power using violence and force.

CHAPTER 10

The Nazi state

THE CENTRAL ROLE OF HITLER

A portrait of Hitler painted by Heinrich Knirr in 1937.

In the Nazi state, Hitler made laws. He was the supreme master in the Nazi state. Around him were many institutions, which competed for his attention and influence. As the state developed, so laws were increasingly made by Führer decrees (*Erlasse*) which Hitler would sign or by Führer orders that were spoken. Hitler's authority came from his position at the centre of the Nazi movement. His was the final word in any dispute. In all policies he considered essential, Hitler made the key decisions, from the Night of the Long Knives in 1934 to the invasion of Poland in 1939 and the launching of the Final Solution in 1941. The problem was that at a lower decision-making level, Hitler's orders were often contradictory. Lammers, head of the Reich Chancellery, found it increasingly difficult to sort out the contradictions in government, partly because he had only joined the Nazi party in 1932 and therefore lacked influence over the party.

THE RELATIONSHIP BETWEEN PARTY AND STATE

Structure

The Nazi party was organised as a complex hierarchy with Hitler at the head of the movement. Below him in the hierarchy were 32 *Gauleiters* (district leaders), 760 *Kreisleiters* (circuit leaders), 21,000 *Ortsgruppenleiters* (local group leaders), 70,000 *Zellenleiters* (cell leaders) and 700,000 *Blockwarten* (block wardens). By 1938 the party had a membership of 5 million and there were some half a million party officials. Hitler's aim was that the party would involve itself in every aspect of German business and social life.

Führer Adolf Hitler	The undisputed leader of the party
Reichsleitung der NSDAP (Reich leadership)	Several Reich leaders had specific responsibilities, such as the party treasurer, and the Führer's deputy in charge of party affairs
Landesinspekteur (regional inspector)	Originally there were nine regional inspectors, each with responsibility for a *Gau*, but they were eventually replaced by the *Gauleiter*
Gauleiter (district leader)	There were 36 leaders of *Gaue* or districts, such as Saxony or Swabia. The number grew with the inclusion of Austria, Sudetenland and Danzig
Kreisleiter (Circuit leader)	The next lower administrative unit, equivalent to a rural council
Ortsgruppenleiter (local group leader)	Leaders responsible for a town section
Zellenleiter (cell leader)	Based on a neighbourhood (4 5 blocks of households) or employment unit
Blockwart (block warden)	The lowest officials just above the ordinary member
PG-Parteigenosse (Party comrade)	The ordinary members

The organisation of the Nazi Party.

As is shown above, the organisation of the Nazi Party was an important reason for the Nazis coming to power. However, the party's role in the running of the country after 1933 was poorly defined. The Law to Ensure Unity of Party and State of December 1933 did little to clarify the different roles each was expected to take. In a speech to *Gauleiters* on 2 February 1934, Hitler stressed the role of the party as being limited to spreading propaganda and supporting the government. But this line was partly due to Hitler's concern about the attitude of the establishment. Once the party had been purged at the Night of the Long Knives in June 1934, Hitler stressed that it was not to be powerless. In particular he saw it as an alternative to the civil service in terms of making policy and seeing that it had been carried through.

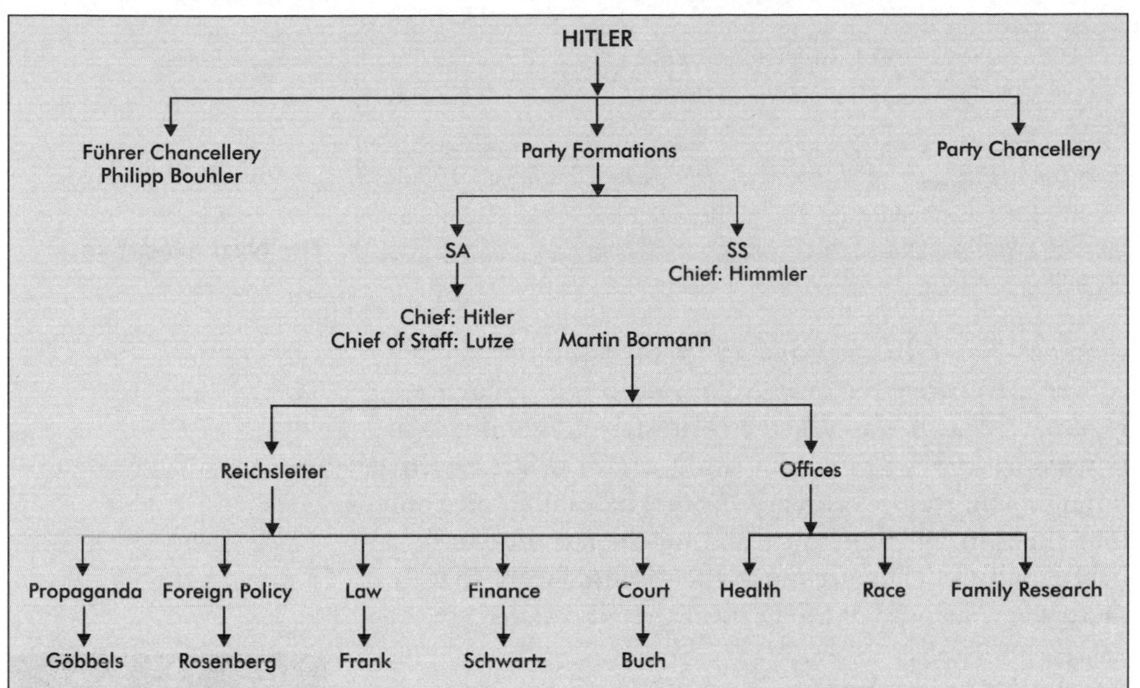

The structure of the Nazi Party.

However, throughout the period there was considerable rivalry between the party and the state which was never resolved. In 1934, by the Law for the Reconstruction of the Reich, Wilhelm Frick tried to put the newly created Reich Governors under the control of the Ministry of the Interior. It did not work. In most areas the Reich Governor argued bitterly with the head of the state government, the Minister-President. At a more local level, the party held greater sway through the offices of the *Gauleiters* who had often built up impressive local power bases. The district party leaders (*Kreisleiters*) also had political influence at a local level, especially after being given the right to choose local mayors by the Reich Local Government Law of January 1935.

KEY TERM

Cabinet Government In a cabinet government, a decision is made after discussion between the members. All members of the cabinet are then expected to accept the decision.

The decline of cabinet government. The traditional means of running the country was by **cabinet government**. Hitler's first cabinet included many non-Nazis, such as Alfred Hugenberg as Economics Minister (until June 1933). In the first year, Hitler accepted the cabinet as the formal means of government: in 1933 it met 72 times. However, by 1935 the Cabinet met only 12 times. Slowly Hitler removed from positions of influence all those who

Party leader and Head of State Adolf Hitler			
Presidential office	*Reich chancellery*	*Party chancellery*	*Führer's personal secretary*
Dr Meissner	Dr Lammers	Rudolf Hess	Philipp Bouhler

The Nazi executive.

were not Nazis. In 1937 and 1938, the last of the conservatives were removed from positions of influence – Hjalmar Schacht was sacked as Minister of Economics in November 1937, Konstantin von Neurath was removed as Foreign Minister in February 1938. The cabinet met only four times in 1936 and once and for the last time in February 1938. The decline in the cabinet meant that there was a vacuum at the heart of the Nazi state.

The Reich Chancellery. The Reich Chancellery, the head of which was **Hans-Heinrich Lammers**, took on this cabinet role as the co-ordinator of government. The role of the Reich Chancellery was to draw up legislation. The influence of Lammers in the years leading up to the Second World War was very great because he controlled the flow of information to Hitler. However, the Chancellery's position at the heart of government was weakened by new ministries which tended to act more independently than the old traditional ministries. By 1936 the police powers of the SS concentrated under Himmler meant that Lammers no longer had control of such issues. This was also the case with Hermann Göring, whose control of the Economics Ministry as part of the Four Year Plan office (set up in 1936) gave him sufficient political influence to go straight to Hitler.

KEY PERSON

Hans-Heinrich Lammers was an important part of Hitler's inner circle of advisers. He was a much trusted legal adviser of Hitler.

In 1943 Lammers was appointed to the Committee of Three which was to help Hitler in his role as Führer. Therefore he was close to the centre of the regime.

Rudolf Hess and Martin Bormann. From 1934 Hitler gave more personal power to the 'Führer's Deputy for Party Affairs', Rudolf Hess, and indirectly to his Chief of Staff, Martin Bormann. From 1934 Hess had the power to supervise new laws. From 1935 he could have a say over new appointments. As a result Hess and Bormann succeeded in asserting the dominance of the party over the state civil service. Bormann set up his own party organisation, rivalling that of the Reich Chancellery. There were two main departments of Bormann's organisation:

- Department II ran party affairs
- Department III managed party–state relations

From 1937 all state officials were made directly responsible to Hitler and party membership had become compulsory for civil servants by 1939.

The growth in power of Martin Bormann. Hess managed to strengthen the party's position before 1939. The Second World War saw this trend continue with the party reaching new heights of power and influence. On 30 August 1939 the Ministerial Council for the Defence of the Reich was set up. In September 1939 leading *Gauleiters* became Reich Defence Commissioners and began to assume total control in their regions. In May 1941, Hess flew to Scotland in an attempt to make peace with Britain. This left Bormann with considerably greater influence in charge of the Party Chancellery. He formed the Committee of Three with Keitel and Lammers and attempted to use this to try to isolate rivals.

KEY TERM

Führer's Secretary was an extremely important role in the Nazi state. It gave Martin Bormann considerable power because he was so close to the Führer. Although some leading Nazis, such as Albert Speer, had access to Hitler without going through Bormann, most had to go through the Führer's Secretary. As a result, the influence of Lammers in particular lessened towards the end of the war. The party, as represented by Bormann, had triumphed over the civil service in terms of influence.

In 1943, Bormann became Hitler's personal secretary – the **Führer's Secretary** – which again strengthened the party in its relations with the state. However, much of Bormann's energies were spent trying to protect his position and influence from the challenges of Albert Speer and Heinrich Himmler. As a close friend of Hitler and the mastermind behind the mobilisation of the economy, Speer shared Bormann's access to Hitler. In 1943, Bormann tried to turn the *Gauleiters* against Speer but the attempt failed to undermine Hitler's confidence in his favourite minister. Such rivalry weakened the Nazi state.

The SS ('Schutzstaffel')

The SS was the most powerful and most sinister element of the Nazi movement. Originally formed as Hitler's elite bodyguard in 1925, it was turned into a formidable private army by its leader Heinrich Himmler. The SS was modelled on the Jesuit Order of the Catholic Church. Its members were subjected to strict discipline. They were

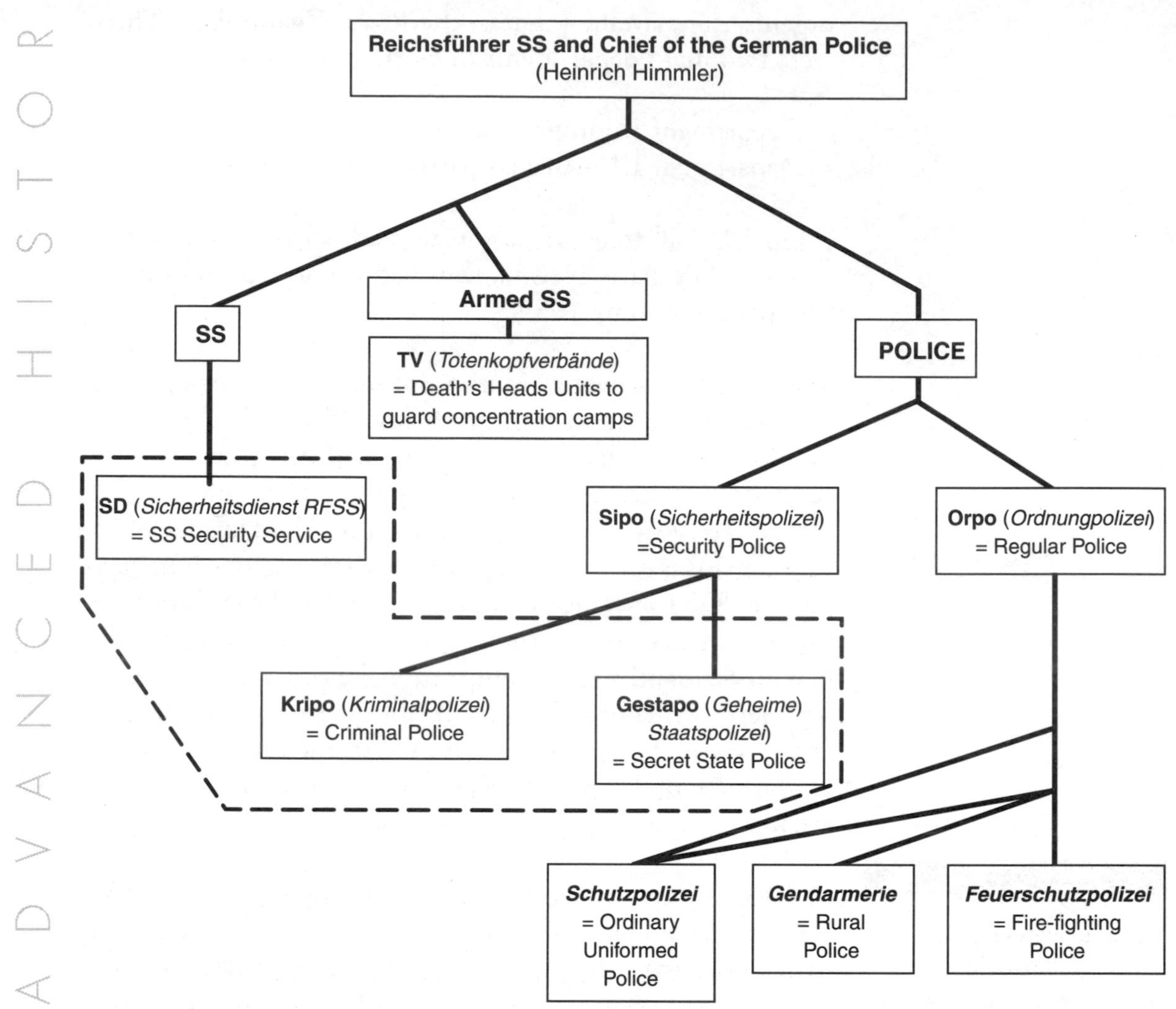

The structure of the SS.

expected to show complete obedience to the Führer. The SS were the racial elite of the Nazi Party. By the SS Marriage Order, which was issued by Himmler in December 1931, all members of the SS were expected to marry Aryan (racially pure) wives.

The role of the SS. After the Night of the Long Knives in June 1934, the SS became the main police arm of the Nazi Party with the aim of eliminating all opposition within the state. This task became the specific responsibility of the SS Security Service (SD) and the Gestapo.

- The SD was formed by Himmler in March 1934 and was placed under the command of Reinhard Heidrich. It was the intelligence arm of the SS with the special task of maintaining the security of Führer, party leadership, Nazi Party and Reich. Although the SD was supposed to operate under the authority of the Minister of the Interior, Frick, in reality it was controlled entirely by Heidrich and Himmler. Throughout the Nazi regime it had the power of arrest, detention and execution.

- The Gestapo undertook the role of a secret police force. In April 1933, Göring incorporated the Prussian political police into the Gestapo and set up their new offices on the Prince Albertstrasse in Berlin. In April 1934, Göring appointed Himmler head of the unified political police force. This was important as it gave Himmler and the SS some control over the state police. In 1936 any confusion was resolved when Hitler appointed Himmler head of the German police. In 1939 the Reich Security Head Office (RSHA) was formed, which brought together the Gestapo and SD under the central leadership of the SS. By 1939, in its role as the political police force, the Gestapo became the most important element in the state's security system. It played a key role in eliminating opposition through creating an elaborate terror machine. Those suspected of opposition to the regime or those **denounced** (informed on) by their neighbours often ended up imprisoned in one of the many concentration camps run by the SS. The Gestapo played a significant role in most of the major events in the development of the Nazi state from Hitler becoming Chancellor to the crushing of resistance in occupied Europe during the war. Even at the end of the war in 1945 there were around 40,000 Gestapo officers.

KEY TERMS

Denounced By a decree of March 1933, it became a crime to attack the government. From 1935 this was extended to attacks on the party. Many German towns had few Gestapo officers, e.g., in 1935 the number of officers in Hanover was 42. This meant that people denouncing their neighbours as suspects played a vital role in the creation of a police state. In many cases these denunciations were for personal reasons rather than because any crime had been committed.

The **concentration camp system** was set up to imprison the opponents of the Nazi state. The first camps at Dachau, Buchenwald and Sachsenhausen housed communists and Jews, but camps were soon being used for all opponents of the regime.

The extent of SS influence. Himmler's organisational skills and his closeness to Hitler resulted in the spread of SS influence and power. Eventually the SS controlled a vast economic empire, had influence in military and foreign affairs, controlled the **concentration camp system** and organised the extermination of the Jews. In many senses it became a 'state within a state'. Himmler wanted the SS to be financially independent of the state. As a result the SS created a huge concentration camp system in which

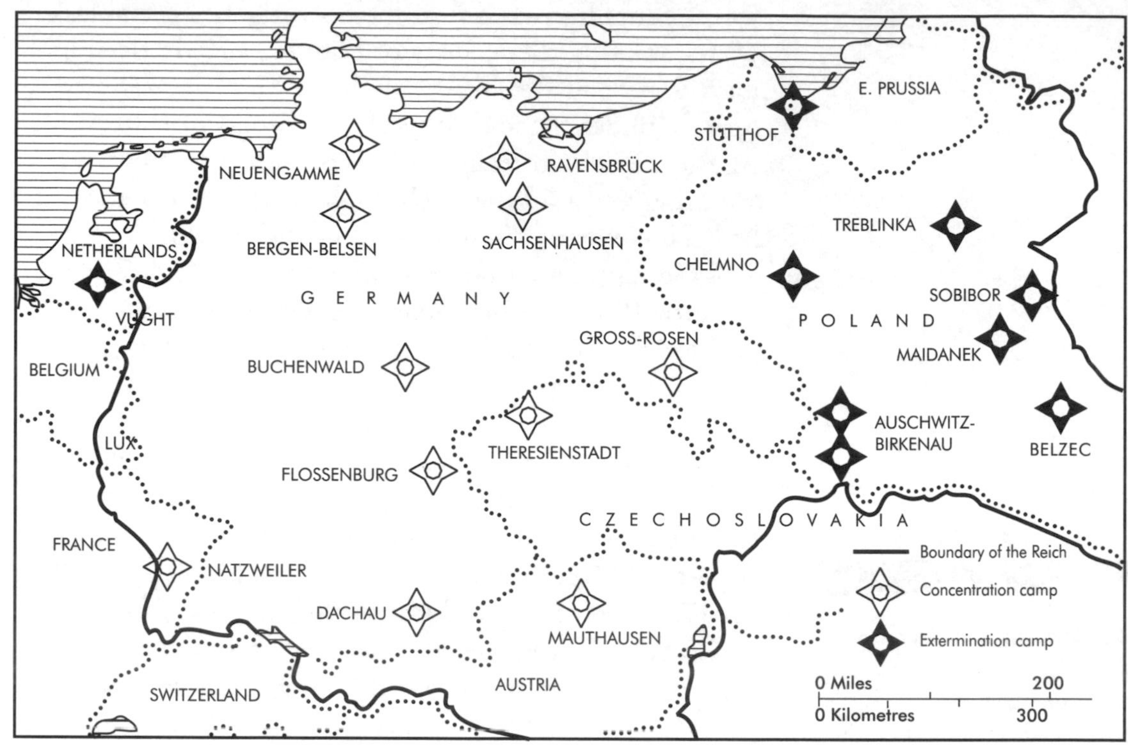

The Nazi concentration camp system.

enemies of the Nazis could be imprisoned and their labour exploited.

The concentration camp system grows. The SS assumed complete command over the running of the camp system after the Night of the Long Knives in 1934. The camps were filled with those the Nazis considered undesirable or 'asocial'. This included political opponents, gypsies, homosexuals and Jews. In 1938 the German Quarrying Company (DEST) was set up to exploit the labour of the camps' prisoners. The war saw a huge increase in the numbers of inmates, including Russian prisoners of war and resisters from across Europe. New camps were set up, including Auschwitz in 1940 where, from 1941, those spared the gas chambers were put to work at the Buna factory belonging to IG-Farben. Many opponents were arrested under the ***Nacht und Nebel*** decree issued by Hitler on 7 December 1941. In 1942, the concentration camp system was reorganised. The SS Economic and Administrative Head Office (WVHA) was set up to oversee the work of the forced labour camps. The camps chosen

KEY TERM

The **'Nacht und Nebel'** (Night and Fog) decree of December 1941 allowed the seizure from their homes of any 'persons endangering German security'. The SD implemented the decree. It is not known how many disappeared as a result.

solely as extermination centres, e.g. Sobibor, Treblinka, Maidanek, were run separately. By mid 1944 the SS controlled 165 labour camps from which workers were used in a range of industries from chemicals to textiles and agriculture to quarrying.

The growth of the Waffen SS. To build his racially motivated 'Great Germanic Empire' Himmler established a 'second army' which rapidly grew into the Waffen SS. By 1939 it had a membership of 23,000 and had broken free of army (*Wehrmacht*) control. This was because the army had been weakened during the Blomberg–Fritsch affair in 1938 (see page 138). Himmler saw the role of the Waffen SS as a political one. In a post-war Europe it would be at the centre of a mass army which would control the new German Reich. Therefore, numbers of the Waffen SS were allowed to expand to the extent that it was no longer an elite: by 1944 it had recruited over 800,000 soldiers, both German and non-German.

For Himmler, the most important mission for the SS was the war against the Jews (see section on Jewish policy on page 133). The SS took direct responsibility for this in 1938. **Adolf Eichmann**, who was in charge of subsection IV-B-4 of the SS Reich Security Office, drew up plans for the transportation and emigration of Jews. SS *Einsatzgruppen* (action squads) began to eliminate Jews in Poland in 1939 and more systematically in Russia in 1941. In 1941, Himmler and Heydrich devised their 'Final Solution', the total extermination of all European Jews by ordering their gassing in specially built concentration camps.

The last months of the war. As the Allies closed in on Germany, so Hitler attempted to strengthen the role of the party in relation to the state. He also attempted to mobilise further enthusiasm for the war. In July 1944, Göbbels was appointed as **Reich Plenipotentiary for Total War Mobilisation.** Although there was little active enthusiasm for the regime by the end of the war, the attempted assassination of Hitler in July 1944 met with little public approval.

KEY PERSON

Adolf Eichmann had a deep-rooted hatred for the Jews which partly came about because of taunting from school friends about his 'Jewish' appearance. He had the responsibility for the transportation of Europe's Jews to their death. In 1946 he fled to South America but was captured by Israeli secret agents in 1960, flown back to Israel, tried and executed.

KEY TERM

As **Reich Plenipotentiary for Total War Mobilisation**, it was the task of Göbbels' to mobilise the remaining population capable of fighting into army ranks. The initiative to find extra personnel at a local level was given to *Gauleiters* and other party officials.

In September 1944 the Allies entered Germany. The regime responded by strengthening the party's role further and, as the Allies crossed the Rhine, the party was placed in control of the newly created ***Volkssturm***. In the last months of the war, the state disintegrated as Germany collapsed. The regime began to reflect this state of collapse. In March 1944, Hitler issued a destruction order to prevent materials or industry falling into the hands of the advancing invaders.

KEY TERM

The **Volkssturm** was the German Home Guard raised at the end of the war. It accepted all able-bodied men who were not already conscripted into the armed services. Most members of the *Volkssturm* served in their local districts but some were drafted to the Western or Eastern fronts.

Himmler and Göring both attempted to succeed Hitler. Only Göbbels and Bormann stayed loyal to the end. On 29 April, Hitler dictated his private will and testament and his political testament. In the latter document, Hitler expelled from the party Göring and Himmler who had attempted to make a separate peace with the Allies. Hitler committed suicide on 30 April 1945.

SUMMARY QUESTIONS

1 Describe the power of the SS in the Nazi state.

2 Explain Hitler's role as a dictator in the Third Reich.

CHAPTER 11

Economic policy, 1933–45

INTRODUCTION

The economic situation in Germany in the early 1930s was very poor. Unemployment was as high as 8.5 million in 1931 and businesses collapsed along with consumer confidence. The domestic economy was very weak before the Wall Street Crash of 1929, in 1928 there were already 3 million unemployed. The collapse in the world markets made conditions worse.

RECOVERY, 1933–6

Work schemes and the reduction in unemployment

The most important challenge facing the Nazis on taking office was to reduce unemployment. Within the first year, legislation and initiatives were introduced which dealt effectively with the numbers of Germans out of work. The work schemes first used by Papen and Schleicher in 1932–3 were extended by the Law to Reduce Unemployment of June 1933. These ***Arbeitdienst*** (work schemes) were part of an overall job creation plan which included the building of new roads, the *Autobahnen*. The so-called 'Battle for Work' was extended by the government lending money to private companies so that they could create jobs.

State investment. Initial state investment was poured into work creation schemes in the period 1932–5, in all some 5 billion RM. In June 1933, the first law was passed releasing the money for the building of the first *Autobahn*. The nature of the work creation projects reveals much about the regime's priorities. The Labour Service and Emergency Relief Schemes which put thousands back to work were **labour intensive**. The regime's attempts to reduce unemployment were successful. In 1933 the

KEY TERMS

'Arbeitdienst' was the main element of the Nazis' plan to reduce unemployment. In 1935 the Nazis made the *Arbeitdienst* compulsory for all unemployed between 19 and 25. The main area of employment was in agriculture.

Labour intensive This is when many people are employed rather than using machinery to do the same work. In the early years of the regime, technological advancement was not a priority for the regime. This was because new technology often reduced the need for workers.

percentage of those unemployed was 25.9. This figure had fallen to 7.4 per cent by 1936. This fall was partly helped by an improvement in the world economy as a whole. However, this is not as important a factor as the growth in state investment in explaining why unemployment fell.

Restoring confidence in the countryside. Unemployment was not the only problem facing the new regime. The desperate state of the peasantry, who had suffered from the collapse of agricultural prices between 1929 and 1933 was dealt with in two ways.

- The Reich Food Estate, created in September 1933, took control of the overall planning and organisation of agriculture.
- In the same month, the Reich Entailed Farm Law attempted to enhance the security of peasant ownership of land.

Because Germany did not have much foreign currency to pay for imports of food, the regime launched a 'Battle for Production' in 1934 and 1935 to increase the production of grain. However, this drive was not so successful because of a lack of new machinery and labour, and poor harvests.

A Nazi poster advertising the new 'Autobahnen' in Germany in the 1930s.

Hjalmar Schacht and the New Plan

In May 1933, Hitler appointed **Hjalmar Schacht** as President of the Reichsbank. One of the main reasons for the depth of the German depression in the period 1929–33 was the over-reliance on foreign capital. So it is not surprising that one of Schacht's first acts was to increase state control of foreign trade. In the summer of 1934 Schacht was made Minister of Economics. He promptly introduced the 'New Plan' in September 1934 which gave the government extensive powers to regulate trade and currency transactions. This New Plan was introduced in the face of a foreign exchange crisis (which was the result of Germany importing more goods than it exported). As Germany's economy had collapsed on the back of world depression, so the aim of the New Plan was to make it independent of that system. In 1934 Schacht also proceeded to negotiate a series of trade agreements with countries in South America and south-eastern Europe

KEY PERSON

Hjalmar Schacht was a very important figure in the Nazi economic recovery. A Nazi supporter from the early 1930s, Schacht used his influence as an ex-president of the Reichsbank to help Hitler into power. In March 1933, Schacht was appointed president of the Reichsbank and from August 1934 to November 1937 he was Reich Minister of Economics. Schacht continued to serve the regime although he had doubts about the Night of the Long Knives, the regime's anti-Semitism and the stress the regime placed on rearmament. See also page 30.

which were aimed at preventing Germany running up a huge foreign currency deficit whilst still being able to procure essential raw materials. Those countries involved would be paid for their goods in Reichsmarks.

Mefo bills. Schacht also created a policy aimed at encouraging the growth in demand in the economy. This was done by the introduction of Mefo bills. These were bills issued by the government as payment for goods. They were then held by investors or banks and could either be exchanged for cash or held for up to five years, earning four per cent interest a year.

1936–9: REARMAMENT OR CONSUMPTION?

Guns versus butter?

Hitler's main long-term objective was to create an economy which could support sustained rearmament. By 1936 the economy had recovered to such an extent as to make this possible. However, there were problems which potentially could prevent this happening. By 1935, Germany was still importing large amounts of foodstuffs such as butter and vegetable oil. The 'Battle for Production' begun in 1934 aimed to increase the production of foodstuffs in Germany. However, this was not so easily done. Agriculture suffered from a lack of machinery and, increasingly, manpower. The head of the Reich Food Estate, Walther Darré, asked Schacht for foreign currency to import such foods, the alternative being the introduction of rationing. But Germany also needed to import raw materials such as lead and copper to sustain rearmament. The crisis grew worse by 1936 as Germany used up its reserves of raw materials and was now forced to buy raw materials, such as oil, on the open market for cash. The problem facing Schacht was the fact that Germany could not afford to import large quantities of food and raw materials for rearmament. The only politically acceptable answer to this problem was to cut imports and embark on a policy of greater self-sufficiency.

Self-sufficiency in synthetic fuels. In April 1936, Hermann Göring was appointed Commissioner of Raw Materials, giving him responsibility for making the German economy self-sufficient. This was to be partly achieved by manufacturing rubber and oil synthetically. The manufacturing company IG-Farben persuaded the Nazi regime that such a process was possible. In 1933 the government signed the Feder-Bosch agreement with IG-Farben which set a price for synthetically produced oil and guaranteed it a market. The problem was that the process of synthetically producing oil was expensive. Such considerations were secondary in the minds of those such as Hermann Göring who, as head of the German air force, the Luftwaffe, enthusiastically welcomed any possibility of producing fuel in Germany for his planes.

The Second Four Year Plan, 1936-40

The Second Four Year Plan was based on the policy of **autarky**. Göring set up a separate organisation for the Four Year Plan which was to become the most important of the departments concerned with the economy. One of the casualties of Göring's rise in influence in the economics sphere was Schacht. Worried by the pace of rearmament and bitter at his loss of influence, Schacht resigned as Minister of Economics in November 1937 to be replaced by Walther Funk. From this moment on, Göring took full control of the economy. Targets were set by Göring for the increased production of oil, rubber and steel. The construction of the huge ***Reichswerke Hermann Göring*** at Watenstadt-Salzgitter was testament to the drive to produce essential war goods in Germany. In 1937–8, money spent on the military rose to 10 billion RM and by 1938–9 this figure had risen to 17 billion RM. On top of that the state spent considerable sums on the manufacture of synthetic goods.

The limitations of autarky. However, the policy of self-sufficiency was not a complete success. By 1938 Germany's balance of trade deficit had risen to 432 million RM. One reason was that the regime did not want to squeeze the consumer too much. The thinking behind this was political. The Nazis had come to power partly as a result of economic depression. Hitler, in particular, was acutely aware of how unpopular the regime might become if basic consumer goods were unavailable. Therefore, although

KEY TERMS

Autarky means self-sufficiency. Although Germany had reserves of many natural raw materials, it still had to import food and essentials such as oil.

'Reichswerke Hermann Göring' was a huge national business organisation which could control the development of industry.

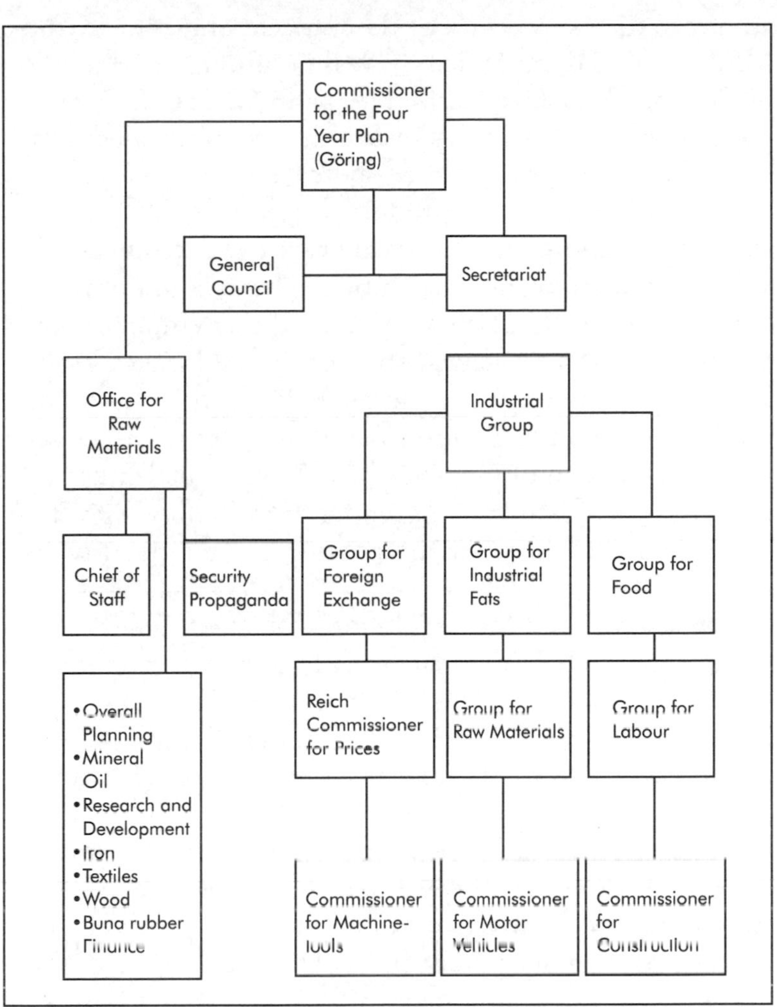

The organisation of the Second Four Year Plan.

consumer spending power did not rise significantly from 1936 to 1939, neither did it decline. This was because full employment meant Germans were prepared to spend money despite wage and price controls.

THE ECONOMY, 1939–45

Organisation of the war economy

The outbreak of war in September 1939 saw the responsibility for the planning of the German war economy shared among competing agencies. At the Ministry of War, General Thomas led the economics section in charge of the armaments programme. Yet such was the overlap in the Nazi state that he had rivals for administrative supremacy of the war economy, chiefly the Ministry of Economics led by Walther Funk and the office of the Four Year Plan led by Hermann Göring. In March 1940, however, a Ministry of Munitions was created under Fritz Todt which went some way towards ending the confusion in this area of production. In June 1940, France surrendered and plans were made to use the resources of the already significant Nazi empire. The invasion of the Soviet Union in 1941 aimed to extend that empire – but the prospect of a prolonged struggle on the Eastern Front led to the rethinking of economic policy. The invasion of the Soviet Union, Operation Barbarossa, began on 22 June 1941. By the end of October the **axis** forces had swept to the outskirts of Moscow. As winter drew in, however, it became apparent that the momentum was temporarily lost.

KEY TERM

Axis The axis powers were Germany, Italy and Japan.

Rationalisation and the appointment of Speer. On 3 December 1941, Hitler issued the Führer Order on the Simplification and Increased Efficiency in Armaments Production which ordered Todt to rationalise the armaments industry. Thereafter there was a significant change in priorities. Industry accepted responsibility for raising levels of production with central direction coming from Todt's ministry. In February 1942, Albert Speer was appointed Todt's successor in the post of Minister of Armaments and War Production. This marked the beginning of the campaign for a total war, which was so markedly different from the official attitude in the early days of the war. In particular, Speer developed Todt's plans for rationalisation of industry and the more efficient control of raw material distribution.

Economic change and labour shortages, 1939–41. This is not to suggest that the economy had not already undergone a significant readjustment from 1939 to 1942, **military expenditure** alone rising from 17.2 billion to 55.9 billion RM. The demands of war resulted in a shift of labour, investment and priorities towards munitions, for example, the numbers working in aircraft manufacturing doubled between 1939 and 1941. However, such were the demands of war that a shortage of labour became apparent in its early days. By May 1940 there were 3.5 million less workers in the workforce than a year before. This shortfall

KEY TERM

Military expenditure Of the rise in military expenditure, perhaps as much as 75 per cent was due to the increase in military personnel *not* armaments. Therefore, the figures are somewhat misleading and need to be treated with care.

was partly made good by the use of French prisoners of war, some 800,000 by October 1940, and other nationals (mainly Poles) which made a total of around 2 million foreign workers in Germany by the end of the year. This was not enough to meet the growing demand, with 1.7 million workers drafted into the armed forces in 1941 and a further 1.4 million called up between May 1941 and May 1942. Such a shortage produced urgent measures. In February 1941, General Thomas had called for the use of more rational measures of production to increase efficiency. Yet even this would not be enough. Following on from a decree in the Netherlands in February 1942, the so-called Plenipotentiary General for Labour, **Fritz Sauckel**, issued a compulsory labour decree for all occupied countries in August of the same year. In September, **the Vichy government** in France established compulsory labour for men and women between the ages of 18 and 65. Such measures brought in around 2.5 million new workers and by the end of 1942 there were some 6.4 million foreign workers in Germany toiling for the Reich.

KEY PERSON

Fritz Sauckel was an important figure from 1942 until the end of the war in the effort to import foreign labour. He had been *Gauleiter* of Thuringia and was recommended for the job of Plenipotentiary General for Labour by Martin Bormann.

KEY TERM

The Vichy government The government which ruled the unoccupied part of France after the armistice with Germany in 1940. Its leader was Marshal Pétain. In reality, it did what the Nazis demanded of it.

Women and the workforce, 1942–5. Despite a reluctance to conscript women, the pressures on the economy led to a gradual rethink. In January 1943, women between the ages of 17 and 45 were obliged to sign up for work, although out of this only some 400,000 were finally recruited. The preference of employers and the Nazi hierarchy was still for foreigners to be employed. However, the percentage of women in the labour force as a whole was 41.5 by 1944. Their inclusion was made necessary by the turn in fortunes of the army: in January 1943 the German army surrendered at Stalingrad and losses in the army were running at 150,000 a month. Against this background, a campaign of total war was launched by the regime.

The move to total war. The move to total war was signalled by Göbbels in a speech at the Berlin Sportsplatz in February 1943. He called for universal labour service and the closure of all non-essential business. Such a move to improve production and productivity was reinforced by the appointment of Speer as Reich Minister for Armaments and Production in September 1943. This post gave Speer responsibility for all industrial output and raw materials and into these areas of the economy he introduced reorganisation and rationalisation. An example was the Armaments Commission set up in 1943 to improve the cooperation and coordination between the design and manufacturing processes in munitions. The economy became more productive as the war continued despite the ever greater numbers of forced labourers. By 1944, 29.2 per cent of all industrial workers were foreign, and in all areas of work a total of over 9.3 million by the summer of that year. By 1943, up to one-third of all miners was from occupied countries, in particular those in the East.

Increase in worker productivity. Although foreign worker productivity was as much as 50 per cent lower than that of the German worker, changes in work methods, increased mechanisation, better distribution of materials, a more equitable wage structure for German workers and the introduction of mass production techniques resulted in significant increases in productivity.

- One of the most impressive examples was the use of production-line assembly in the manufacture of the Panzer III tank in 1943, which cut by 50 per cent the man hours needed in its assembly.
- In the manufacture of munitions, output per worker rose by 60 per cent between 1939 and 1944 despite the disruption caused by allied bombing.
- Although the numbers in the industrial workforce increased by only 11 per cent between 1941 and 1943, the production of all weapons grew by 130 per cent in the same period.

1944: Göbbels and Speer's influence increases. In 1944 the war deteriorated considerably for the Nazis on all fronts. In the east, by the summer months the Russian army had pushed the German army back to the Polish border. The Allies continued to make slow progress in Italy and forces were landed on the Normandy coast in France in June. The following month, an attempted assassination plot against Hitler resulted in the appointment of the trusted Göbbels to the post of Reich Plenipotentiary for Total War Mobilisation. This gave Göbbels even greater control over production and allowed Speer more scope for change.

This was because in the permanent infighting that characterised the Nazi state Speer was a close ally of Göbbels. Speer's methods of rationalisation and his seemingly non-ideological approach won him many enemies. Based mainly at the Ministry of Economics, Nazis such as Franz Heyler, who was State Secretary at the Ministry, and his deputy Otto Ohlendorf represented the more radical wing of the party led by Himmler or Martin Bormann.

1945: THE ECONOMY COLLAPSES

As the Allies crossed the borders of Germany in early 1945, Hitler's demands for a policy of 'scorched earth' and the destruction of all industry was resisted by Speer. It was apparent that defeat was inevitable and Hitler ordered the evacuation of all in the path of the advancing armies. From January 1945 the German economy was in a state of collapse, partly as a consequence of invasion but also due to exhaustion and the effects of the allied **bombing campaign**. Indeed the bombing campaign had reduced production of essential war materials by anything up to 40 per cent in 1944. The use of foreign labour was of even

KEY TERM

Bombing campaign The effectiveness of the allied bombing campaign has been the source of dispute amongst historians. There is little doubt that the campaign acted to stiffen rather than break the morale of the German people. However, the bombing campaign was essential in limiting the increase in production caused by Speer's rationalisation programme.

The German city of Wesel after the Allied bombing in the Second World War.

greater importance as all able-bodied German men were called to the front. In an attempt to increase their productivity, marginal improvements were made in the living conditions of the foreign labour force on the insistence of Fritz Sauckel, Plenipotentiary General for Labour. From 1943 to the end of the war, 2.5 million extra foreign workers were employed and these, as with the others who had survived the brutality of their working conditions, were categorised by race. In an attempt to increase production, however, Sauckel sought to improve the situation of all workers with regard to pay and overtime. In March 1944, all eastern workers were given the same pay and benefits as other foreign labourers. This was all comparative since conditions for the vast majority of foreigners working for the Nazis were appalling and deteriorated even further during 1945.

SUMMARY QUESTIONS

1 Explain the main themes of the German economy 1933–9:
- rearmament;
- consumption;
- employment.

2 List the main features of the German war economy.

CHAPTER 12

Society

'VOLKSGEMEINSCHAFT'

KEY TERM

'Volksgemeinschaft' was the term the Nazis used to describe the racially 'pure' and harmonious national community they promised.

The working class

It was Hitler's aim to create a genuine ***Volksgemeinschaft***. To do this it was important to win the support of the working classes. Hitler recognised that this would be his greatest domestic challenge. Although some skilled workers had supported the Nazis before 1933, most unskilled workers had been committed to the socialist SPD and communist KPD. In 1933 the still powerful trade unions had, in theory, the means to resist Hitler. The SPD and KPD did attempt to oppose Hitler's coming to power in 1933 but they were easily repressed by the Nazi reign of terror which followed. Many working-class leaders were the first victims of concentration camps.

KEY PERSON

Robert Ley A loyal supporter of Hitler, Robert Ley was the leader of the DAF with wide-ranging powers.

The DAF. Hitler wanted a disciplined workforce which would not challenge his dictatorship or threaten his plans for rearmament with excessive wage demands. On the day after the May Day holiday in 1933, the offices of the trade unions were ransacked. Within a few days 169 trade unions were under Nazi control. Independent unions were abolished to be replaced on 10 May by the **German Labour Front** (DAF) led by **Robert Ley**. In many factories radical Nazi organisations, the National Socialist Factory Cells or NSBO, were set up. Their main objective was to spread Nazi propaganda in the workplace. At its peak in the 1930s, the DAF had around 20 million members.

Employment schemes, 1933–6. Hitler attempted to win the support of the workers by a combination of material improvement and state welfare. The economic recovery after 1933 and the creation of around six million jobs was vital in attracting working-class support to the regime. Thousands of workers found employment in the public works schemes, labour service or, after 1935, in the army.

A 'Kraft durch Freude' poster.

There was significant expansion in training schemes for the unskilled and in apprenticeships for working-class school leavers. In addition, the regime provided 60,000 new housing units for workers and doubled the number of paid holidays.

State paternalism. From 1933 workers were compensated for the loss of political rights and wage freezes by state paternalism. This means the state saw itself as the sole protector and provider for all workers. In November 1933 Robert Ley established two new organisations:

- *Schönheit der Arbeit* (Beauty of Labour) was set up to persuade employers to improve working conditions in factories. This was done by promoting schemes highlighting the benefits of better lighting, ventilation, cleanliness and the potential benefits of giving workers wholesome meals.
- *Kraft durch Freude* (Strength through Joy) offered to reward loyal workers with evening classes, recitals and art exhibitions, theatre trips, sporting competitions and package holidays. By 1938 around 180,000 workers had been on a *Kraft durch Freude* sponsored cruise and ten million (one-third of the workforce) had enjoyed a state financed holiday.

KEY PERSON

Benito Mussolini was the Italian fascist leader who had been in power since 1922. At first, Hitler adopted some of the Italian fascists' ideas.

Labour relations. In January 1934 the Law for the Ordering of National Labour set out the Nazi vision of labour–employer relations. Modelled on **Mussolini**'s Labour Charter, it established the idea of a plant community in which the workers were a retinue following a plant leader. Factory conditions would be inspected by Trustees of Labour and disputes would be resolved by Courts of Honour. The new system called for all workers to work together for the common good of the nation.

Worker discontent. Most workers enjoyed real wage rises after 1933 and skilled workers prospered with a return to full employment by 1936. At the same time the working week increased from an average of 44 hours in 1933 to 60 hours in 1944. Industrial accidents and industrial related illnesses rose by 150 per cent between 1933 and 1939. Despite the repression and the fall in unemployment, there was some working-class unrest.

- There were strikes at Russelheim and Berlin in 1936 and a party report from Nuremberg found open insubordination, sabotage (the deliberate destruction of equipment), go-slows, absenteeism and a rapid turnover of staff.
- Whilst few workers risked open defiance, there was by 1936 an increasing sense of boredom, mistrust and indifference to the regime among the working classes.

- Despite the economic recovery, many workers resented the regimentation and regulation of their lifestyle and mistrusted state propaganda.

However, Hitler always remained vigilant to the mood of the working classes and was aware of their apathy towards the regime, especially in Berlin. His attempt to instil some militaristic spirit by marching troops through Berlin in 1938 was a complete flop and there was certainly no popular enthusiasm for war in 1939.

The working class during the war years. The regime was successful in sustaining working-class morale during the first three years of the war. This was largely due to the spectacular successes of the German army until 1941. It was also due to the fact that the workers suffered relatively little material hardship. Fear of working-class opposition forced the regime to adopt a wage freeze in September 1939, rather than wage cuts. Night work and holiday bonuses were quickly restored after workers responded to their abolition with absenteeism. The system of food and clothing rationing was accepted with little opposition from workers. The system avoided the injustices and **profiteering** of the First World War and was relatively generous. However, working-class morale declined significantly following the winter of 1941–2.

KEY TERM

Profiteering is when people make a profit out of war. In their propaganda before coming to power, the Nazis attacked those who profited from the First World War.

The battle to keep morale high, 1942–5. The failure to defeat the Soviet Union and the declaration of war on the United States in December 1941 alarmed public opinion. There was growing exhaustion and increasing criticism of state propaganda. But allied air raids from the spring of 1942 helped to generate a degree of popular solidarity and bolstered the determination to 'stick it out' (*ausharren*). The Propaganda Minister Joseph Göbbels was particularly effective in raising working-class morale by visiting bombed out towns such as Dortmund, which was destroyed in May 1943, or Hamburg, which was heavily bombed in July 1943. Nonetheless not even his spectacular **'Total War' speech** in February 1943 could disguise the problems facing Germany after the disaster of Stalingrad. By 1944 the shortage of supplies, and the growing sense that distribution of goods, was becoming more unfair led

KEY TERM

The **'Total War' speech** was made by Göbbels in Berlin on 18 February 1943. The speech contained many of the main points of Nazi propaganda in the latter part of the war: the demand for total war, and policies against communism and the Jews.

Göbbels speaking in February 1943.

to a growing black market (trading in goods without state control). However, despite all these problems and the collapse in morale, there was hostility to the assassination attempt on Hitler's life in July 1944.

The middle class: the 'Mittelstand'

The *Mittelstand*, comprising groups such as small business owners, traders, craft workers, clerks and shopkeepers, was Hitler's most committed group of supporters. From the start the regime did attempt to fulfil some of its election pledges to the *Mittelstand*.

- The establishment of new **department stores** was banned on 12 May 1933.
- Half the consumer cooperatives were forced to close by 1935.
- Competition in craft trades was curbed by the introduction of new regulations.
- Cut-price competition between businesses was banned.
- State and party agencies gave preferential treatment to small businesses.
- The state made available low interest loans and a share of confiscated Jewish trade.

KEY TERM

Department stores were particularly important to the *Mittelstand*. The increase in their numbers in the 1930s threatened the businesses of many German shopkeepers.

Problems for the 'Mittelstand'. After 1933, the *Mittelstand* benefited from the return of business confidence. However, their status was not significantly raised during the pre-war years despite the actions listed above. Hitler's first priority was the creation of jobs and the maintenance of low prices, both of which were more effectively provided by larger firms. In July 1933, the deputy Führer Rudolf Hess defended supermarkets from attacks by party activists and restrained the Nazi Combat League of Tradesmen. Small traders continued to be outpriced by department stores and were squeezed between the Reich Food Estate, which controlled agricultural prices, and price freezes in the shops. By 1943 a quarter of a million small shops had gone out of business.

The policy of rearmament after 1936 and the switch to a total war economy after 1941 both favoured big business. Craft industries could no longer compete with the wage rates of big businesses. The number of self-employed craft workers fell by half a million between 1936 and 1939.

'Blut und Boden' means 'Blood and Soil'. An example of a poster glorifying the peasant farmer.

Rural 'Volkgemeinschaft'. Nazi ideology glorified the peasant farmer as decent, honest, uncorrupted and racially pure. They put forward a policy of 'Blood and Soil' in an attempt to protect a healthy and economically secure rural community. The Nazis thought this was essential if they were to provide cheap food for the cities and if they were to safeguard a racially pure stock. The Nazis undertook a series of measures to protect the rural economy.

- After coming to power the Agriculture Minister Alfred Hugenberg attempted to honour Nazi election promises by increasing tariffs on imported food and by cancelling farmers' debts.
- The regime attempted to safeguard small and middling sized farmers by the Reich Entailed Farm Law of 29 September 1933. The new law identified farms of around 30 acres as being hereditary farms which had to be passed on to the eldest son without being divided up. Farmers were offered financial support to stay on the land and many were exempt from insurance payment. As a result of the Farm Law and an improvement in the economy, mortgage interest payments were cut by £280 million between 1934 and 1938. The tax burden on farmers was cut by £60 million in the same period.

- Farming was regulated by the **Reich Food Estate** which became a huge organisation. Its role was to supervise the country's 3 million farms, half a million retail stores and 300,000 food processing businesses. The Reich Food Estate fixed agricultural prices and wages, set production quotas, dictated crop rotation and allocated scarce resources.

As a result of state direction and the general improvement in the economy, farming income did recover from the post-1929 levels. However, it fell again after 1937 as labour costs rose and prices were fixed. Farming wages could not compete with industrial wages after the return to full employment in 1936. In the late 1930s, as social amenities and marriage prospects were poor, the long-term drift from the land accelerated.

The Nazis and the landowners. At first many of the rural elite were quite hostile to the regime. Owners of large estates resented interference from Nazi *Gauleiters* and they did not enjoy being forced to invite local Nazi leaders to their social gatherings. But the local elites succeeded in maintaining their economic and social status. The elimination of the communists and the disciplining of the workforce secured their position. Despite some talk in Nazi circles of land redistribution, this never became official policy. Indeed, it was the landowners who benefited most from the annexation of Western Poland in 1939.

WOMEN AND NAZISM

Women and family

Nazi ideology stressed that women should be confined to a purely domestic role in society. Their duty was to produce healthy Aryan children, uphold conservative principles and comfort their husbands in their service to the state. These ideas were advertised by the Nazi slogan of ***Kinder, Küche, Kirche.*** The first step taken by the regime to bring women into line with Nazi ideology was the creation of the **Women's Front** (*Frauenfront*) by Robert Ley on 10 May 1933. All 230 women's organisations in Germany were to expel their Jewish members and integrate into the

KEY TERM

'Kinder, Küche, Kirche' was the central theme of the Nazi policy towards women. Meaning 'children, kitchen, church' it was aimed at encouraging women to concentrate on working in the home.

Nazi propaganda picture showing the Nazi ideal for women.

Women's Front or face being disbanded. Most organisations happily obliged, pleased to support a regime they saw as nationalistic and supportive of the traditional role of women.

The attack on women at work. The new regime lost no time in shaping their negative policy towards women. Particularly under attack were educated women in professional jobs.

- In 1933, nearly all the 19,000 female civil servants in regional and local goverment lost their jobs as did around 15 per cent of women teachers.
- By early 1934 there were no women left working in the Prussian civil service. The three per cent of lawyers who were women faced a decline in their status.
- From 1936 no woman could serve as a judge and women were no longer accepted for jury duty.
- However, the regime was careful not to upset the women's organisations which had so willingly joined the Women's Front. In 1934 the Minister of the Interior, Wilhelm Frick, responded to widespread unease about the sacking of women teachers by reversing the policy, at least temporarily.
- As the economic situation improved and unemployment fell, so the situation of women in most professions (apart from the law) improved, despite the regime's official line on women in work. In 1930, five per cent of all doctors were women, by 1939 this figure had risen to seven per cent.

The number of women in employment generally remained low in the first years of the regime. The economic improvement after 1933 was at first fuelled by the rearmament based industries and therefore did not have too much of an effect on women in work. However, conscription of men and then the return to near full employment created a labour shortage, which meant that the regime began to try and persuade women to go back to work. Between 1933 and 1939 the number of women working increased from 11.6 million to 14.6 million. This shows a contradiction between Nazi ideology and reality.

Factors affecting women and work during the war. The needs of the German economy for more labour during the war were not solved by the conscription of women. Between 1939 and 1944, 200,000 extra women entered the workforce. There were many factors which prevented the number of women at work rising dramatically.

- The refusal of Hitler to allow conscription of women was ideologically based, the Nazi view of the role of women revolving around *Kinder, Küche, Kirche*

('Children, Kitchen, Church'). Even with the move towards total war, the registration of women for work in January 1943 had little effect and in all only some 400,000 women were recruited for work. The failure to mobilise more women created significant ideological tensions within the Nazi leadership.

- There was a shortfall of some four million workers in the economy by 1944, but still over 1,360,000 women were in **domestic service**. Attempts by Speer to change this in September 1944 had little effect because of the number of exemptions allowed (such as for those who petitioned to keep their servants) and the fact that Hitler still refused to accept the full-scale mobilisation of women.
- Nazi policy on women was to have consequences for women and work. As women had been very much encouraged to marry and raise families, so the numbers of women in such a situation had risen dramatically. Nearly one million more children were born in Germany in 1939 than six years previous. Similarly, a far higher proportion of women between the ages of 25 and 30 were married by the eve of the war, the difference between 1933 and 1939 being 9.2 per cent. A great disincentive to work was the benefits paid to wives of soldiers, which meant that they could resist the temptation to supplement their husbands' pay. All of this made the conscription of women harder and further complicated the labour crisis.
- However, the issue of women's labour is a complex one. Ideology played a role in the state's attitude towards women but it was not the most important factor in limiting the increase of women in the wartime labour market. What is often ignored is that the proportion of women in the workforce at the start of the war was relatively high *despite* Nazi ideology. It was significantly higher than that in Britain – in May 1939, 37.3 per cent of German women went out to work as opposed to 26.4 per cent of their British counterparts. Of those between the ages of 15 and 60, 52 per cent of women were working and an astonishingly high 88.7 per cent of single women were in employment. The reason for this is that, by 1936, levels of employment were high and women were needed to work. Also wages did not increase significantly and many families wanted a second income.

KEY TERM

Domestic service meant working as servants in other people's houses. The majority of domestic servants worked as maids.

	May 1939	May 1940	May 1941	May 1942	May 1943	May 1944
Agricultural	6,495	5,689	5,369	5,673	5,665	5,694
Industry/Handicrafts/Energy	3,836	3,650	3,677	3,537	3,740	3,592
Commerce/Banking/Insurance/Transport	2,227	2,183	2,167	2,225	2,320	2,219
Domestic service	1,560	1,511	1,473	1,410	1,362	1,301
Administration/Services	954	1,157	1,284	1,471	1,719	1,746
Total	14,626	14,386	14,167	14,437	14,806	14,808

German women in employment, 1939–44.

As is shown in the table above, large numbers of women worked in agriculture. In 1939 they comprised 36.6 per cent of the workforce and their importance grew with conscription of men into the army. By 1944, 65.5 per cent of the agricultural workforce were women (this figure applies to native-born Germans). Similarly, the high proportion of women employed in textiles in 1939 (58.2 per cent) could not be spared to other areas of war work, such as munitions, given the demands on the industry and the effects of male conscription. So ideology was not the sole reason why women were not fully mobilised into essential war work from 1939. The proportion of women already in the workforce was high to begin with.

KEY TERM

Pro-natalism was a policy encouraging the birth of children. Hitler saw the responsibility of women as bearing and bringing up the future leaders of Nazism.

Pro-natalism. Almost immediately after coming to office the regime embarked on a **pro-natalist** policy aimed at women.

- In 1933 **marriage loans** of up to 1000 RM (around one-fifth of the average worker's annual pay) were offered to newly-weds on the grounds that the wife would not work outside the home and that neither of the couple were Jewish. The loan was interest free and to be repaid over a period of eight and a quarter years. The loan was partly funded by a bachelor tax of between two and five per cent of salary. For each child born to couples taking part in the marriage loan programme, the amount to be repaid was reduced by 25 per cent. There was no doubt as to the popularity of the marriage loans: by 1937 700,000 married couples had received a loan.

- Parents could deduct 15 per cent from their taxable income for every child they had. Those with six children or more paid no personal taxation.
- **Mother's Day** was changed to Hitler's mother's birthday (12 August), which was a national holiday.
- **Family allowances** were set up to help those on low incomes. In 1935 low income families were given grants of up to 100 RM per child. In 1938 child allowances were increased for those on incomes lower than 650 RM a month, 10 RM a month for every third and fourth child and 20 RM for each child thereafter.
- The status of mothers was raised by a series of propaganda campaigns. An example was the introduction of the **Mother's Cross** in 1939 for those with large families.

However, despite these incentives the **birth rate** did not respond positively to Nazi policy. Abortion was made illegal in 1933 by Article 218 of the Civil Code, but the numbers of women seeking to terminate their pregnancies remained high, perhaps as many as half a million in 1936. Indeed the birth rate remained fairly constant throughout the 1930s after an increase in 1933–4 (it is likely that that increase was due to the end of the depression). Nazi propaganda seems to have had some effect on women but not as much as the regime would have hoped. This was possibly because propaganda stressed that it was women's responsibility to bear children not for reasons of personal happiness but out of duty to the state. But there were other factors which kept the birth rate depressed. There was a shortage of houses, and labour service and conscription kept many young men away from home. The number of marriages went up from 516,800 in 1932 to 740,200 in 1934 but this also was as much to do with the ending of the depression as the introduction of marriage loans.

'Lebensborn' (Fountain of Life). Hitler was obsessed with race and his belief that the main function of women was to bear children resulted in the *Lebensborn* programme. Organised by the leader of the SS, Heinrich Himmer, it encouraged German women to bear the children of SS officers whether they were married to them or not.

KEY TERMS

The Mother's Cross was awarded to mothers who had given birth to a certain number of children. A woman with four children received a bronze cross, with six a silver cross and with eight a gold cross.

The **birth rate** is the number of children born per year per 1,000 people.

Year	Marriages per 1000	Divorces per 10,000 existing marriages	Births per 1000	Live births
1933	9.7	29.7	14.7	971,174
1934	11.1	37.0	18.0	1,198,350
1935	9.7	33.0	18.9	1,263,976
1936	9.1	32.6	19.0	1,277,052
1937	9.1	29.8	18.8	1,277,046
1938	9.4	31.1	19.6	1,348,534
1939	11.1	38.3	20.3	1,407,490

Population statistics, 1933–9.

German girls in the League of German Girls (BDM) were educated in their duty to Germany to have Aryan children. During the Second World War the *Lebensborn* programme was extended to include the kidnapping of Aryan-looking children from all over occupied Europe. The *Lebensborn* programme was unpopular with many Germans who objected to its immorality.

Divorce. The Nazis claimed to be supporters of the traditional family but, as the above table shows, the divorce rate rose between 1933 and 1939. Whilst the Nazis stressed the dominance of the man in a marriage, they also made it easier for him to divorce his wife. In 1933 and 1934 the number of divorces rose as judges granted the right to legal separation on racial grounds. In 1938 the divorce law was reformed further to give men more grounds on which they might divorce their spouses, including immorality, racial incompatibility and refusal to have children.

KEY PERSON

Gertrud Scholtz-Klink's role as leader of the Nazi women's organisations was to make sure that these organisations accepted the party line at all times.

Women's organisations. In 1934 **Gertrud Scholtz-Klink** was appointed National Women's Leader of the Third Reich. It was her task to indoctrinate German womanhood. Under her leadership over 1.5 million women attended maternity school and 500,000 women studied home economics between 1933 and 1938. Similarly, Scholtz-Klink organised the *Frauenwerk* organisations in which four million women participated. She was in overall charge of the women's division of the Nazi Labour Front which had five million members. The

Nazi welfare organisation, the NSV, had over 25,000 advice centres by mid 1938.

YOUNG PEOPLE

The indoctrination of young people was an important element in the Nazi dictatorship. To establish a **Thousand Year Reich** Hitler aimed to educate all young people 'in the spirit of National Socialism'. The aim of such education was to train young people into certain roles: boys into soldiers, girls into submissive wives and devoted mothers. To achieve these aims the regime first encouraged from 1933, and then conscripted from 1939, German youth into huge state run organisations.

KEY TERM

Thousand Year Reich Hitler's vision of a Nazi state which would last a millennium.

Boys

From 1933, boys aged 10–14 years old joined the DJ – German Young People (*Deutsches Jungvolk*). When aged 14 they joined the HJ – Hitler Youth (*Hitler Jugend*). From 1933 the leader of the HJ, **Baldur von Schirach**, was given the responsibility of coordinating all youth groups and bringing them under the control of the HJ. By 1935, some 60 per cent of all German youth belonged. Enormous pressure was put on parents to allow their children to join. In 1936, the HJ became the only organisation which could organise all sports activities for young people up to 14 (later extended to 18). On 1 December 1936, the HJ became a department of state. However, even though all boys were expected to be members of the HJ it wasn't made compulsory until the Hitler Youth Law of 25 March 1939. The HJ offered a wide range of activities to its members, from outdoor activities to music. For many young people it was an excellent chance to enjoy the outdoor life but the degree of regimentation and the overtones of militarism offended many. During the war the HJ undertook many tasks connected with the war effort. Hitler appointed Baldur von Schirach Youth Leader of the German Reich in June 1933.

KEY PERSON

Baldur von Schirach was a very important figure in Germany before the war. As the leader of Germany's youth he had a key role in building the Thousand Year Reich. In 1941 he was made *Gauleiter* of Vienna.

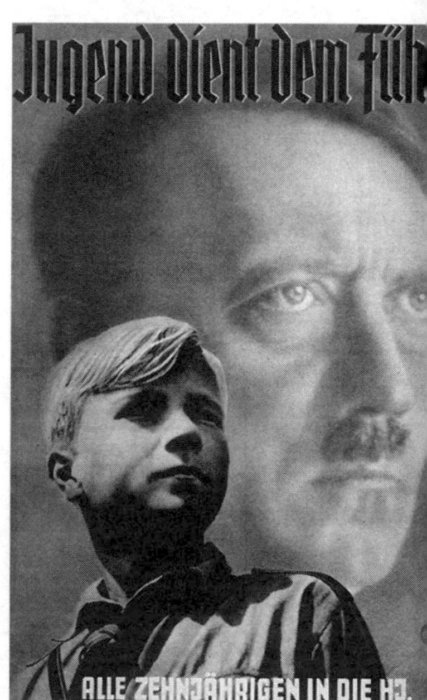

The Hitler Jugend.

Girls

At the age of 10 girls joined the JM – League of Young Girls (*Jüngmädelbund*) – and at 14 they were expected to become members of the BDM – League of German Girls (*Bund Deutscher Mädel*). By 1936, the BDM had a membership of over two million girls. The rules on membership were similar to those of the HJ. Until 1939 it was still not compulsory, although to opt out was frowned upon. Girls in the BDM were taught to accept the role of mother and wife in their future adult life. At the age of 17, girls in the BDM could join up to the Faith and Beauty organisation. Set up in 1937, it specialised in education in domestic science and preparation for marriage.

Education

Hitler's remark 'whoever has the youth has the future' is a useful guide to the importance the Nazis placed on education. In February 1933, Hitler appointed **Bernhard Rust** Prussian Minister of Education and Minister of Culture. A year later he promoted him to the post of Reich Minister for Science, Education and Culture. It was Rust's task to begin the purge of the teaching profession which would make the Nazification of education possible (changing the curriculum and teachers to promote Nazi values). Jewish teachers were fired immediately as were all those of suspect politics. The party tightened its control of teachers through encouraging membership of the National Socialist Teachers' Alliance (NSLB). By 1937, some 97 per cent or 320,000 teachers had joined. This organisation took specific responsibility for indoctrinating teachers in Nazi ideology. By 1939, nearly two-thirds of the NSLB membership had been on courses. Many teachers were keen members of the Nazi Party and most willing to pass on its ideology. In 1936, 32 per cent of NSLB members were party members. The regime also set up an elite school system consisting of the **Adolf Hitler Schools**, ***Napolas*** and the ***Ordensburgen***. These schools came under the influence of the HJ and the first of them opened in April 1937. The reorganisation of higher education mirrored that of the schools – those teachers who were believed to be unacceptable were purged.

The school curriculum. The Nazis insisted on a revised school curriculum as part of their attempt to control the minds of Germany's young people. The importance of

KEY PERSON

Bernhard Rust Despite his promotion to Reich Minister from 1935, Rust was a comparatively weak figure. Although he attempted to centralise control of education, e.g., from 1937 his ministry had sole control over the appointment of teachers, he soon found other leading Nazis including Göbbels and Schirach interfering in education.

KEY TERMS

Adolf Hitler Schools placed an emphasis on physical education and racial ideology.

'Napolas' were Nazi military academies. Graduates of the Napolas would usually be expected to join the Waffen SS.

'Ordensburgen' were for the elite students chosen from the other two types of schools. The students were given military and political instruction to prepare them for leadership in the Third Reich.

sport was upgraded as was history, biology and German studies.

- Sport was the means by which a new militarily orientated youth could be engineered. The promotion of sport matched the anti-academic nature of many Nazi leaders.
- History was studied as a means of politically indoctrinating Germans about their past.
- Biology became the study of racial stereotypes and the supposed superiority of the Aryan race.
- Mathematics and physics were less easy to manipulate. However, the new textbooks issued to German schools still managed to use these subjects to pass on racial or military messages.
- Religious studies lost time in the curriculum and in 1935 it was dropped as a subject from the school-leaving examinations.

It is not surprising to note that as a result of these changes academic standards dropped, as did the status of teachers. By 1938, there were 8,000 teaching vacancies to be filled.

NAZISM AND THE CHURCHES

Introduction

The tension which existed between Nazism and the Churches was a result of their conflicting ideologies. At its roots, Nazism rejected Christianity as a product of Jewish culture. In 1933, Hitler spoke of 'stamping out Christianity' in Germany. In the Nazi Party programme of 1920, Point 24 spoke of promoting '**positive Christianity**'. What this meant in practice was a rejection of Catholicism and Protestantism. In 1934, the German Faith Movement was set up by the Nazi state to promote the ideals of positive Christianity. It became the state religion and all those in positions of authority such as civil servants were expected to join. It campaigned vigorously against Christian rituals such as prayers in school. Instead, its members attempted to paganise the Christian rituals of baptism, marriage and death. However, in 1939 only five

KEY TERM

Positive Christianity was an idea developed by the Nazi thinker Alfred Rosenberg. It was to be a religion based on racial values, the promotion of the Aryan peoples and a return to the ideas of past Nordic pagan faiths.

per cent of the population were registered as members of the German Faith Movement.

Nazism and the Catholic Church

Early agreement. The fear of the Nazi leadership was that in coming into conflict with the churches they would upset large numbers of Germans. So at the start of the dictatorship, they followed a policy of conciliation and compromise with the churches. For the leaders of the Catholic Church, the most important priority in 1933 was to secure their position. Many bishops feared a repeat of the ***Kulturkampf*** of the early 1870s, which so damaged the Church's power. As a result, between April and July 1933 negotiations took place about the status of the Church in the new Germany. By July 1933 there was agreement between the papal representatives and high ranking German officials including the Vice-Chancellor von Papen. The **Concordat** which was signed included the following points:

- The Catholic Church was guaranteed religious freedom and the right to conduct its own affairs without interference from the state.
- The property rights of the Church were guaranteed as were the legal status of the clergy and the Church's role in the appointment of bishops.
- Importantly for the Church, it continued to have a key role in education.
- In return, Hitler was guaranteed that the Church would not interfere in politics. He also won considerable praise both at home and abroad for his diplomatic success. The Concordat acted to undermine support for the Centre Party.

Growing tension. Such an agreement contradicted Hitler's aim to include the churches in the *Gleichschaltung*, the Nazi process of coordination. It became quickly apparent that Hitler had little desire to respect the Concordat. However, his frustration was that the churches survived as an alternative focus for the loyalty of many Germans. To many in the SA, the Catholic Church was an important enemy. Catholic youth groups were harassed and disbanded as in the case of the Catholic Youth League. The Church was weakened by what could be described as a

KEY TERMS

'Kulturkampf' means a cultural struggle. From 1871 to 1883 the new German state dominated by Otto von Bismarck attacked the privileges and role of the Church in education and social affairs. The May Laws of 1873, which effectively put the clergy under state control were at the centre of the state's attack.

Concordat is the word used to describe an agreement between church and state.

war of attrition waged at local and national level. The Ministry of Church Affairs, created in 1935, further weakened the position of the Church. By the end of 1935, the Catholic organisational network remained intact, yet relations with the regime were far from secure. In a speech to the SS at Vogelsang Castle in 1937, Hitler attacked those who gave their allegiance to organisations other than the party.

Conflict between church and state. However, the Catholic Church's hierarchy was increasingly concerned about Hitler's attitude to organised religion. In response to growing censorship of the Catholic press and harassment of the clergy the papacy decided to speak out. On 14 March 1937, Pope Pius XI issued a papal encyclical, a letter to all Catholic bishops, with the title ***Mit Brennender Sorge*** (*With Deep Anxiety*). Hitler's response was immediate. Religious affairs were removed from the Ministry for Church Affairs and handed to the SS. He demanded that all Germans make a choice between their religion and the regime, e.g., the ranks of the Nazi Party were closed to all but Hitler Youth graduates. All voluntary organisations were closed down. The Nazis also began a campaign to remove crucifixes from the classroom. The opposition this raised, especially in strong Catholic areas, such as Bavaria, caused the campaign to be suspended until the war years.

KEY TERM

'Mit Brennender Sorge' (*With Deep Anxiety*). In the encyclical the Pope condemned the regime's racial policies and the absence of natural law or justice in Nazi Germany. The Pope objected strongly to the regime's persecution of priests and accused it of breaking the 1933 Concordat.

Relationship during the war. Even though the campaign against the Church eased for the first two years of the war, the tension between Church and state remained. On 22 March 1941, Cardinal von Galen led an attack on the policy of executing mentally ill people. Galen's outburst resulted in the euthanasia programme being wound up. However, the Catholic Church failed to speak out against the murder of Europe's Jews. Despite receiving reports from across Europe about the deportation of Jews to the extermination camps, Pope Pius XII chose to remain silent on the issue. However, such silence did not prevent anti-Christians in the Nazi regime, such as Martin Bormann, encouraging attacks on Catholics until 1945.

Nazism and the Protestant Churches

The German Christian Church. In 1933 the Protestant faith was divided into 28 churches with 45 million members. The largest church was the Lutheran Church with 18 million members. These divisions gave Hitler the opportunity to impose his will on the Protestant churches. On 4 April 1933, Hitler appointed **Ludwig Müller** as National Bishop to lead all Protestants in an all-embracing German Christian Church. On 14 July a constitution for the new Church was recognised by the Reichstag. Müller was formally endorsed as the first Reich Bishop after a rigged vote. However, the ideology of this new Church was dominated as much by Nazi ideas as by Protestantism.

KEY PERSON

Ludwig Müller was chosen by Hitler to lead the new Church because of his strong nationalist and anti-Semitic opinions. As a loyal supporter of the regime Müller worked hard to counter the Confessional Church.

Pastor Martin Niemöller and the Confessional Church. As a result of the creation of the German Christian Church 200 pastors led a breakaway church, the Confessional Church in 1934. In all some 7,000 of the 17,000 pastors in Germany joined the Church. Its leaders included **Pastor Martin Niemöller** who insisted that the Church be independent of the state. He helped set up and lead the Pastors' Emergency League in 1934, as an organisation committed to defending the new Church. The Protestant Women's Bureau with 2.5 million members, led by Agnes von Grone, criticised the regime until the organisation was disbanded in 1936. Tensions between the new official Protestant church and the old established Churches were considerable.

KEY PERSON

Pastor Martin Niemöller initially welcomed the Nazi regime because of his opposition to communism. However, his decision to set up the Confessional Church set him in opposition to the regime. Niemöller survived the war and his imprisonment in Sachsenhausen and Dauchau.

The Ministry of Church Affairs. By 1934, Müller had failed to attract any more than 2,000 pastors to the German Christian Church. The regime responded with the demotion of Müller and the creation of the **Ministry of Church Affairs** in 1935, which coordinated the harassment of practising Christians. In 1937, Niemöller spoke out against the regime in a sermon and was arrested and imprisoned in Dachau. During the remaining years of the Third Reich the Confessional Church opposed the regime's attacks on religion. However, it remained silent about the persecution of the Jews of Germany. Many Protestants rejected the state organised German Christian Church but also the Confessional Church. Indeed by 1937 the Protestant churches had lost their ability to defend themselves against the state.

Dietrich Bonhöffer. During the war, the Protestant churches continued to fail to speak out against the regime. However, there were examples of individuals such as Dietrich Bonhöffer, who showed the courage and the conviction to speak out and resist. A leading member of the Confessional Church, Bonhöffer joined the resistance against the Nazis. Although he became a double agent for the Nazi secret service, he was arrested in 1943. Bonhöffer was sent to Buchenwald and then Flossenberg concentration camp, where he was executed in April 1945.

Dietrich Bonhöffer.

SUMMARY QUESTION

Consider all the areas described in the chapter:
- the working class;
- women;
- youth;
- the churches.

Which of these did the Nazis manage to change most by 1939? Explain your answer using evidence from the chapter.

CHAPTER 13

The 'Jewish Question'

DISCRIMINATION AND VIOLENCE

Introduction. At the heart of Nazi ideology was anti-Semitism. After coming to power in January 1933, the Nazis moved to identify and isolate Germany's half a million Jews, discriminate against them with legislation and then attack them with propaganda and physical violence.

Boycott. Almost immediately after Hitler became Chancellor in January 1933, Nazis began attacks against Jews and their property. Although Hitler sympathised with the attackers, the violent means they used were considered a problem by a Nazi leadership that was concerned about its image. The attacks were organised at a local level and often provoked by members of the SA. However, other groups were involved including the violently anti-Semitic Fighting League of the Commercial Middle Class. The attacks were widely reported across the world. In the United States, Jewish organisations responded to events in Germany by attempting to organise a boycott of German goods. Calls from within the Nazi movement for a counter-boycott grew. In response to these calls the regime agreed to a nationwide **boycott** of Jewish businesses on 1 April 1933. However, the boycott was not universally popular. On top of this, SA violence on 1 April provoked widespread disapproval and raised concerns amongst leading Nazis that this disapproval could affect the party politically.

KEY EVENT

Boycott: 1 April 1933
Originally Hitler planned an indefinite boycott (a refusal to buy Jewish goods or deal with Jewish businesses). However, pressure from Foreign Minister Neurath and Reichsbank President Hjalmar Schacht, as well as from the governments of Britain, France and the United States, resulted in the boycott being limited to one day. The boycott was only a partial success. In many areas there was violence but considerable numbers of Germans ignored the boycott.

Further laws to discriminate against the Jews. This violence led the Nazi leadership to respond with legislation that would discriminate against the Jews:

- On 7 April 1933 Jews were banned from jobs in the civil service and on 11 April from the legal profession. This was closely followed by a ban on Jewish doctors

and dentists. At this stage of the regime there were exceptions made, especially of those who had fought for Germany in the First World War.
- In October 1933 the Editors' Law restricted Jewish participation in journalism.
- Throughout 1933 the Nazi leadership had responded to pressure from its rank and file to act against Jews. The alternative was that Jews were attacked at a local level indiscriminately. Another example of this was in April 1933 when the Law Against the Overcrowding of Schools limited the total number of Jewish students to 1.5 per cent of the overall total number of young people being educated. This was in response to the exclusion of Jews from schools at a local level.
- Industrialists, such as **Gustav von Krupp**, who were keen to please the Nazis sacked their Jewish employees. Krupp did so in April 1933.

Violence and the Nuremberg Laws, 1934–5. Propaganda against the Jews flourished after January 1933. The magazines *Der Stürmer*, edited by the violent anti-Semite, Julius Streicher, or Joseph Göbbels' *Der Angriff* pumped out a diet of harsh anti-Jewish propaganda. But by 1934 Nazi leaders were again becoming disturbed by the level of locally inspired anti-Jewish violence. In some areas, such as Franconia where Streicher was *Gauleiter*, the economic boycott against the Jews was semi-permanent. Every now and again there was an outburst of violence against the Jews whipped up by the SA. In Franconia in the spring of 1934, 35 Jews were injured. However, attacks against Jewish businesses damaged the regime's standing abroad and threatened economic recovery. But party activists continued to demand the removal of Jews from German society. The response of Hitler was to have his civil service draft what became known as the **Nuremberg Laws** of 15 September 1935. The main points of these laws were as follows:

- The Reich Citizenship Laws deprived Jews of their German citizenship and their political rights.
- Under the Law for the Protection of German Blood and German Honour, marriage and sexual relations between Jews and Germans were outlawed.

KEY PERSON

Gustav von Krupp was one of Germany's leading industrialists and a key munitions maker. Until early 1933 he opposed the Nazis coming to power. However, once he had been reassured by Hitler that the new regime would follow a policy of rearmament, he became one of its most enthusiastic supporters.

Further discrimination, 1936–8. Following the Nuremberg Laws there was a quiet period for the Jews of Germany. Fear of a boycott of the 1936 Berlin Olympic Games and a wish to ensure the success of the Second Four Year Plan in its first year meant that open attacks on Jews were discouraged. However, harassment of Jews continued at a local level and decrees continued to be passed discriminating against them. In October 1936 a decree was passed banning all civil servants from consulting Jewish doctors. As the economic position of Germany improved from mid 1937, so attacks on the Jews intensified. Those who feared the economic results of attacks on the Jews looked to the Minister of Economics, Hjalmar Schacht, to argue their case. In November 1937 he was forced to resign his post. In December 1937 Hermann Göring ordered that Jewish businesses be restricted in the raw materials they could receive. The *Anschluss*, the union of Germany and Austria, in March 1938 unleashed a wave of attacks against Jewish property in Austria. This triggered Göring into issuing the Decree for the Registration of Jewish Property in April 1938. Furthermore, Jewish professionals were again attacked – from September 1938 Jewish doctors were forbidden to treat Aryan patients. New steps were taken to identify Jews and Polish Jews were expelled from Germany in October 1938.

'Kristallnacht' and its aftermath, November 1938. The murder of a German diplomat, Ernst von Rath, in Paris on 7 November 1938 by a Jew, Hersch Grynszpan, sparked an episode of violent persecution. The Propaganda Minister Joseph Göbbels was determined to use the murder as the way to get back into Hitler's favour after the Führer had expressed disapproval at his affair with Czech actress Lida Baarova. Göbbels encouraged an attack on Jewish shops, homes and synagogues that became known as ***Kristallnacht*** (Crystal Night) because of the glass strewn across the pavements and streets of German towns and cities. Around 100 Jews were murdered and a further 20,000 sent to concentration camps. After *Kristallnacht* the regime introduced new measures against the Jews: Jews were excluded from German economic life (12 November 1938), all Jewish pupils were expelled from school (15 November 1938) and Jewish businesses were closed

KEY EVENT

'Kristallnacht' was an important turning point in the persecution of the Jews. It signalled a much more violent attitude to the Jews by the Nazi regime.

The interior of a synagogue damaged during Kristallnacht.

(3 December 1938). Many Jews emigrated from Germany but many more stayed.

The consequences of 'Anschluss'. The *Anschluss* was to have an important effect on the level of anti-Semitism in Germany. The level of violence and the ferocity of the attacks on Austria's Jews in 1938 was worse than anything experienced in Germany. In particular, Vienna's 180,000 Jews were the targets of regular attacks, as well as having their property looted. After the *Anschluss*, Reinhard Heydrich had set up the Central Office for Jewish Emigration, which was administered by Adolf Eichmann. In its first six months of operation it forced 45,000 Jews to leave Austria. In January 1939, Göring set up a Reich Central Office for Jewish Emigration, which was placed under the control of Reinhard Heydrich. However, events were soon to be overshadowed by the coming of war.

A Jewish person wearing a Star of David.

THE HOLOCAUST, 1939–45

The isolation of the Jews of Germany. In his infamous speech to the Reichstag on 30 January 1939, Hitler predicted that any future war would lead to 'the destruction of the Jewish race in Europe'. The start of the war led to a further tightening of restrictions on the Jews. On 1 September a curfew was introduced for all Jews and on 21 September Reinhard Heydrich ordered the concentration of Jews around railway junctions. At the same time, all radio sets were confiscated from the Jews in Germany. The relentless policy of separating the Jews from mainstream German society continued. In January 1940 all ration books belonging to Jews were to be stamped with a capital J. The aim was to identify Jews and ensure that they did not claim goods barred to Jews, such as leather. On 1 September 1941 all Jews were ordered to wear a Star of David badge, failure to do so leading to immediate arrest and imprisonment. The Nazi obsession with identifying who was a Jew for purposes of persecution continued throughout the war. Even minor points were tackled, such as the law in November 1942 which said that Jews could no longer be given the Reich sports medal. By this time mass murder had already begun in the East. The final humiliation for many German Jews was in April 1943 when they lost their German citizenship.

The concentration of Jews in specified areas began early in the war. On 30 October 1939 Himmler ordered the deportation of Jews from north west Poland, which was now conquered and made part of Germany, to Nazi-occupied Poland, under the General Government administered by Hans Frank. In many of the conquered territories, Jews were put into recreated medieval **ghettos**. In January 1940, Jews were used for slave labour and confined to ghettos in the previously Polish towns of Lodz, Warsaw, Lublin, Radom and Lvov. By the summer of 1940, Reinhard Heydrich was suggesting emigrating the 3.25 million Jews under German control to a suitable territory. The response of the Jewish section of the Foreign Office was to emigrate the Jews to **Madagascar**. Hitler was openly enthusiastic about such a scheme and mentioned it to the Italian leader Benito Mussolini in June 1940.

KEY TERMS

A **ghetto** is an area of a town or city which is separated from the rest of the town by a wall or fencing.

The Madagascar Plan was the forced emigration of the Jews of Europe to the island of Madagascar, 250 miles off the African coast. Madagascar was a French colony and the plan involved the transfer of ownership of the island to Germany. The idea was to emigrate all Jews to Madagascar and place it under the control of Heinrich Himmler. The problem was that the plan required peace with Britain, whose navy controlled the seas around the island.

The destruction of the Jews of Europe, 1941–5.

However, the alternative of mass murder was also being considered.

The 'Einsatzgruppen'. The link between war against the Soviet Union and genocide is clear. In March 1941, Hitler claimed that war with Russia would be one of annihilation and in the same month Heidrich wrote in a letter about the impending Final Solution whilst also encouraging plans for emigration. In June, as Nazi troops swept across the western Soviet Union, SS *Einsatzgruppen* were authorised by Hitler to exterminate Jews in Russia. Eight months later, 700,000 Jews had been murdered. In anticipation of the Holocaust, the Nazis began to convert Auschwitz into an extermination camp in the summer of 1941.

The Wannsee Conference. On 31 July 1941, Göring ordered Heydrich to prepare for the 'sought-for final

KEY TERM

SS 'Einsatzgruppen' were special units of soldiers set up under the direction of the RSHA led by Heydrich. Their task was to supervise and carry out the Final Solution of the Jews by shooting.

Children at Auschwitz in January 1945.

solution of the Jewish question' and in August Eichmann informed the Foreign Office that Jews were no longer permitted to emigrate from German held territory. A conference was called to discuss the 'Jewish Question', meeting at Wannsee in Berlin in January 1942. Chaired by Heydrich, it reviewed the possible alternatives for the removal of Jews from German territory including the emigration option, which was now not considered possible. In December 1941, the United States had entered the war against Germany and the war in the Soviet Union had ground to a halt. The 'solution' was to murder the Jews of Europe by working or gassing them to death. The conference ordered the organisation of the extermination of Europe's 11 million Jews.

Mass murder. In the next few months German Jews were deported to the ghettos in the East and on to the death camps of Belzec, Treblinka, Sobibor, Maidanek and Auschwitz. In all around 303,000 German Jews were deported, the vast majority of them to their death. On 27 November 1944 Himmler ordered the end of the mass murder of the Jews. However, by the time Auschwitz was liberated by Soviet troops in January 1945 approximately six million Jews had been murdered.

SUMMARY QUESTION

Make four columns across a double page with the headings: Identification, Separation, Violence, Extermination. Put appropriate examples from this chapter under each of these headings. Use this information to answer the following question:

How did the process of Nazi discrimination against the Jews take place?

CHAPTER 14

Opposition to the Nazis

EARLY OPPOSITION IN 1933 AND 1934

Some political opponents attempted to prevent the establishment of Hitler's dictatorship. Communist gangs battled with Nazi storm troopers in February 1933 and the Social Democrats opposed the Enabling Act in March 1933. Conservative opponents began to compile dossiers of crimes committed by the regime. Realising that any attempt by conservative politicians to control Hitler was doomed to failure, Vice-Chancellor Franz von Papen emerged as the spokesman of conservative critics. In his speech at Marburg in June 1934, Papen called for an end to the excesses of the regime and a return to normal government behaviour. The significance of such a speech was that it was the first and last example of open defiance until the latter years of the war.

THE NATURE OF OPPOSITION TO THE NAZIS

Rather than a single united movement, opposition came from individuals and underground groups. The KPD (communists) and SPD (socialists) formed small groups, published reports and maintained contact with exiled leaders. Arvid Harnack from the Reich Economic Ministry and Harro Schulze-Boysen from the Air Ministry formed ***Rote Kapelle*** (Red Orchestra). Most important for the communists were the resistance cells set up in factories and coordinated by Robert Uhrig. In the summer of 1941 there were 89 such factory cells in Berlin alone. There were communist resistance cells in other German cities, including Hamburg and Mannheim. They produced papers and pamphlets attacking the regime and calling for acts of resistance. In 1942, the communist resistance united under the leadership of Wilhelm Knöchel. Its main weakness was that it was vulnerable to Gestapo infiltration.

KEY TERM

'Rote Kapelle' (Red Orchestra). This group passed information to the Soviet Union and campaigned for a future German-Soviet partnership. The group was discovered by the *Abwehr*, the army's counter-intelligence agency in 1942. Many of its leaders were executed by being hung on meat hooks.

In 1943 the communist resistance movement was almost destroyed and Knöchel was arrested. Others carried out individual acts of defiance. Herbert Baum led a Jewish communist group which fire-bombed an anti-Russian exhibition in Berlin in 1942. Disillusioned by the inactivity of their leadership, the socialists began to form splinter groups, including 'Red Patrol', 'Socialist Front' and 'New Beginning', which championed a more assertive policy and worked for cooperation with other opposition groups.

Youth groups

Various youth groups attempted to resist the regime. Disaffected working-class youths formed groups such as the Edelweiss Pirates who attacked members of the Hitler Youth. **Hans and Sophie Scholl** led Munich students in the 'White Rose' group which distributed anti-Nazi leaflets and sought to sabotage the German war effort. In 1943 the Scholls led an anti-Nazi demonstration in Munich. As a result they were arrested by the Gestapo, tried and executed in February 1943.

KEY PEOPLE

Hans and Sophie Scholl studied at Munich University under the anti-Nazi professor Dr Kurt Huber. The aim of the White Rose group was to 'strive for the renewal of the mortally wounded German spirit'. After their execution, the Scholls were made into martyrs for the anti-Nazi movement.

The army

The Army was the most powerful non-Nazi force in the dictatorship. Although the army had been reduced to 100,000 by the Treaty of Versailles, it was highly

Hans and Sophie Scholl.

disciplined and continued to hold a privileged place in German society. The role of General von Schleicher and the army in general in the intrigue of 1932–3 (see page 75) shows its influence. Whilst some generals looked down on Hitler because of his background and his rank, many were sympathetic towards his nationalist, anti-communist views and plans for rearmament. The appointment of **General von Blomberg** as Minister of Defence in January 1933 secured Hitler's alliance with the army. It also foiled plans by Generals von Schleicher and von Hammerstein for a putsch (takeover) against the Nazis. However, relations between the regime and the army remained tense as the SA continued to threaten social revolution and the leader of the SA, Ernst Röhm, argued for the absorption of the *Reichswehr* into a 'People's Army'. General Walther von Brauchitsch issued an ultimatum in April 1934 that the army would only support the Nazi regime if the SA were purged. It is not surprising, then, that the army actively supported the Night of the Long Knives in June 1934 and offered a personal oath of loyalty to Hitler in its wake. This meant that any organised opposition to the regime was likely to be isolated. However, the army was now in a strong position.

KEY PERSON

General von Blomberg supported the Nazi takeover of power because he believed that it would strengthen the role of the army. Blomberg was an important figure in the early years of the Nazi state. He persuaded the army to give Hitler the oath of loyalty in 1934. Partly as a result Blomberg was appointed supreme commander of the newly created *Wehrmacht* (army, navy and air force combined) in 1935. Blomberg was dismissed in 1938 after becoming disillusioned with some aspects of Hitler's dictatorship.

The army's confidence in the regime increased with the development of the rearmament programme and the introduction of conscription in March 1935. This increased the size of the army to over 500,000 men, despite the 100,000 limit set by the Treaty of Versailles. In 1936, Hitler ordered the army into the Rhineland that had been demilitarised by Versailles. Such a move was also popular but there were still tensions between army and regime.

The Blomberg–Fritsch Affair, 1938. At the Hossbach Conference in 1937, the record of which is known as the Hossbach Memorandum, Hitler put forward his foreign policy aims. High on the list was the recovery of German lands and peoples lost at Versailles and *Lebensraum* (living space) in the East. Most generals supported such a policy, even at the risk of war with Russia. Some generals including Blomberg, Ludwig Beck and Werner von Fritsch raised doubts about Germany's ability to fight any war. This was because it did not yet have the resources to do so.

However, Hitler reacted angrily to what he saw as criticism. He moved quickly to remove those he believed to be his critics from office. In February 1938, the Minister of Defence and supreme commander of the Wehrmacht, Field Marshal von Blomberg, was forced to resign when Berlin police files revealed that his wife might have worked as a prostitute in the past. On Blomberg's dismissal, Hitler appointed himself supreme commander of the armed forces. Another opponent of Hitler's at Hossbach, General von Fritsch, was forced to resign at the same time over accusations that he had been involved in homosexual acts. Although the evidence was weak, especially in Fritsch's case, Hitler had managed to remove potential critics from the Army's High Command. Hitler appointed the ever loyal General Keitel as Chief of the High Command and General von Brauchitsch as Commander in Chief of the Army. Both had limited powers. To complete the purge, 16 generals were retired and 44 transferred.

Despite this, General Beck did attempt to lead a putsch against Hitler during the Czech crisis of September 1938 which Beck believed might trigger a war against Britain and France. Hesitancy and divisions amongst the conspirators weakened the plan. In any case it was foiled when Britain and France gave in to Hitler's claims at Munich. With the success of blitzkrieg between 1939–41, there were few attempts on Hitler's life.

Operation Flash. After 1940, more generals joined the resistance, including Hans Oster (Chief of Staff, military intelligence), Franz Halder (Chief of the Army's General Staff, 1938–42), Karl von Stülpnagel (Military Governor of France), Erich Fellgiebel (Chief of Communications for the Armed Forces) and leading officers Henning von Tresckow and **Claus von Stauffenberg**. In March 1943, two officers attempted to assassinate Hitler by placing a time bomb on his plane. Known as Operation Flash, the attempt on Hitler's life was masterminded by Major General von Tresckow. He managed to have the time bomb disguised as a bottle of brandy smuggled onto Hitler's plane which was travelling between Smolensk and East Prussia. The attempt failed when the detonator failed

KEY PERSON

Claus von Stauffenberg was a soldier of distinction who became disillusioned and disgusted with Hitler and the Nazi regime. He was a leading conspirator in the attempt to kill Hitler in July 1944. He was shot on the same day as the assassination attempt.

The scene after the attempt on Hitler's life.

to go off. Luckily for the conspirators, the bomb was not discovered.

The Kreisau Circle

As the war turned against Germany, so more members of the military establishment were drawn together in opposition to the Nazi leadership. The most significant group was the Kreisau Circle led by Helmuth von Moltke and Peter von Wartenberg. In August 1943, they drew up their *Basic Principles for the New Order* which was a blueprint for a new German state based on democratic values. By 1943 the group had some twenty members including Social Democrat Julius Leber and Deitrich Bonhöffer.

The July Plot, 1944. From the ranks of the Kreisau Circle came many of the conspirators in 'Operation Valkyrie', the most serious attempt to assassinate Hitler. The aim of the plot was to replace Hitler with a provisional government led by General Beck. On 20 July 1944 a bomb left by Claus von Stauffenberg exploded at Hitler's headquarters at Rastenburg. Unfortunately for the conspirators, the briefcase carrying the bomb had been moved from its position where it might well have killed Hitler. As a result Hitler suffered only minor injuries. Some 200 conspirators were ruthlessly tracked down, arrested and executed. Many were hung with piano wire at Plötzensee Prison in Berlin. The list of those killed included Stauffenberg, Beck, Dr Leber, Father Alfred Delp and Admiral Wilhelm Canaris. Others, including General Rommel and Major General von Tresckow, committed suicide.

SUMMARY QUESTIONS

1 Why was the army opposition to Hitler so limited in the period 1933–9?

2 Describe the opposition to the Nazi regime during the war.

CHAPTER 15

Foreign policy and the road to war

Throughout his political career, Hitler's foreign policy objectives remained constant and clear. They were clearly expressed in *Mein Kampf* and numerous articles and speeches. Hitler believed in the following:

- **Versailles.** Hitler despised the Treaty of Versailles and saw it as a national humiliation. He promised that if he came to power he would tear up the treaty, end Germany's reparation payments to the Allies and restore Germany's borders to how they had been in 1914.
- ***Lebensraum.*** In *Mein Kampf* and elsewhere he argued that the Aryan race demanded *Lebensraum* (living space) in the East. This living space would be in what is now Poland and Russia.
- **Nationalism.** Hitler was a nationalist who believed that Germany should be respected diplomatically. He also believed strongly in the union of German-speaking peoples. This would include a union between Germany and Austria, the country of his birth.
- **Anti communism.** He hated communism and promised the destruction of that ideology worldwide, if he came to power.
- **Economic expansion.** Hitler's economic policy of rearmament meant that Germany needed raw materials such as coal, iron ore and oil. It also needed to increase its industrial capacity. Therefore, Hitler's foreign policy aims were geared to ensuring a guaranteed supply of materials.

Within a year of his appointment as Chancellor, Hitler had withdrawn Germany from the Disarmament Conference and the League of Nations. From the start, the regime took very little note of international convention or agreements. The League of Nations had been weakened by the actions of Japan in Manchuria in 1931–2. By leaving the League, Hitler made it clear that Germany would have to be dealt with by individual members of the world community. However Hitler needed to avoid any foreign conflict until the regime was secure at home. In 1934, he signed a ten-year Non-Aggression Pact with Poland which ensured the security of Germany's eastern borders. Of particular importance was the fact that this treaty broke the French system of alliances in eastern Europe.

The Austria crisis of 1934. The Treaty of Versailles had banned political union between Germany and Austria. However, such a union was one of Hitler's cherished ambitions. From 1933, Hitler backed a campaign by Austrian Nazis to undermine the government of that country, led by Engelbert Dollfuss. Their actions included blowing up strategically important buildings and attacking important government officials. On 25 July 1934, Austrian Nazis murdered Dollfuss. However, their attempted take-over of power was foiled by government troops led by Dr Kurt von Schuschnigg. The affair raised the possibility of Nazi intervention in Austria. This was made impossible by the actions of **Mussolini** who deployed 40,000 troops along the Austrian border.

KEY THEME

The attitude of Mussolini. Italy's northern borders are shared with Austria, amongst others. The Italian leader, Benito Mussolini, did not relish the possibility of German troops on Italy's northern borders and acted fast to deter Hitler from making any move. Mussolini twice received visits from Dr von Schuschnigg in the autumn of 1934 to show his support for Austrian independence.

The destruction of the Treaty of Versailles

- **The Saar, 1935.** As stated above, Hitler's aim was to destroy the Treaty of Versailles and to restore to Germany what he believed rightfully belonged to Germany. In January 1935, a **plebiscite** (vote) was held in the Saarland over whether the region should return to German control, stay under League of Nations jurisdiction or be transferred to French control. The vote was legitimate under the terms of the Treaty of Versailles and was carried out by the League of Nations. The Nazis campaigned for a vote to join Germany. The electors of the region responded with a 90 per cent 'yes' vote. On 1 March the Saarland was formally reabsorbed into the German Reich. Up until this point, Hitler had been wary of upsetting Britain and France. However with the plebiscite won, it opened the possibility of further territorial gain.
- **Rearmament and conscription, 1935.** The Treaty of Versailles had limited the size of the *Wehrmacht* as well as Germany's navy and air force. In March 1935, Hitler announced that Germany formally renounced the

KEY TERM

A **plebiscite** is a vote, usually on a single issue.

KEY THEME

Conscription and Versailles. At the heart of Nazi policy was the destruction of the Treaty of Versailles. From 1935, Hitler undertook policies which would destroy the Treaty, e.g., conscription, remilitarisation of the Rhineland, restoration of Germany's 1914 boundaries and union with Austria. By the 1930s Britain and France were not prepared to challenge Hitler for fear of provoking another war.

KEY TERMS

The **Stresa Conference** of April 1935 was called with the aim of establishing a common front against Germany. The signing of the Anglo-German Naval Agreement undermined this common front.

Ethiopian crisis, 1935–6. In 1935 Mussolini ordered the invasion of Ethiopia in Africa. The League of Nations condemned Mussolini's actions and imposed limited sanctions on Italy.

sections of the Treaty of Versailles concerned with its disarmament. Immediately he reintroduced **conscription and rearmament**. The *Wehrmacht* was to increase in size to 36 divisions. Hitler justified his actions by arguing that both France and the Soviet Union were increasing the size of their armed forces against the spirit of the Treaty of Versailles. France reacted strongly to German rearmament and encouraged Britain and Italy to protest. The three countries met at the **Stresa Conference** in April 1935. In April 1935 the League of Nations also criticised Germany's rejection of the Treaty of Versailles. However, Hitler saw that there was not a solid alliance formed against Germany. Britain was interested in protecting its empire and, in June 1935, signed a separate Anglo-German Naval Agreement with Germany. This allowed Germany a navy 35 per cent of the size of the British fleet. It was the willingness of the Allies to deal separately with Germany that allowed Hitler to expand unchecked.

- **Rhineland, 1936.** One of Hitler's most dangerous political gambles was the remilitarisation of the Rhineland in March 1936. The *Wehrmacht* was not of any great strength and would not have been able to resist French intervention. However, Hitler was prepared to take the risk and ordered German troops into the region. This was another violation of the Treaty of Versailles and a challenge to the French. However, the French did not respond militarily. The diplomatic world was distracted by the **Ethiopian crisis** and Britain was not prepared to introduce sanctions against Germany.
- **Danzig, 1933–9.** One of Hitler's most common criticisms of the Treaty of Versailles was the creation of the Polish Corridor and the placing of the port of Danzig into League of Nations administration. In 1933, the Nazis in Danzig won 39 seats out of 72 in the senate that ran the port. Two years later, in 1935, they won 43 seats. Encouraged by Hitler, the Danzig Nazis slowly undermined their opponents and, as the influence of the League of Nations declined, so their ability to restrain the Danzig Nazis disappeared. By 1938, 70 seats in the senate were held by Nazis, laws against Jews had been passed and, to all intents and purposes, the city had become part of the German Reich. These measures show

the extent that Hitler and his party were prepared to go in destroying the Treaty of Versailles.

- *Anschluss* **(union with Austria), 1938.** In March 1938, Hitler fulfilled a long-cherished personal ambition by invading Austria and proclaiming *Anschluss* (union) between Germany and Austria. Mussolini's opposition was reduced by Italy's involvement in the **Spanish Civil War** and Mussolini's desire to develop a strong alliance with Germany, which had begun in 1936 with the formation of the **German–Italian axis**. Therefore, when Schuschnigg visited Italy in 1937, Mussolini informed him that Austria could not rely on Italian support in a war against Germany. Hitler continued to pressurise the Austrian government. In February 1938, Schuschnigg visited Hitler and agreed to amnesty Austrian Nazis in prison. Internal chaos and pressure from the Nazis resulted in an ultimatum presented to the Austrian government in March 1939. The Nazi Arthur Seyss-Inquart seized the chancellorship and German troops invaded on 12 March. A plebiscite on *Anschluss* was held in Austria in April 1938 with a 99.75 per cent 'yes' vote. Again British and French protests at the undermining of the Treaty of Versailles were half hearted. Hitler had managed to destroy the Treaty of Versailles while the leading democracies continued to believe that a policy of appeasement was the only way to deal with the successive crises.
- **Czechoslovakia, 1938.** After *Anschluss* with Austria, Hitler turned his attention to Czechoslovakia. Before 1919, the provinces which made up Czechoslovakia were part of the Austro-Hungarian Empire. Therefore there was a considerable German-speaking minority in Czechoslovakia, called the Sudeten Germans. Hitler believed that these three and a half million Sudeten Germans, who were concentrated near the borders with Germany and Austria, should become part of the German Reich. However, Czechoslovakia was attractive for Germany in other ways; it was rich in raw materials and the Skoda engineering company was one of the largest in Europe.

In February 1938, Hitler promised protection to German minorities outside the Reich's borders. This was a clear

KEY THEMES

The Spanish Civil War 1936–9. In 1936 army officers disillusioned with the democratic regime in Spain, attempted a coup d'état. Led by Generals Mola and Franco they asked for military and financial support from sympathetic non-democratic powers Italy and Germany. Hitler's response was immediate. He sent a squadron of planes to ferry the main body of the rebel army from Africa to mainland Spain. For the next three years, Hitler supported the rebels with troops and credit. The most infamous incident of Nazi involvement was in 1937 when the German *Condor Legion* bombed the undefended Basque town of Guernica.

The **German-Italian axis** was formed in 1936, as a result of the Ethiopian crisis. In response to British and French criticism of his action in Africa, Mussolini concluded that an alliance with Italy's ideological partner, Nazi Germany, was more suitable. The axis of 1936 resulted in the military alliance, the **Pact of Steel** signed in May 1939.

Czechoslovakia's allies. Since its foundation in 1918, the Czech Republic had looked to Britain and France to protect it. In 1935 it also signed a protective alliance with the Soviet Union.

signal that he was preparing to interfere in the affairs of Czechoslovakia. The *Anschluss* with Austria in March 1938 completely changed the situation as the new German Empire surrounded Czechoslovakia on three sides. In April 1938, the Sudeten German leader, Konrad Henlein, presented a series of demands to the Czechoslovak government, led by Dr Milan Hodza. Known as the **Karlsbad Programme**, the demands were entirely unacceptable and immediately rejected. This was despite encouragement from Czechoslovakia's allies, Britain and France, that they should accept. Throughout the summer negotiations continued between the government and Sudeten leaders. As tension rose all major powers put their armed forces on alert; in September 1938 Britain held naval manoeuvres and France called up its reserves. On 12 September, Hitler increased the tension by demanding self-determination for the Sudeten Germans. In September he twice met the British Prime Minister, Neville Chamberlain, at Berchtesgaden and Godesberg. Hitler demanded the following:

KEY THEME

The **Karlsbad Programme** included full autonomy for predominately Sudeten regions, reparations for any damages suffered to Germans since 1918, a revision of Czech foreign policy and full cultural freedom.

- Czechoslovak surrender of predominantly Sudeten territories
- Plebiscites to be held in areas with large Sudeten minorities by November.

Britain and France both wished to appease Germany, but Chamberlain and the French Prime Minister, Daladier, found these proposals unacceptable. Eventually Hitler was persuaded by Mussolini to hold an international conference on the issue.

The Munich Conference, September 1938

The conference was held to resolve the Czechoslovakian crisis. While Britain, Italy, France and Germany were represented, Czechoslovakia was not. The agreement that was signed at Munich represented a considerable diplomatic victory for Hitler. Although some people in Britain and France protested against the destruction of the last democratic country in central Europe, there was considerable relief in those countries that war had been avoided. The conference concluded that:

- German occupation of mainly Sudeten areas was to take place at the beginning of October 1938.
- In all, Germany gained 10,000 square miles containing 3.5 million inhabitants of which 700,000 were Czechs.

The annexation of the remains of Czechoslovakia, March 1939. Hitler's ambitions for territory beyond the limits of the Treaty of Versailles and Germany's racial borders became apparent in March 1939. He summoned the Czech President **Hacha** to Berlin and informed him of his plans to incorporate the remains of Czechoslovakia into the German Reich. On 15 March, the Czech provinces of Bohemia and Moravia became German provinces, to be followed the next day by Slovakia. More than any other action, the destruction of Czechoslovakia proved to the outside world that Hitler's ambition lay in achieving *Lebensraum*. And Hitler did not stop there. In the same month, he put pressure on Lithuania to give up Memel and made demands concerning the Polish Corridor. In response to such aggression, Britain and France promised help to Poland in March 1939 if it was invaded by Hitler.

KEY THEME

Hitler's demands to President **Hacha** in March 1939 could not have been clearer. Hitler told him that he should 'place the fate of the Czech people . . . trustingly in the hands of the Führer.'

Nazi–Soviet Pact, 1939. Throughout the 1930s, Hitler's foreign policy had been fiercely anti-communist. This was seen in Germany's involvement in the **Spanish Civil War** between 1936–9. However, in August 1939, Hitler sent his Foreign Minister von Ribbentrop to Moscow to sign a non-aggression pact with the Soviet Union. Such a move was greeted with amazement across the diplomatic world. The main points of the pact ensured that Germany could attack Poland without provoking a response by the Soviet Union. On 31 August 1939 the Supreme Soviet of the Soviet Union finally agreed the terms of the treaty. The following day Hitler invaded Poland.

KEY THEME

All through the **Spanish Civil War** Germany sent help to the Nationalists led by Franco. This involvement in Spain was part of Hitler's commitment to fight what he saw as the spread of communism. A further example of this commitment was the signing of the Anti-Comitern Pact with Japan in November 1937. However, this treaty was also an extension of the German–Italian Axis formed in October 1936.

THE OUTBREAK OF WAR

In September 1939, Poland was invaded and quickly conquered by the German armed forces. The declaration of war had brought Germany into conflict with Britain and France. However, Hitler was to show little restraint. By the end of 1940, France, Belgium, Holland, Denmark,

Norway and Luxembourg had been invaded and overwhelmed. Not only had Versailles been avenged, but also European domination achieved. Only Britain managed to hold out. This was partly due to the defeat of the Luftwaffe in the Battle of Britain of 1940, but also because Hitler turned his attention to his main goal, the destruction of the Soviet Union. German forces invaded Russia on 22 June 1941. The date for invasion might have been earlier had the German army not invaded the Balkans in April 1941 to support their defeated Italian allies.

Operation Barbarossa

Despite the signing of the Nazi–Soviet Pact in August 1939, Hitler had always intended to invade Russia. For Hitler, Russia was not only a strategic threat to his European empire but it was the birthplace of Bolshevism and international Judaism. By invading Russia Hitler intended to:

- win *Lebensraum* for German settlers;
- use the large reservoir of Slav labour;
- exploit oil reserves in the Caucasus and
- exploit the grain supply from the Ukraine.

Operation Barbarossa began with a force of three million troops. They were mainly German but some were from Germany's allies including Italy, Hungary and Romania. The attack took place along three fronts; the northern was to capture Leningrad, the centre to capture Moscow and the southern to overrun the Ukraine and Crimea and to drive on to the Caucasus. Hitler hoped to repeat the spectacular triumphs of his blitzkrieg against Poland in 1939 and against France in 1940. The Germans made rapid advances along all three fronts. By November 1941, Leningrad and Moscow were under siege and three million Soviets had been taken prisoner. However, the vast distances, poor roads, partisan activity and the scorched earth policy of the retreating armies delayed the German advance. By December heavy snow and freezing temperatures brought the Germans to a standstill 30 miles west of Moscow. Hitler had sent his troops into Russia totally unprepared for such extreme conditions. He also underestimated the strength and resistance of the Red Army. Even more decisive was the ability of the Soviets to

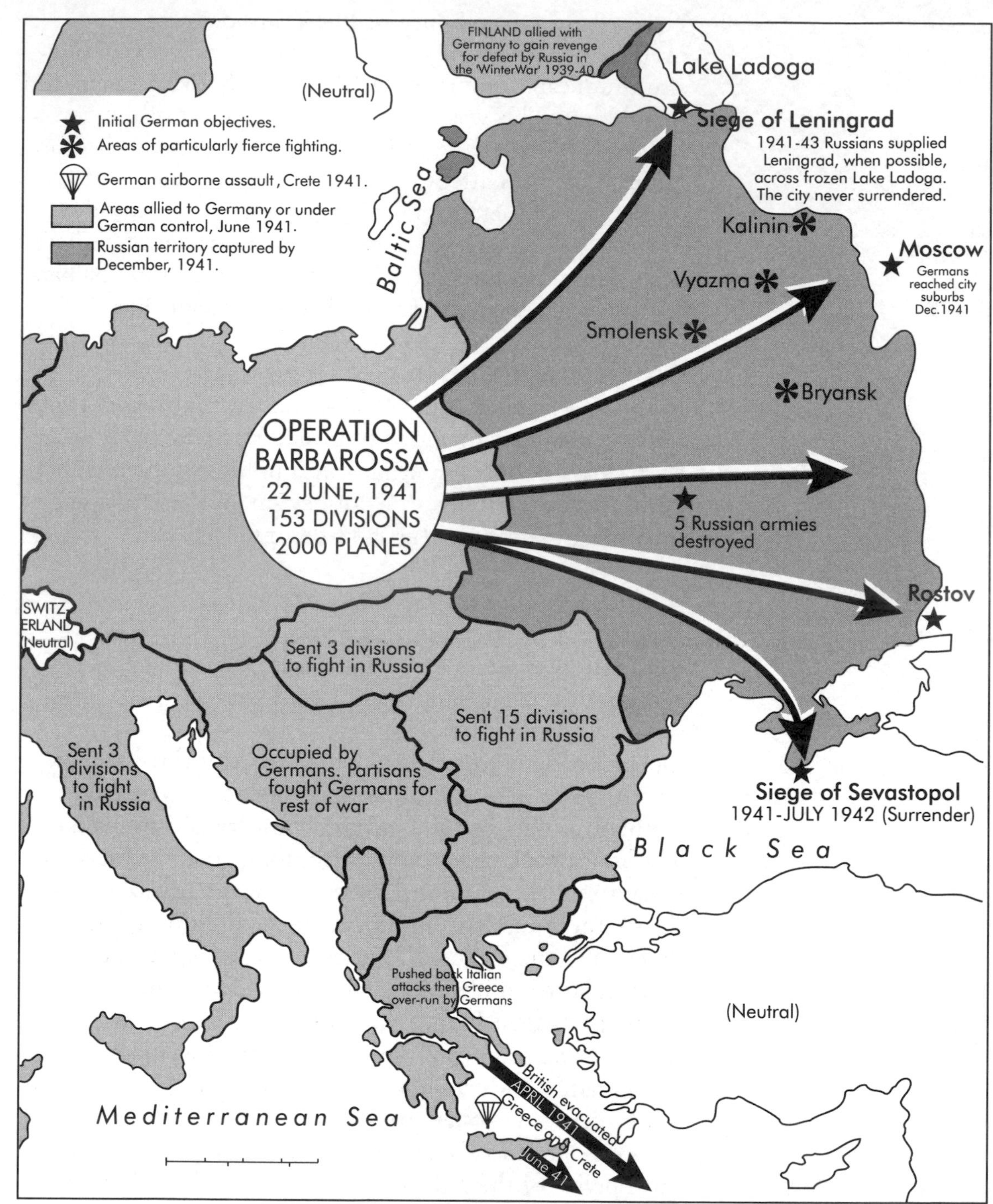

The Russian Front.

uproot 1,500 key factories in 1941–2, transport them and their workforce thousands of miles east of the Urals and reassemble them to become more productive than the German economy by late 1943. On 6 December 1941 the

The siege of Stalingrad.

Russians counter-attacked under General Zhukov, an action which at least halted the German advance.

Stalingrad. In June 1942 the Germans launched a huge summer offensive to capture the Caucasus oilfield. Hitler also ordered the Sixth Army to capture the strategically important city of Stalingrad which guarded the Volga River. The city was besieged from September and bitter street fighting continued throughout the autumn. Stalin was determined to hold on to the city that bore his name and Zhukov organised heroic resistance of the city. On 19 November, the Red Army launched a counter-offensive which trapped the Sixth Army in a giant pincer movement. Although Hitler ordered the Sixth Army's commander, General von Paulus, to fight to the death, on 31 January 1943 he surrendered. The Red Army captured some 92,000 men including 24 generals. The defeat at Stalingrad was one of the most important turning points of the war. The Russians exploited their success with a crushing victory in an enormous tank battle at Kursk in July 1943. This victory paved the way for the Red Army's liberation of Eastern Europe and entry into Germany.

North Africa

German troops led by **General Erwin Rommel** invaded North Africa in April 1941 in support of their defeated

Italian allies. After a series of impressive victories, Rommel's Afrika Korps drove towards Egypt in May 1941 besieging the important town of Tobruk. The British led by General Auchinleck counter-attacked in November and forced Rommel back to El Argheila. As British forces were weakened by the need to reinforce the Far East campaign against Japan, Rommel was able to capture Tobruk and 30,000 prisoners on 21 June. However, the German advance was halted in October 1942 when the British Eighth Army led by General Montgomery inflicted a heavy defeat on Rommel at El Alamein. In November 1942, an Anglo-American force led by General Eisenhower landed behind Rommel in Morocco in Operation Torch. In May 1943, the remains of the Axis forces (Germany, Italy and Japan) in North Africa surrendered.

KEY PERSON

General Erwin Rommel
Known as the Desert Fox, Rommel led the Afrika Corps with distinction from 1941 to 1943. He then became leader of Army Group B in Italy. By 1944, Rommel had become disillusioned with Hitler. Although not part of the plot to kill Hitler, he was named as part of the conspiracy and committed suicide.

Italy

Allied troops invaded Sicily in July 1943 and crossed to mainland Italy in September. In the same month the deposed Italian dictator Benito Mussolini was rescued by German troops led by Captain Skorseny and was taken to Berlin. As the new Italian government surrendered to the Allies, German troops led by Field Marshal Kesselring seized many important Italian cities and strategic points. The allied advance was slow and was held up at Salerno, Anzio and Monte Cassino. Rome was only captured in June 1944 and German troops fought on in Italy until May 1945.

Defeat on the Western Front

British and American troops invaded France on 6 June in Operation Overlord. Led by Generals Eisenhower and Montgomery, some 326,000 troops were landed along the five Normandy beaches. The Americans on Omaha beach encountered severe German resistance, but Hitler was slow to reinforce the Normandy sector. In June, American troops captured Cherbourg and cut off 50,000 crack German troops in the Falaise Pocket. British troops suffered heavy casualties as they advanced through the difficult Bocage countryside of Normandy. Outnumbered, the German troops fell back. Paris was liberated on 24 August and Brussels and Antwerp in the first week of September. The allied advance then slowed as supplies

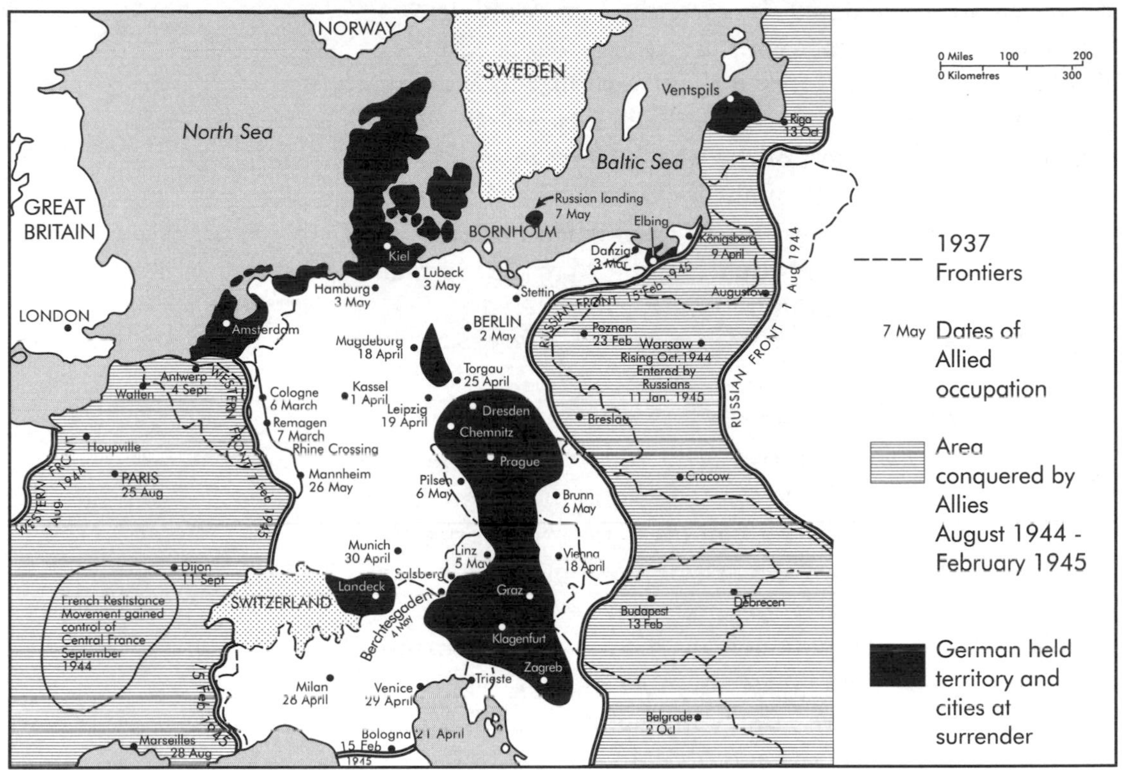

Map showing positions at German defeat in 1945.

were exhausted and German troops rallied to defend German soil. In an attempt to accelerate allied progress General Montgomery launched the doomed Operation Market Garden at Arnhem. Hitler hoped to repeat the victory of 1940 by launching an attack through the Ardennes Forest on 16 December 1944. In the Battle of the Bulge, the German advance was halted and the allied advance resumed. The American troops crossed the Rhine on 22 March 1945 and 320,000 German troops surrendered in the Ruhr in early April. On 25 April, American and Soviet troops met at Torgau on the River Elbe.

War in the East

Following the victory at Kursk, Soviet forces drove the Germans back to the River Dneiper and cut off those units in the Crimea. In the north, the siege of Leningrad was finally broken in January 1944 and western Russia was liberated by July. By the end of 1944 the whole of Russia had been liberated and Germany's allies Romania and

Bulgaria had surrendered. In 1945 the Red Army drove into Germany to be met with fierce resistance. Led by Zhukov, Soviet forces crossed the River Oder in March and began the final assault on Berlin. The battle for Berlin was one of the bloodiest of the war as German troops bolstered by SS soldiers fought for every street. The city was virtually overwhelmed by 30 April when Hitler committed suicide in his bunker. On 7 May the German government, led by Admiral Dönitz, surrendered unconditionally.

The bombing of Germany

Initially the air campaign had little impact on the German war effort. Until 1942 raids were few and inaccurate and merely served to stiffen German resistance. In February 1942 the RAF launched the first of many mass raids. On 30 May Cologne suffered the first thousand-bomber raid. In July 1943 over 50,000 civilians died in the firestorm in Hamburg and an even greater number died in the firestorm which followed the bombing of Dresden on 13 February 1945. By the end of 1943, the Luftwaffe's strength was severely depleted. In 1944 the allied air offensive intensified. In January and February over 1,000 German planes were destroyed and vital machine plants in Schweinfurt and Essen crippled. The precision bombing against targets in the Ruhr did have an important damaging effect on the German war economy to the extent that by 1945 Speer recognised that defeat was inevitable.

SUMMARY QUESTIONS

1 From this chapter, identify two 'turning points' of the war. Explain your choices.

2 Describe the events of the campaign in the East.

AS ASSESSMENT – NAZI GERMANY 1933–45

Sources exercise in the style of Edexcel/OCR.

Exercise 1 The rise in support for the Nazi Party in the 1920s and 30s.

Reading. Before answering the questions you should read Chapter 8 (pages 64–78) and pages 165–174.

Study Sources A to E and then answer Questions 1–5.

Source A

The National Socialists are neither Socialists or in any true sense national. The name 'Socialist' is used as bait to the working men for a movement that has anti-communism as its inspiration. To Hitler's party flock young people of the featherbrained, unbalanced type – students, clerks and others who have lost their economic security. In his speeches Hitler asked that the German nation be cleansed of all non-Aryan elements. He says that Germany would be free of all its ills if Jewish economic power were destroyed. However, he argues that first of all accounts must be settled with what he calls the traitorous Jewish Socialist leaders who have plunged the German people into misery.

Adapted from a report by Paul Gierasch, a German journalist writing about events in Munich in November 1923.

Source B

During the 1920s I began a searching inquiry into the Jewish question. It became clear to me that international Marxism and the Jewish problem are increasingly bound together. In this I recognised the cause of the political, moral and cultural decay of my Fatherland. I studied the solutions proposed by various parties and convinced myself that the Nazi programme is absolutely necessary for the rebirth of Germany.

Adapted from a 1934 'life history' written by a young Nazi. The competition for which the 'life history' was written was organised by the Ministry of Propaganda.

Source C

A Nazi propaganda poster.

Source D

In his latest speeches Hitler has largely dropped the anti-Semitic passages. Now his speeches amount to little more than a repetition of his charges against the 'November criminals' and the 'Marxists' governments of the last fourteen years. These are based on deliberate lies. The average Nazi audience is made up very largely of young people under 30 who appear to be ignorant of the most basic historical facts, who believe Hitler when he declares the revolution of 1918 led to Germany's defeat – the 'stab-in-the-back' legend – and believe him, too, when he claims that the present unemployment is the work of successive left-wing governments.

Adapted from a report written by the British ambassador in Berlin in 1933 for the British government.

Source E

There is little doubt that Hitler's insistence on 'legal' means gave the NSDAP movement a legitimacy that it lacked in the 1920s...Although the Nazis picked up a significant number of votes from those who had previously voted for the middle class parties such as the DVP or DNP, it is wrong to assume that it lacked a broad social base. By the early 1930's the Nazis were the only party that could present itself as a national one that could cut across class and interest lines. This was due to the attractions of the Nazis as a party of protest and lofty but ill-defined ideals such as *Volkgemeinschaft* (the concept of national community). Nazi policy was vague but deliberately so, style being more important than substance. It was this which made the Nazis successful electorally.

A crucial factor in the rise to power of the Nazis was the ability of the party to expand and provide a political home for the discontented, particularly after the crash of 1929. The use of rallies, speeches, lectures and 'aeroplane campaigns' in certain areas were effective in raising the profile of the party and increasing the vote at elections...The depression and economic crisis that followed the crash in 1929 did not in itself bring the Nazis to power. What it did was create the possibility, the opportunity and the context in which Nazi propaganda would not fall on deaf ears.

Adapted from Martin Collier and Philip Pedley *Germany, 1919–45* published in 2000.

Questions

1 Study Source D. According to this source, why did some young people support the Nazis in Germany in the early 1930s?

How to answer this question. The question is asking you to show that you understand the source. Therefore you must do the following:

- Provide some explanation which answers the question.
- Extract brief quotes from the source to back up what you are saying.

Style. Here is an example of the style you should use:

According to the British ambassador many young people were easily deceived. He writes that they were 'ignorant of the basic facts'. Those who were deceived supported the Nazis as they accepted the Nazi explanation for Germany's problems; for example the myth that Germany was defeated in 1918 after the revolution 'the stab in the back legend'. The Nazis also gained support by playing on fears of unemployment in 1933 by blaming it on 'successive works of left-wing governments'.

2 Study Source A and use your own knowledge to answer the question. What did the Nazis mean by 'non-Aryan' elements' in the 'German nation'?

How to answer this question. The question is asking you to explain the key term of 'non-Aryan'. Therefore you need to respond with a thorough explanation which takes in at least some of the following points:

- 'Non-Aryan' within the 'German nation' was used to describe those who were living in Germany but did not belong to the 'Aryan' racial group as defined by the Nazis.
- A 'non-Aryan' was someone who did not match the physical appearance of a member of the Nordic *Herrenvolk*. The defining traits of a 'non-Aryan' would be that he/she would believe in 'foreign' ideas such as democracy or internationalism.
- To the Nazis, the Jews were the most obvious and hated 'non-Aryan' group within Germany. Such a doctrine was the product of Hitler's obsession.

3 Study Sources A and D and refer to both sources in your answer. 'Hitler's speeches did not change much in content from 1923–33'. To what extent do you agree with this statement?

How to answer this question. You need to look for examples in the sources of change and continuity. The question asks you to use the sources and you need to focus on what they say in your answer.

Plan. Before you write you need to come to some kind of conclusion about how you will answer the question. An example might be along the lines of the following:

- This statement is not convincing. There are examples of continuity in Hitler's speeches between 1923–33. However, the change in circumstances and audience meant that his speeches changed significantly in content.
- You should also underline in the source examples of change and of continuity.

Style. Make sure that you quote from the sources when making your point. Below is an example of the style you might adopt in answering this question.

In 1933 the priority of the regime was to consolidate power and encourage economic recovery. Therefore for the time being, Hitler reduced the number of attacks on Germany's Jews in his speeches, as Source D pointed out 'Hitler has largely dropped the anti-Semitic passages'. This was a significant change from the days out of power of 1923 when Hitler felt free to urge that Jewish economic power 'was destroyed'.

4 Study Sources B and C. How valuable are these sources to an historian studying the reasons why people supported the Nazis in the 1920s and early 1930s?

How to answer this question. When answering a question about the value of a source you should try to avoid generalisations about the type of source and you should concentrate on more than its content. Instead you should ask yourself the following questions:

- What is the situation of the author of the source?
- What is the purpose of the author in producing the source?
- What are the limitations of each source as well as their positive points?

Style. Try to refer to the sources when possible to back up your ideas. To gain top marks you need to ensure that you cover both sources. Below is an example of the style you might chose to use.

Many young Germans were taken in by Nazi propaganda and Source B is a clear example of this. The source is also valuable as evidence of the simple nature of the Nazi message which appealed to the young. The source also valuable as one written by a middle class author as it indicates the fears of that class the Nazis were able to exploit for votes 'the political, moral and cultural decay of my Fatherland'. However the value of the source is limited by the fact that it was submitted for a competition organised by the Ministry of Propaganda. The author has remained anonymous and the source represents more the view the Ministry wanted to portray as much as that of the individual.

5 Use your own knowledge and Source E to explain why support for the Nazis grew so rapidly in the period 1929 to 1933.

How to answer this question. This question asks you to analyse the reasons why support for the Nazis grew in the years before they came to power. To reach full marks you will need to do the following:

- Look for a variety of reasons to explain why support for the Nazis grew. Prioritise your most important reasons.
- Use information from both the Source and your own knowledge.
- Plan your line of argument first and what you are going to put in each paragraph.

Plan. You might use these points of argument in your plan.

- The growth in support for the Nazi party must be placed into the context of economic crisis, in particular in the aftermath of the collapse of 1929. As the effects were felt across Germany, so the electorate became more receptive to the message of those who offered a radical solution.
- The Nazis were well organised, used new and powerful propaganda techniques and were ideologically flexible.
- Their appeal was reinforced by the apparent 'legality' of the Nazi assault on power in the late 1920s and early 30s in contrast to the attempted putch of 1923.

Exercise in the style of Edexcel (unit 3). Using a source as a stimulus.

Exercise 2 Life in Nazi Germany, 1933–9.

Reading. Before answering this question you should read pages 97–101 and pages 187–193.

Study Source A and then answer Questions 1 to 3 which follow the source.

Source A

Under the Nazis there has been much invisible unemployment. The number of unemployed Jews is great, but these are not counted as unemployed. Another source of 'invisible unemployment' has been the wholesale discharge from paid work of women whose husbands are employed, and of unmarried men under twenty five. None of these are included among the unemployed in the official statistics. Part-time workers are counted as fully employed. 'Artificially created' work accounts for some of the employment. The reintroduction of conscription has taken hundreds of thousands of men off the labour market. In 1935 came the increase in employment due to rearmament: this of course is dependent on the continuance of rearmament at the same lively rate.

Adapted from an article in the magazine *Foreign Affairs* written by the American Norman Taylor in 1936. Taylor was an expert on German affairs.

Questions

1 How much does the author of this source rate the achievements of Nazi economic policy? Use the source and explain your answer fully.

How to answer this question. The question wants you to focus your answer on Source A.

- In asking you to explain your answer the question is also hoping that you will explain the author's view of the Nazi achievements by using your own knowledge.
- You should quote from the source whenever possible. However you should ensure that your quotes are short and to the point.

Style. You need to answer the question directly. Here is an example of a sentence showing how you might do that.

The tone of this extract is dismissive of Nazi economic 'achievements'. In particular the author cast a serious doubt on the means by which the Nazis have reduced unemployment. He is damning of the labour schemes, the Arbeitdeinst, which he dismisses as 'artificially created'. He also highlights the strong link between military policy, i.e., rearmament and conscription, and the reduction in the numbers of the unemployed.

2 What were the main aims of Nazi economic policy in the period 1933–39?

How to answer this question. Although there is a source at the start of the exercise, the question does not ask you to use it if you do not want to. Instead the source can act as a stimulus; it can give you a clue to at least a part of your answer. In this case it mentions the reduction of unemployment which was one of the main aims of Nazi economic policy.

The question here wants you to describe the main features of Nazi economic policy. It would be a good idea for you to organise your description thematically. Themes you might include are:

- rearmament, autarky, reduction of unemployment, maintenance of living standards.

3 Did Nazi economic policy improve or worsen the lives of the German people in the period 1933–39? Explain your answer.

How to answer this question. For this question you are to use the source but only as a stimulus. The question asks for an analytical answer. therefore you need to do the following:

- Answer with a strong line of argument and make a clear judgement which comes down on one side or the other of the question.
- Show that you understand that various groups within society saw their lives improve but for some their lives worsened.
- Use well selected evidence to back up your argument.

Exercise 3 Essay questions.

Question 1 in the style of AQA.

1 How did the relationship between the German Army and Hitler change in the period 1933–38?

Reading. To answer this question you need to read pages 136–138 and pages 182, 230–232.

How to answer this question. This question asks you to analyse the change in the relationship between Hitler and the army. The emphasis of the essay is on the concept of change and you need to produce an argument which focuses on this specifically.

Plan. You need to plan your essay to avoid simply running through a narrative account of the relationship between the German army and Hitler in the period in question. You need in particular to identify the points of argument which would allow you to do this. here are some examples:

- The relationship between army and Hitler changed considerably as Hitler consolidated his power after 1934.
- Hitler's expansionist foreign policy caused tension between leading army generals and himself which was counter balanced by foreign policy success and the popularity of rearmament.

Content. You must ensure that the content you use covers the whole period in question. Those who focus on an important period moment such as the summer of 1934 stand to be penalised. You should make reference to the following in your essay:

The role of Hindenburg in 1933 and the importance of his death in 1934, the significance of the Night of the Long Knives, rearmament, the importance of Hitler's consolidation of power and his domestic and foreign policy successes, the 'Hossbach' conference of 1937 and Blomberg-Fritsch affair. You might also refer to the examples of opposition up to 1938.

Question 2 in the style of AQA.

2 The role of Hitler was the most important factor in the development of the one party state in Germany by 1939. Explain why you agree or disagree with this statement.

Reading. Before answering this question you should read pages 81–96, 135–140 and 175–186.

How to answer this question. You need to work out clearly in your mind what you think is the most important reason for the development of a one party state. In your answer you should give a balanced explanation which will create links between Hitler and other factors.

Plan. You must identify your main points of argument. Below are examples of the type of points you might make:

- The role of Hitler as dictator is crucial in the creation of a one party state in Germany and the statement is accurate to a considerable extent. Of importance in aiding Hitler was state propaganda.
- However the weakness of opposition and the role of the army, civil service and judiciary are of real importance in explaining why Germany developed into a one party state.
- One must also place the actions of Hitler into the context of economic improvement which reduced the scope for opposition.

Question 3 in the style of OCR.

3 The increase in the popularity of the Nazis by the late 1930s in Germany can be explained by the following factors:

- The weaknesses of the Weimar Republic
- Nazi economic policy and its consequences
- Nazi social policy
- Hitler's leadership and Nazi propaganda

a Choose any two factors from the above list. Explain how they helped increase the popularity of the Nazis in the late 1930s.

Reading. This question is very wide ranging in its scope. Before answering this question you should have read pages 87–101, 107–126 and looked at pages 175–209.

How to answer this question. To answer this question, and questions of a similar style, you need to do the following:

- You should check the period in question. Although the question mentions 'popularity' and the Weimar Republic the question is about the 'late 1930s' and **not** the Nazi rise to power.
- You are being asked to show a high degree of understanding. Therefore you will need to analyse the importance of your two chosen factors. You must not simply

describe the factors. For top marks both factors must be linked to popularity at the end of the 1930s.

Plan. In your plan you should try and refine your argument by showing that the factors you have chosen led to popularity. However they did not mean that the Nazis were popular with all Germans by the late 1930s.

Here are examples of points you could make in your introduction and you can expand upon throughout your answer.

- Economic changes and the return to near full employment won the regime considerable support. However static living standards and the prioritisation of rearmament over consumption meant that for some that support was qualified.
- The regime gained support from some groups of Germans as a result of their social policy. However, the failure of the regime to transform German society and the exclusion of some groups meant that popularity was not uniform.

Style. *The most significant aspect of Nazi economic policy which led to considerable public support was the reduction in unemployment. By 1936 almost all Germans enjoyed by having a job. This was a political priority for the regime and essential in winning it widespread working class support. Training schemes for the unskilled and apprenticeships for working-class school leavers were significantly expanded. Most workers were earning 20 per cent more by 1939 in real terms compared to 1933 and though non-skilled workers saw little or no such increase, most accepted this in return for job security and improved social benefits . . .*

If there was a social transformation during the Nazi dictatorship then it can be detected most easily in the ideas and attitudes of young Germans. It was in youth policy that the regime had its greatest successes and won most popularity. Thousands of young people were taken in by the excitement of hiking, camping, competitive sports, marching in smart uniforms or simply by a yearning to belong. By 1939 seven and a half million young Germans were active participants of the Hitler Youth. Education submitted passively to nazification. Teachers were heavily over-represented in the Nazi Party and schools purged the dissident minority. However the regime's popularity did decline by 1939 as young people became disaffected by growing regimentation, petty restrictions and ineffective and ageing youth leaders. Around 10 per cent of German youth rejected the Nazi youth organisations despite considerable pressure to join. Similarly Nazi social policies did not appeal to those excluded for the Nazi racial ideal and in particular Germany's young Jews.

b Compare the importance of at least three of these factors as contributions to the popularity of the Nazis in Germany in the late 1930s.

How to answer this question. The key to answering this type of question is to compare the difference in importance of the factors. To gain the top level you must do the following:

- You should plan an argument before you start and then follow that argument throughout your answer.
- You must provide enough evidence to back up your answer.
- Try and link the factors together. Where you can, try and evaluate the relative importance of the factors.

Plan. In your plan you should identify the main points of argument which will help answer the question. You should also include a list of what you are going to write about in each paragraph.

- The image the regime's propaganda painted of Hitler was important in maintaining its popularity. This was primarily due to the regime's sensitivity to popular opinion.
- However most important in securing the regime's popularity were the economic changes which took place between 1933–39.
- Whilst the regime did influence attitudes through its social policy, it did not affect a social transformation.

Style. The style of writing below attempts to do what has been suggested in the section above.

There is no doubt that the Nazi dictatorship gained the support from many women. The vision promoted by 'Kinder, Kirche, Kuche' attracted sympathy from women who supported a return to more traditional values. Marriages increased by 130,000 per annum, births by over half a million per annum between 1933 and 1939. Women were barred from professional employment and a sixth had left all employment by 1937. Nazi womens organisations such as 'National Socialist Womanhood' and 'German Women's Enterprise' were enthusiastically supported. However such success however represented not so much a social revolution as an attempt to return to traditional values. The direct impact of Nazi social policy was limited. In particular earlier marriages and a rising birth rate was related more to the increasing prosperity not to social policy.

A2 SECTION: WEIMAR AND NAZI GERMANY

Introduction

Since 1945 there has been considerable historical research and debate about the nature of Nazi Germany. The following sections attempt to concentrate on the main areas of debate.

- **Section 1: Why did the Nazis come to power?** attempts to clarify the reasons why the Nazis came to power in Germany in 1933.
- **Section 2: The Nazi State** looks at the complex nature of the Nazi state and Hitler's role in its creation and management.
- **Section 3: Nazi economy** discusses the extent and nature of the Nazi economic recovery and the economic priorities of the Nazi leadership.
- **Section 4: Nazi society** examines the extent to which the Nazis managed to create a 'social revolution' in Germany between 1933 and 1945.
- **Section 5: The Holocaust** attempts to discover why the Holocaust took place and the role leading Nazis took in its planning and execution.
- **Section 6: Opposition to the Nazis** attempts to look at the scale of opposition to the Nazis, the effectiveness of the resistance and the reasons for opposition.
- **Section 7: Expansion and aggression: German foreign policy, 1933–45** looks at the motives behind German foreign policy in the period and Hitler's manipulation of events before and during the Second World War.

SECTION 1

Why did the Nazis come to power?

KEY POINTS

The explanation for the rise of the Nazi Party should be divided into three factors:

- **Crisis in the Weimar Republic.** The emergence of a previously marginalised organisation should be placed into the context of the growing crisis of the Weimar state. The turning point or catalyst that translated this crisis into widespread lack of confidence in the established political system was the economic collapse of 1929.
- **Nazi Party organisation and discipline.** That the Nazi Party was to become the beneficiary of this discontent was due to its organisational strengths and ideological flexibility which enabled it to become the natural focus for the hopes of the millions of disenchanted Germans. Yet this on its own does not explain why the Nazi Party was on the verge of seizing power in 1933.
- **The role of President Hindenburg.** The main factor leading to the rise of the Nazis was the destruction of the Weimar democracy by the establishment between 1930 and 1933. Led by President Hindenburg, the aim behind such a policy was the restoration of authoritarian government. As part of this process Hitler was appointed Chancellor and it was in this political environment that the Nazi Party flourished. It was from this base that Hitler indeed restored authoritarian rule within Germany, but not in the manner his sponsors had anticipated. The rise of the Nazi Party was not inevitable, but essentially reliant on the conditions of the establishment's making.

HISTORICAL INTERPRETATIONS

KEY TERM

Structuralists are those who believe that things happen because of the political, economic, military or other structures in a country.

Much debate has revolved around the causes of the failure of the Weimar Republic which created the conditions in which the rise of the Nazis became possible. On the one hand, the **structuralists**, such as **Richard Bessel** (1990) argue that the Weimar Republic was structurally weak and therefore bound to fail. This argument began with the claims of **W. Conze** (1954) that the Weimar political system was doomed to failure because of its built-in weaknesses. One of the main weaknesses was the state of the Weimar economy identified by **K. Borchardt** (1982).

Against this side of the debate is the view of the **intentionalists** that the failure of the Weimar state was not inevitable. Historians such as **E.J. Feuchtwanger** (1993) have argued that whilst there were weaknesses in the Weimar democracy, it wasn't doomed to collapse as it did. **John Hiden** (1996), who argues that the Weimar state proved itself to be stronger than has been previously portrayed, backs him up. Hiden's arguments follow the line first advocated by **K.D. Bracher** (1955) that the fatal problems of Weimar were the result of the manoeuvrings of President Hindenburg, rather than the weaknesses of the democracy.

KEY TERM

Intentionalists believe that things happen because of the intentions and actions of certain individuals.

There is now considerable agreement that the Nazi rise to power was the result of a number of interrelated factors. The difference between historians is often in the different emphasis they give to different factors. One area of debate that is keenly contested is the question of who voted for Hitler. The commonly held assumption that the Nazis relied on the middle classes for their support has been challenged by more sophisticated research. Indeed, it is argued by those such as **R.F. Hamilton** (1982) or **J.W. Falter** (1984) that the Nazis gained support from across a wider social spectrum. Another area of debate has been over the help given by business to the Nazi Party on its way to power. In numerous works, **H.A. Turner** (1985) has argued that this help was modest. This view has been dismissed by **D. Abraham** (1987), who follows more closely the line taken by **D. Stegman** (1973) that the links between industry and the rise of Hitler were far more important than Turner is prepared to accept.

WERE THE NAZIS BROUGHT TO POWER?

The destruction of democracy. The Nazis were brought into power in 1933 by an establishment that believed it could use the Nazi organisation to maintain its power and influence. President Hindenburg, Papen and others had come to rely on the Nazis, due in the main to the disintegration of the democratic system that they had engineered from 1930 onwards. The aim of this elite (which included many in the army) was the destruction of the hated Weimar Republic and the isolation of the equally despised SPD. This was achieved due to a mixture of reasons.

- They were helped by the considerable cynicism or distrust attached to the traditional democratic parties as a result of economic collapse of 1929 and the inability of the system to tackle the root causes of the depression. This manifested itself at the ballot box, the DVP vote, for example, falling to 1.2 per cent of the vote in July 1932, as opposed to 10.1 per cent eight years earlier.
- Secondly and most importantly, the presidential powers built into the constitution and in particular Article 48 gave Hindenburg the

constitutional framework to undermine the democratically based constitution.

Attempt of the establishment to use the Nazis. Hitler became Chancellor in 1933 because of the belief of Hindenburg and others that once the Weimar Republic had been undermined a new more authoritarian regime could be installed peacefully. This could only take place if it had a base of popular support. It was this popular support which only the NSDAP on the right of the political spectrum could provide. Therefore, the main reason for the Nazis coming to power was that the destruction of the democracy by the establishment left a political vacuum it could not itself fill. The establishment attempted to use Hitler and his party to give itself legitimacy for a new authoritarianism. In reality it served only to legitimise Nazism.

Hindenburg's undermining of democracy. A key moment in the process in the Nazi rise to power was the establishment of the Brüning government in March 1930 after the collapse of the 'Grand Coalition' government which had included the SPD. This government was the first to be based on presidential and not parliamentary power. Reichspresident Hindenburg made it very clear from the start that if the minority government was defeated or suffered votes of no confidence at the hands of the Reichstag, then the Reichstag would be dismissed and Germany would be governed by decree. Brüning's first cabinet had minority support from the centre parties but was defeated comprehensively in July 1930 over part of its financial bill. In attempting to pass the legislation by decree, the government was defeated again by 236 to 221 votes. This was within the constitutional rights of the Reichstag as defined by part of Article 48 of the constitution. Hindenburg's response was to dissolve the Reichstag. This is a crucial moment in the Nazi rise to power. It is the most obvious point at which the President and his advisers openly showed their contempt for not only the constitution, but also the Reichstag and the Weimar democracy. It also marks the shift from parliamentary government to presidential government. It was the latter which created Hitler's path to power as it gave the Nazis a 'legal' route to success that Hitler so needed.

THE DESTRUCTION OF DEMOCRACY

Papen's coup in Prussia, July 1932

The appointment of Hitler as Chancellor was part of an acceptance amongst the establishment that a return to a more authoritarian form of rule was desirable. The Nazi rise to power should be seen as part of a wider trend. Evidence of this can be seen in Papen's *coup d'état* against the Prussian government in July 1932. Although the action to depose the government was done in the name of the constitution (Article 48) its legality was highly questionable. The takeover of power, in what had been the cradle of social democracy, was met with little resistance. As neither the Prussian government, SPD or trade unions resisted the takeover of power, so a precedent was set.

Prussia 1932 as a precedent. The new Prussian regime was created as an authoritarian one with a political police that no longer served the Weimar state but obeyed the orders of Papen and his appointees. This paved the way for the actions of Göring who, as Reich Commissioner of Prussia from January 1933, embarked on an immediate programme of arrests, purges and intimidation which had only a flimsy basis in law. The point is this, the actions of Papen the previous July had ensured that Göring's programme could be undertaken under a pretence of 'legality'. This was because any legality as defined by the Republic's constitution had effectively been destroyed. It was therefore possible for Göring to use the political police to arrest communists and even, in February 1933, order by decree the recruitment of SA and SS members into that police force. By 1933 the emergency powers of the constitution had been used to destroy the Prussian constitution. The Nazi inspired decrees of 1933 that destroyed the foundations of the Republic, such as that of 28 February which enabled interference in local government and suspended basic rights, were possible because the trend to undermine democracy had been growing for at least three years. The Nazis were able arbitrarily to seize power in all German states, such as Bavaria, Hamburg or Hesse, from February to March 1933 onwards by means that were fundamentally unconstitutional but had the appearance of being legal. A typical example was the appointment in March of NSDAP Reich Commissar Karl Krogmann in Hamburg after the SA/SS had taken over the town hall and central government had placed pressure on the democratic government to resign.

HOW IMPORTANT WAS POLITICAL INTRIGUE IN EXPLAINING THE NAZI RISE TO POWER?

The misjudgement of Papen and Hindenburg in believing that they could control and use the Nazi movement is crucial in explaining the Nazi rise to power. However, this has to be put into the context of the time. From 1930 onwards, government was conducted by **intrigue** and deals, an example being the removal of Gröner and Brüning from office by Hindenburg and his political allies in May 1932. Brüning was to be followed as Chancellor by Papen in June 1932. His hold on power was always weak because he did not have a power base in the Reichstag. Attempts to rewrite the constitution to pave the way for a more authoritarian form of government were blocked by General von

KEY TERM

Intrigue is when individuals or groups plot against others.

Schleicher. Schleicher's government followed that of Papen and from December 1932 to January 1933 he attempted to be more conciliatory towards the left and appeal to the wider population as a whole.

The role of business in bringing the Nazis to power. It is difficult to underestimate the fear of communism among Germany's business classes in the 1920s and early 1930s. This is the context of the attraction of Hitler for many who would have otherwise felt his personality and tactics repellent. Hitler's strong anti-communist and anti-Weimar credentials help to explain why, in 1929, Alfred Hugenberg was prepared to offer the Nazis a national platform for the first time by inviting them to join the right wing coalition the 'Reich Committee for a Referendum to oppose the Young Plan'. This committee contained respected national political figures of the right, including Franz Seldte of the Stahlhelm movement (the foremost nationalist ex–servicemen's organisation). The campaign in favour of the 'Freedom Law' gave Hitler media exposure and considerable legitimacy. The result was clear at the ballot box; in the state election in Thuringia in December 1929 the Nazis polled 11.3 per cent.

However admiration on the conservative right for Hitler and his party was not universal. By late 1932 many feared the potential destructiveness of the Nazi party and the unpredictability of its leader. Despite fears about the democratic views of General Schleicher (to many he was known as the 'Red General'), he was preferred to Hitler, as was von Papen. The business interests which actively supported Hitler revolved around the Cologne banker Baron Kurt von Schröder and the **Keppler Circle**. There was also keen lobbying in favour of Hitler from landowner organisations such as the *Reichslandbund* (Reich Agrarian League). The influence this small group was to have on leading politicians was crucial. Initiatives were undertaken by von Schröder to create an alternative government of the right that included the NSDAP. These initiatives were centred on von Papen who resented his treatment at the hands of von Schleicher the previous year. It was Schröder who persuaded von Papen to meet with Hitler at his house in Cologne in January 1933. The negotiations which took place eventually resulted in Hitler becoming Chancellor. Although one must not exaggerate the role of Schröder and his associates, he was influential at a critical moment in Germany's history. Individuals, therefore, had an important role to play in creating the political circumstances in which it became desirable on their part to bring the Nazis into power.

KEY TERM

Keppler Circle. Named after businessman Wilhelm Keppler, this group was set up to advise Hitler on economic affairs.

WHAT WAS THE NAZIS' ELECTORAL APPEAL?

Introduction. At no point did the Nazis achieve an electoral majority; even in March 1933 they gained only 43.9 per cent of the popular vote.

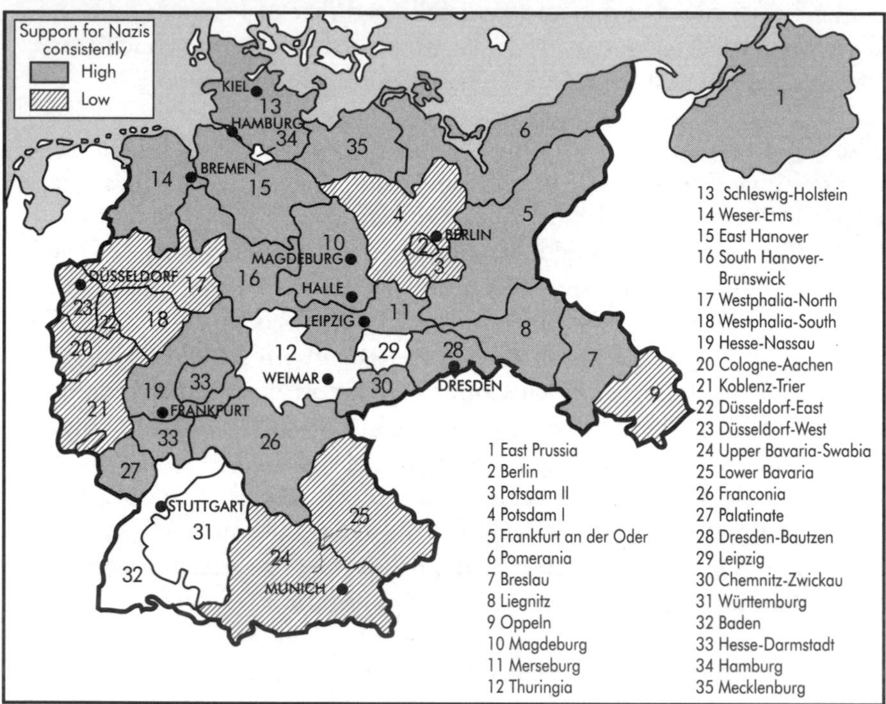

Nazi Party electoral support, Reichstag elections 1924–32.

It has been often rightly pointed out that the Nazi vote fell in 1932, from 37.3 per cent in July to 33.1 per cent in November, and that the appointment of Hitler as Chancellor was at a stage when the Nazis were declining electorally. Yet this misses the point, for by 1932 elections were not the means by which power was gained, such was the extent to which the Reichstag had already been undermined. However, Nazi electoral success was an important factor for the establishment in their dealings with the Nazis.

The attraction of the Nazis for the establishment. The Nazis came to power, therefore, because the elite saw them as the means by which the Republic and the left could be destroyed. There is little doubt that Hitler's insistence on 'legal' means, rather than those that failed so dismally in 1923, gave the NSDAP movement a legitimacy that it lacked in the 1920s. This legitimacy was enhanced by Schleicher and Papen, who were prepared to ignore the violence and illegality of Nazism as the movement was a bulwark against the left.

The significance of the Nazis as a national party. What made the NSDAP such an attractive ally was its nature as a mass movement and the broad base of its electoral support. This was unique in a party system where the other parties represented their own interests. The established view is that the Nazi vote was primarily that of the middle class, the *Mittelstand* of civil servants, officials and those damaged by the economic instability of the Republic. Although the Nazis picked up a significant number of votes from those who had previously voted for the middle-class parties such as the DVP or DNP, it is wrong to assume that the party lacked a broad social base. The Nazis failed to attract significant votes from the industrial working class, but the DNVP had gained over 2 million worker votes in the 1924 election and it is to be assumed that the Nazis attracted these as voters at the turn of the decade. The Nazi vote was weakest in urban areas: in Berlin in November 1932 the left (KPD and SPD) took 54.3 per cent of the vote. However, by the early 1930s the Nazi Party was the only party that could present itself as a national one cutting across class and interest lines. This was due to the attractions of the Nazis as a party of protest and lofty but ill-defined ideals, such as *Volksgemeinschaft* (the concept of national community). Nazi policy was vague but deliberately so – style being more important than substance. Yet it was this which made the Nazis successful electorally and, as a result, so attractive to the ruling establishment which shared their critique of Weimar and the desire to destroy democracy.

WHAT WAS THE IMPORTANCE OF NAZI PARTY ORGANISATION AND DISCIPLINE IN ITS COMING TO POWER?

KEY TERM

The **crash of 1929** was the collapse of the German economy which resulted in high unemployment

Restructuring and growth. A crucial factor in the rise to power of the Nazis was the ability of the party to expand and provide a political home for the discontented, in particular after the **crash of 1929**. This should be put down to the flexibility of the party structure as created and developed in the 1920s. After a poor showing in the December 1924 elections the party was reorganised and centralised. The index of all members which was most useful in mobilising support in the years of increasing electoral success between 1929 and 1933. Perhaps the most significant step was the assertion of complete obedience to Hitler, the *Führerprincip*, announced at the party conference at Bamberg in February 1926. It gave the party the internal discipline and cohesion which would make it electorally attractive to Germans discontented with the overt political wrangling and division of other Weimar parties. However despite the other administrative and organisational reforms of these years, e.g., the creation of the Hitler Youth in 1926, the Nazis performed poorly in the election of May 1928. Indeed it received only around 800,000 votes (2.6 per cent) and 12 seats in the new Reichstag.

There were other administrative and organisational reforms undertaken in these years. In 1926 the Hitler Youth and the Nazi Students' Association were founded. At the Nuremberg Party Congress in 1927, further reorganisation took place with unsuitable *Gauleiters* (Nazi regional bosses) being replaced and the central bureaucracy further reorganised. Despite such changes, the performance of the party in the election of May 1928 was dismal, registering only around 800,000 votes (2.6 per cent) and gaining only 12 seats in the new Reichstag.

The importance of the Nazis as a mass movement. Despite electoral disappointment in the late 1920s, the reorganisation of the Nazi party into a mass movement was to have very important consequences. October 1928 saw the creation of the first Nazi professional body, the Association of National Socialist Jurists. This was to be followed in 1929 by similar bodies for doctors, teachers and students which were to give the Nazi movement credibility and distract from the more unpleasant image conjured up by SA violence. It was this structure which enabled the party to rapidly transform into a mass movement and to spread propaganda at elections. Most importantly, the existence of groups to represent specific sections of the community gave the party the wide base which was at the root of its appeal to the establishment which wished to use that base for its own brand of authoritarian rule. There are many examples of these organisations, among the most important being the *Agrarpolitische Apparat* (AA) founded in 1930 to draw a largely discontented peasantry into the movement. Not only did it achieve its aims within a relatively short space of time but it managed to infiltrate and dominate other important agrarian-based organisations such as the *Reichslandbund* which was important in pressing for Hitler's appointment in 1932–3. Part of the work of the AA – as envisaged by its founder Walther Darré – was to create a network of party members to undertake propaganda activities.

Propaganda and advanced electioneering techniques. This local activity effectively complemented the 'saturation' propaganda tactics devised by Göbbels. The use of rallies, speeches, lectures and **'aeroplane campaigns'** in certain areas was effective in raising the profile of the party and increasing the vote at elections. In particular, the tactics of identifying and then targeting certain groups within regions brought rich electoral rewards. This was the case in the local election in Saxony in 1929 in which the poorer farmers were targeted and constituted 14.4 per cent of the votes received, which was a significant improvement on the 1929 election. Similarly, the Nazis were successful in attracting the support of the young and particularly students, in 1930 over two-thirds of members being under 40 years old. Without electoral success in the early 1930s the Nazis would not have been in a position to challenge for power nor would that power have been offered to them.

KEY TERM

Aeroplane campaigns Hitler was the first politician to recognise the use of the 'whistle-stop' campaign style. He would fly into certain regions, show his face and depart. In that region, however, an impression was made.

The leadership of Hitler. The successful electioneering and propaganda of the Nazis and a dedicated and growing party membership were important factors in the rise of Nazi fortunes. Equally important was the discipline that Hitler imposed on the SA, first with the appointment of Captain von Pfeffer in 1926, but continuing until 1933. This is despite numerous instances when local SA leaders rebelled against central control. A clear example was in March 1931 when Hitler accepted a decree requiring police permission for rallies, thereby angering SA leaders such as Walther Stennes into open revolt. That Hitler was seen to be dealing effectively with the more radical party members, such as Strasser or Stennes, was important in securing confidence in Hitler's leadership and his commitment to 'legal' means of gaining power.

HOW IMPORTANT WAS THE CRASH OF 1929?

Introduction. The depression and economic crisis that followed the Wall Street Crash in 1929 did not in itself bring the Nazis to power. What it did was create the possibility, the opportunity and the context in which Nazi propaganda would not fall on deaf ears. It also acted as the trigger for the destruction of the Republic.

The psychological effects of the depression. The psychological effects of the wholesale collapse of the German economy from 1929 onwards should not be underestimated, especially with the problems of 1918–23 so fresh in the mind. It was unemployment and financial insecurity that so undermined confidence in the current structures. By 1933, one in three German workers was unemployed, yet it was not these who formed the bedrock of growing Nazi support. The main support came from those who believed that without political change then they, too, might well suffer a collapse in living standards. Such groups are detailed above, the *Mittelstand*, a peasantry threatened with worsening economic conditions and so on. What the depression did was to harden opinion, and increase the popularity of those who offered radical solutions to the economic problems. This is why the intended authoritarianism of Hindenburg was widely accepted, why the vote for the KPD rose from 1928 onwards (from 3.2 million in 1928 to 5.9 million in November 1932). It also helps to explain why there was so little resistance to the coup in Prussia in 1932 – the SPD and unions being significantly weakened by unemployment. Such was the depth of contempt for existing structures, that in order to dismantle the political system the establishment undoubtedly used the economic crisis. As a result, Brüning was unable to introduce measures to stimulate the economy, such as public works schemes. Instead the economy lurched into a crisis which resulted in the banking collapse of 1931 and the subsequent flight of capital.

KEY TERM

Hoover moratorium In June 1931 the US President Herbert Hoover proposed suspending all German reparation payments for a year. This led the way for the ending of reparations in July 1932.

The crisis and the rise of the Nazis. The worsening conditions helped further to prompt the subsequent **Hoover moratorium** and the suspension of reparation payments in 1932. The point should be underlined, however, that such a policy created the conditions in which the Nazis flourished with their condemnation of the present and their promises of a utopian future. There is a strong correlation between the years of Brüning's economic stewardship and the rising fortunes of the Nazis in elections. So whilst the economic conditions were not created by the establishment, their role in perpetuating the crisis for their own political ends was to have a real influence on the rise of Nazi popularity. The economic crisis crystallised the fears of those who feared social collapse and disorder. This again benefited the Nazis despite the fact that the actions of the SA were often the cause of that disorder. A prime example was the street violence in Berlin in June/July 1932 between the SA and KPD in which around 100 were killed. Such a threat simply strengthened Hitler's position as the leader who could control the SA and thereby prevent anarchy.

CONCLUSION

- The rise of the Nazi Party must be placed into the context of economic crisis, in particular in the aftermath of the collapse of 1929. As the effects were felt across Germany, so the electorate became more receptive to the message of those who offered a radical solution.
- Added to this factor was the organisational strength and ideological flexibility of the NSDAP. Its appeal was reinforced by the apparent 'legality' of the Nazi assault on power in the late 1920s and early 1930s in contrast to the attempted putsch of 1923.
- Yet none of this is sufficient to explain why the Nazis were brought into and then reinforced in power. The answer lies in the ideological and political aspirations of the German establishment. It not only destroyed the foundations of democracy by the use of presidential government but also attempted to use the NSDAP as the tool by which authoritarian rule could be re-established.
- The economic crisis was the pretext for the decline in the power of the Reichstag, but as discussed in the previous chapter, the expansion of executive power began well before 1929.

Without doubt the Nazi Party's message and tactics brought it to the brink of power. That was achieved, however, due to the misjudgement of an elite rather than to the misplaced votes of a desperate electorate. The Nazi movement and its popular base were co-opted by an elite that believed it could use them to its own ends. As hindsight shows, this was a mistake of monumental proportions.

SECTION 2

The Nazi state

INTRODUCTION

The nature of Hitler's regime is much more complex than the image of an all-powerful dictator projected by Nazi propaganda. Hitler's character, ideology and his legal seizure of power all meant that his authority was initially controlled. His dictatorship was limited by constitutional checks, the influence of members of the elite such as Papen and by dissident factions within the Nazi movement. Even when the events of 1934 had served to contain these elements, it is clear that the Nazi state was not a well-ordered monolithic structure but a collection of competing bureaucracies and power blocs over which Hitler presided. It should be stressed, however, that such a system did not weaken Hitler's personal dictatorship. He remained the source of ideology and the arbiter of all decisions. In this sense he was a strong dictator.

Key points
- Hitler's power was limited between 1933 and 1934.
- Hitler was able to establish a powerful dictatorship by August 1934 and absolute power by 1938.
- Hitler's authority was not seriously challenged until the last days of his dictatorship.

HISTORICAL INTERPRETATIONS

Historians are agreed that the Third Reich was not the ordered, efficient, centralised government depicted in Nazi propaganda. Instead it was a fragmented and often chaotic system of competing personal empires and bureaucracies. The debate amongst historians arises over the interpretation of this system. The traditional interpretation is that Hitler was a strong dictator, that his intentions were paramount and that he directed his subordinates by a deliberate policy of divide and rule in the German dictatorship. This is the view of historians such as **Karl D. Bracher** (1970), who in *The Nazi State* calls Hitler the 'master in the Third Reich' and is supported by **Norman Rich** (1973–4), **Eberhard Jäckel** (1977–8) and **K. Hildebrand** (1984).

'Structuralist' historians who believe that Hitler's power was limited by competition from rival elites and factions have challenged this. **Hans**

Mommsen, for example, argues (in Hirschfield, ed., 1986) that he was 'unwilling to take decisions, frequently uncertain, exclusively concerned with upholding his prestige and personal image – a weak dictator'. **Hugh Trevor-Roper** (1947) who believed that 'Hitler remained to the end the sole master of the movement that he had himself inspired and founded and which he was himself, by his personal leadership, to ruin' supports this view.

HOW STRONG WAS HITLER'S DICTATORSHIP 1933–4?

Introduction. Hitler succeeded in eliminating any serious threat to his personal dictatorship by his accumulation of power between January 1933 and August 1934. He achieved this by the destruction of the constitution, tactical alliances with key institutions (e.g., the civil service, army and judiciary), the suppression of all civil liberties and the purge of his own dissidents in the SA.

President Hindenburg offered Hitler power in January 1933, not as a dictator but as Chancellor of a democratic state. However much the constitution of the Weimar Republic had been compromised since 1930, there were still checks and balances that restrained his authority. Indeed it was an accepted element of the conspiracy by the conservative elites which manoeuvred Hitler into office that he would be constrained by the constitution and kept weak.

Initial constitutional checks on Nazi power. Constitutionally the cabinet, the Reichstag, the federal states and the President limited Hitler's power. There were only three Nazis in a cabinet of twelve: Hitler himself, Hermann Göring, Minister without Portfolio, and Wilhelm Frick, Minister of the Interior. The other nine were conservatives, including the Vice-Chancellor, Franz von Papen, who believed that they had cleverly imprisoned Hitler and plotted to abandon him as soon as economic and political stability were restored. The Reichstag in which the Nazis, though the largest party, held only 196 out of 584 seats also restrained Hitler. The federal states, represented by the Upper House, the Reichsrat, could also block decrees by central government. The most important constitutional check to Hitler was, however, President Paul von Hindenburg, an aristocratic conservative who despised Hitler. He had the constitutional right to dismiss the Chancellor and, more importantly, had the command of the army.

The collapse of the constitution. It should be stressed, however, that these constitutional limitations were, even as early as January 1933, largely theoretical. Indeed, the rapid destruction of the constitution within the first few weeks of the dictatorship is a testimony to its feebleness. The use of violence had been a key part of the Nazi seizure of power and the incorporation of Nazi storm troopers into the Prussian police in February institutionalised the use of terror. The State of Emergency declared on 28 February following the Reichstag fire suspended civil liberties and led to the arbitrary arrest, imprisonment and beating of thousands of dissidents. Hitler made it clear that the elections of March 1933 would not change the composition of his government, but were intended merely to demonstrate popular support for the new regime. His personal dictatorship was further strengthened by the Enabling Act on 23 March 1933 that gave Hitler four years of unrestricted power. His dictatorship was also strengthened by the abolition of all other political parties in July 1933 and of the Reichsrat and state parliaments in January 1934.

Checks to Hitler's power in 1933–4. By the beginning of 1934, Hitler's position appeared much more secure than a year before. The cabinet met 72 times but was unable to exert influence over Hitler, the Reichstag was a 'rubber stamp' and opposition parties had been abolished. The press was censored, the trade unions were abolished and the Nazis had forged an alliance with the Catholic Church. It should be stressed, however, that Hitler's dictatorship was not yet absolute. His power was limited by the independence of the civil service, the Catholic Church, by tactical alliances with conservatives, business and the army, by dissident factions within his own party, and by the authority of Hindenburg. Hitler was keen to avoid a revolutionary assault on the state bureaucracy which continued to enjoy a degree of autonomy after the Nazi seizure of power. Whilst the Nazi Party was a highly effective electoral machine it was unable to manage a state as complex and advanced as Germany. The party was too big, too radical, too splintered to formulate and execute policies. Hitler may have claimed in July 1933 that the party had become the state, but he also conceded that its primary role was in education and propaganda. By contrast, the civil service had great expertise and was highly professional. Most civil servants were conservative and looked to Vice-Chancellor Franz von Papen to defend their independence against the radicalism and illegality of Nazi extremists.

Church and political elite. The Catholic Church was also able to enjoy a wide degree of autonomy from the state and continued to have important control in education and youth organisations. More importantly, Hitler's dictatorship in 1934 depended on his tactical alliances. The Commemoration Day at Potsdam on 21 March 1933, at the opening of the Reichstag, was a clear attempt to consolidate his alliances with conservative and nationalist parties whose support he needed to secure a two-thirds majority for the Enabling Act. However, these alliances were by no means sure. In 1934 conservatives claimed that Hitler was intent on a personal dictatorship. The most damming criticism came from Franz von Papen who, at Marburg (May 1934), denounced the brutality and illegality of the regime.

Industrialists and army. Leading industrialists such as Fritz Thyssen and Alfred Krupp gave financial support to the Nazis and played a key role in Hitler's appointment as Chancellor. Hitler's first speech was intended to consolidate this close relationship with business, which now demanded that Hitler establish stability and curb his radical elements. Hitler needed the support of business to establish economic recovery and was therefore prepared to allow Schacht to defend their independence. Leading generals also demanded the crushing of the SA as a price for their support for rearmament. Many older, aristocratic generals despised Hitler as a **Bohemian** corporal and were repelled by the brutality and lawlessness of the SA.

KEY TERM

Bohemian was the term given to someone who originated from Bohemia, the province in which Hitler was born.

The Night of the Long Knives. Hitler established his supreme command over such dissident elements by purging the SA during the Night of the Long Knives on 30 June 1934. Röhm and about 400 SA leaders were eliminated. Hitler also eliminated conservative dissidents such as Jung and Bose as well as old rivals such as General von Schleicher and Gregor Strasser. Hitler's last remaining rival, Hindenburg, died on 2 August 1934. Hitler immediately abolished the position of President and assumed all the authority, including crucially the command of the army. Hitler consolidated his command of the army by exacting from it an oath of allegiance.

HOW LIMITED WAS THE NAZI DICTATORSHIP AFTER 1934?

Introduction. In theory Hitler's dictatorship was absolute by August 1934. Hitler had the power to make all laws, dismiss the Reichstag, appoint all ministers, army officers, state governors, party and government officials, decide foreign policy, declare war and make peace. In practice, the dictatorship continued to exert its power **pragmatically** and to work with elites within the civil service, business and the army. There is no doubt, however, that these constraints were gradually shed and that by 1938 Hitler had established his complete control over the state.

KEY TERM

Pragmatically means that decisions were made based on political needs, e.g., the importance of keeping the army happy.

The role of popular opinion. Despite the establishment of one-party rule and suppression of civil liberties during 1933, Hitler did not ignore popular opinion. He was determined that his election pledges of 1932 would be honoured so that his image as a messiah or saviour of the people would be sustained. For Hitler, his pact with the people was paramount to his charisma and cult of leadership. He believed himself to be a man of the people, the symbol of the National Will and the leader of the National Revolution. Throughout his regime Hitler was sensitive to

A 'Kraft durch Freude' (Strength through Joy) poster promoting holidays for workers.

popular opinion. He did rule by coercion, but he also craved consent. Posters, radio, newspapers and film promoted policies and rallies, demonstrations and processions reinforced ideology. State initiatives such as 'Strength through Joy', 'Beauty of Labour' and 'Winter Help' were set up to show the state's concern for all Germans, including the disadvantaged and working class. Of course, such campaigns excluded Jews and other supposed undesirables. However, these popular campaigns promoted an ideological image of a *Volksgemeinschaft*. They were designed to win popular approval for the state.

This popular approval was tested by the use of plebiscites (votes by all electors) such as those following Hitler's abolition of the presidency in 1934 and the *Anschluss* with Austria in 1938. Gestapo and party officials were often asked to report on public morale. Sensitivity to popular opinion may also have determined the course of policy-making. It is clear for example that the need to create employment after 1933 required a tactical alliance with business and conservative interests, and the postponement of any radical anti-capitalist reform. Similarly the perceived need to satisfy consumer demand necessitated only a limited economic mobilisation for war until 1942. Popular opinion was also important in the suspension of the euthanasia programme (the organised murder by the state of Germany's physically and mentally disabled) in 1940 following its denunciation by Cardinal von Galen. The campaign against the Jews was also partly determined by popular opinion. Hitler realised that there was no popular demand for a coercive policy against the Jews and the hostile reaction to the *Kristallnacht* violence in 1938 convinced him that future policy had to be secret.

Such examples of public interest do not indicate a serious weakening of Hitler's dictatorship. Indeed it was one of Hitler's great strengths that he was so alert to popular sentiment. He was never beholden to it, but it was good politics to respond to it. Ultimately Hitler was able to achieve his objectives irrespective of popular opinion.

WHAT WAS THE ROLE OF THE CIVIL SERVICE?

Introduction. Between 1934 and 1938 Hitler was able to establish his authority over the civil service. It was possible for civil servants to check the arbitrary violence of the party's radicals by constructing a legislative framework. In 1936 the War Ministry extended the decree banning civil servants from consulting Jewish doctors to cover pharmacists and hospitals.

The weakening of the civil service. The civil service's anti-Jewish measures were limited in their scope. However, these initiatives were tolerated because they were in line with party policy. It is inconceivable that policy could be developed against Hitler's wishes. The civil service, though nominally autonomous, shared much of Hitler's conservative and nationalist ideology and willingly accommodated itself to the new regime. The Law for the Restoration of the Professional Civil Service (7 April 1933) purged Jews and political opponents. Thereafter the civil service was progressively Nazified or bypassed by party agencies.

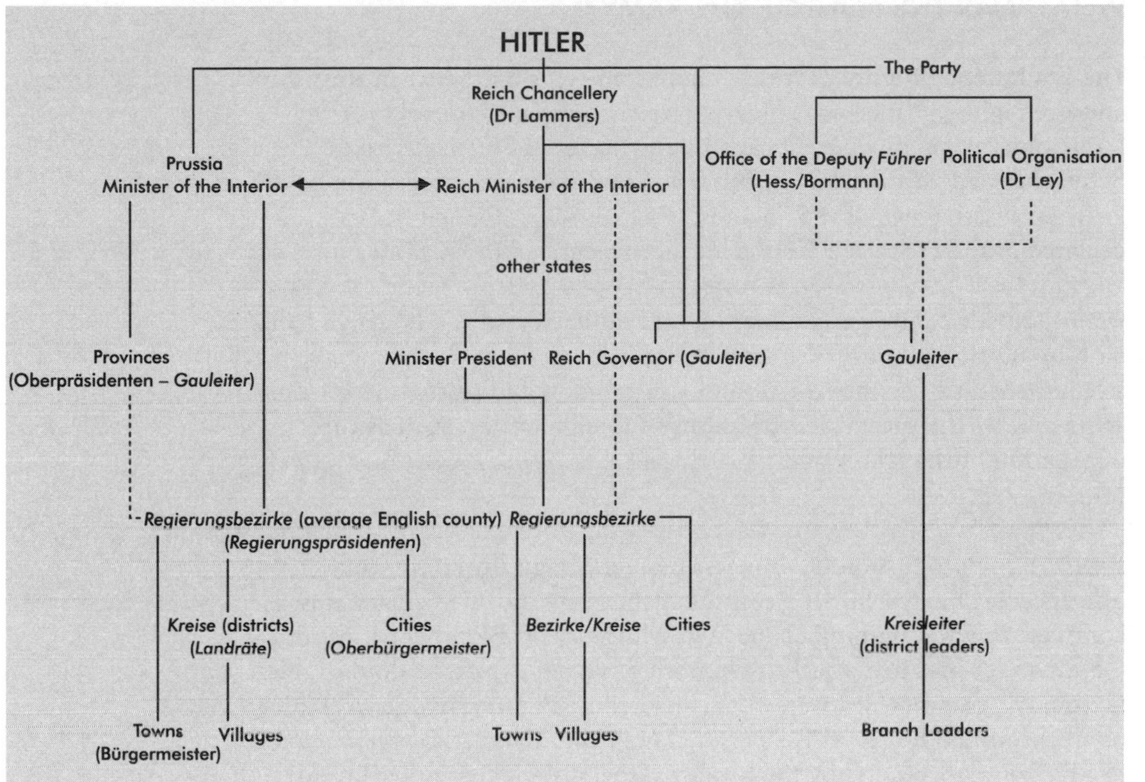

The structure of Nazi institutions.

The increasing dominance of the party. Hitler's second-in-command, Rudolf Hess, vetted all appointments and promotions from September 1935. All officials were made directly responsible to Hitler in 1937, and party membership became compulsory in February 1939. Not only was the civil service weakened, but also it was increasingly shadowed by parallel Nazi institutions. The party had already developed an extensive bureaucracy before its seizure of power. This was refined and expanded by Martin Bormann who was Hess's deputy in the party hierarchy and who established Department III to check and bring about the subordination of the civil service.

Hans-Heinrich Lammers, the head of the Reich Chancellery, remained in position until the end of the regime. In 1943 he became a member of the powerful 'Committee of Three' with Keitel and Bormann. He was, however, marginalised. Bormann had ensured that he was excluded from all key decision-making. The point to note therefore is that in the competition between party and state, the party apparatus was clearly dominant.

WHAT WAS THE ROLE OF THE ARMY?

The limitations of army power. Despite some tensions between the army and the regime, Hitler was able to exert his complete control by 1938. Some older generals were shocked by the murder of Generals von Schleicher and von Bredow in July 1934 and there was opposition to the growing interference of the SS and the expansionist foreign policy declared at the Hossbach Conference in November 1937. Hitler's authority was not, however, threatened by such dissent. Many officers were sympathetic to the nationalism and militarism of the Nazis and the oath of allegiance bound the army to the regime. That alliance was strengthened by the introduction of conscription and rearmament from 1935 and by the spectacular triumphs of foreign policy, such as the occupation of the Rhineland in 1936 and the *Anschluss* with Austria in March 1938.

By 1938 the promotion of younger, more ideologically committed officers consolidated Hitler's control of the army. His supremacy was completed by the purging of the War Minister von Blomberg and the Commander-in-Chief von Fritsch, both of whom expressed doubts about Germany's readiness for war. Hitler made himself Commander-in-Chief of all the armed forces with a personal high command (*Oberkommondo der Wehrmacht*) headed by the loyalist General Keitel. Another loyalist, General von Brauchitsch, was appointed Commander-in-Chief of the army and 16 Generals were retired and 44 transferred. The collapse of a plot led by General Beck to arrest Hitler in the summer of 1938 (in opposition to the policy on Czechoslovakia) demonstrated the impotence of the army. It is clear that Hitler took personal control of foreign policy from the outset and made all the key decisions without any interference. It is here that his strength as dictator can be most clearly demonstrated.

WAS HITLER'S DICTATORSHIP THREATENED BY RIVAL NAZIS?

Other power bases within the Nazi movement. By devolving power, Hitler's style of dictatorship did create the potential for rivals to challenge his authority, but after 1934 no other Nazi was able seriously to threaten Hitler's exercise of supreme power. The complexity of Hitler's system of government did encourage initiatives from competing levels of authority: regional Nazi officials, high-ranking bureaucrats, and, of course, from the Nazi elite. At the local level, the *Gauleiters* demanded autonomy within the party and were given sweeping executive powers in wartime. They were protected at the highest level by Bormann and were able to wield absolute power within their region. During the war they began to undermine Speer's efforts to control the supply of raw materials and sometimes commandeered supplies en route to other regions. At national level, Nazi officials such as Philipp Bouhler, head of Hitler's Chancellery, was able to exert a decisive influence upon the development of policy. By selecting and supporting a petition in 1938, Bouhler successfully promoted the policy of child euthanasia.

Marginalisation of potential threats. Such initiatives were, however, only successful if they won Hitler's active support. A more important potential threat to Hitler's authority came from other leading Nazis. The elimination of Ernst Röhm and the purging of the SA in June 1934 removed the most serious threat to Hitler, but he continued to be surrounded by ambitious and powerful henchmen. Some of the empires created by Hitler were politically insignificant or were held by Nazis of limited ability and imagination and so, like Robert Ley's Labour Front or Baldur von Schirach's Youth Organisation, were easily marginalised.

The importance of the SS. There were, however, empires of strategic importance led by Nazis of stature and ruthlessness which were able to play a major role in policy-making. The most important power bloc within the Third Reich was the SS empire of Heinrich Himmler which embraced a wide range of responsibilities of police, security, racial policy, resettlement and foreign policy. It even developed its own army, the 'Waffen SS'. It emerged in some respects as a state within a state.

Other powerful Nazis. Other principal power blocs were the Four Year Plan office of Hermann Göring, the culture and propaganda empire of Joseph Göbbels and the party machine led by Rudolf Hess and, more importantly after 1941, by Martin Bormann. Given the nature of the regime it was possible for these Nazi leaders to build up vast power. They were all ideologically committed to Nazism and knew they were carrying out policies favoured by Hitler. They were ruthless in enhancing their own position at the expense of their rivals, and as their responsibilities were so ill-defined, there was limitless scope for intrigue, ambition and opportunism. It was possible for the Nazi elite to promote policy without Hitler's direct authorisation. Göbbels, for example, was able to launch the attack on the Jews during *Kristallnacht* without first seeking Hitler's approval. As Hitler became obsessed with the military campaign after 1939, the scope for initiative and intrigue increased further. Himmler and Reinhard Heydrich played a key role in the escalation of Jewish persecution that culminated in the extermination of Jews from October 1941. Göring's growing rift with Hitler even led him to betray the plan to invade Russia in June 1941 to the Allies.

The emergence of Martin Bormann. By 1941 Martin Bormann emerged as the most powerful of the Nazi henchmen. Together with Keitel and Lammers, he had established a new Chancellery in 1941 that controlled all access to Hitler and was responsible for the daily routine of business.

Bormann gained an unparalleled control of patronage and information that made him, according to Hitler's Minister of Munitions, Albert Speer, more powerful than Hitler. Bormann exploited this exalted position ruthlessly. He deliberately stirred up tensions between the *Gauleiters* and Speer in 1943, he appointed Himmler to the doomed position of Head of Army Group Vistula in 1945 and denounced Göring as a traitor in April 1945.

The collapse of Hitler's authority in 1945. It is clear that by April 1945 Hitler was only nominally in command of his regime. A recluse, almost a fugitive after the bomb plot of July 1944, his health was deteriorating rapidly and his mood was increasingly bleak. By April 1945 his subordinates openly challenged him. On his own initiative Himmler ordered the mass slaughter of Jews to be stopped and proposed the surrender of the German armies in the West. He even offered himself as a leader of a reconstituted Germany. Göring also attempted to oust Hitler as Führer in April 1945. Even the loyalist, Speer, attempted to assassinate Hitler in February 1945.

Maintaining power by 'divide and rule'. It should be stressed that until the collapse of the regime, his subordinates did not threaten Hitler's dictatorship. Hitler's policy of devolving power was partly a product of his belief in Social Darwinism (that the strongest would win at the expense of the weak), but was in part a deliberate strategy of 'divide and rule'. More likely, however, the system of dispersing power was not deliberate. Like much of Hitler's state, it was a system that evolved in an ad hoc way but was encouraged as it suited Hitler's needs. Constant feuding sapped the energies of potential rivals. Hitler avoided the squabbling and preserved his charisma through staying detached from arguments. By encouraging empires that overlapped and often conflicted, Hitler was able to curb over-powerful subordinates. Instead, he liked to present himself as the referee settling debates over various initiatives.

The loyalty of his subordinates. Hitler was well served by those around him. However much initiative they were allowed, they were, until the end, fanatically loyal and always sought to translate his visions into specific policies. Promotion depended on Hitler's patronage and officials and ministers at every level worked assiduously to promote his wishes. Göbbels in advocating the *Kristallnacht* violence, and Himmler and Heydrich in advocating in 1941 the policy of the extermination of the Jews, were fully aware that they were championing policies favoured by Hitler. It is equally clear that no subordinate, no matter how powerful, was able to promote a policy against the wishes of the Führer.

Hitler as a dictator. The key point to note is that Hitler exerted a dominant influence over policy-making throughout his dictatorship. It is true that his style was unconventional; he was lazy, he slept until midday, and he spent most afternoons walking, eating and watching films. Moreover he hated meetings, he rarely wrote orders and was away from Berlin for long periods. Dictators, however, do not need to act in the same way as leaders of democratic governments. Hitler was able to demand absolute subservience in three ways.

- Firstly, because his subordinates were totally committed to his ideology.
- Secondly, because of the emphasis placed upon loyalty. Insubordinate colleagues such as Röhm and Strasser were ruthlessly eliminated whilst ultra-loyalists such as Bormann and Himmler rose from obscurity as *Gauleiters* to figures of national prominence.
- Thirdly, Hitler ruled by the 'Führer Principle' – his will was law and the source of all executive authority. The Nazis promoted Hitler as the embodiment of the state that was the living organism of the German people. This domination of the state can be demonstrated in two respects – his close direction of questions of personal interest and by the central role of *his* ideology during the regime.

Hitler's influence on crucial decisions. It is clear that on issues of personal interest Hitler's role was decisive. The sterilisation programme of 1933, the final draft of the Nuremberg Laws of 1935 and the adoption of the child euthanasia programme of 1938–9 were results of Hitler's personal authorisation. Moreover, Hitler took the key decisions in 1941 which authorised the extermination of the Jews. Similarly, he took complete control of foreign policy, determining the timing of the reoccupation of the Rhineland in 1936, the *Anschluss* with Austria in 1938, the occupation of the Sudetenland in 1938, the invasion of Czechoslovakia and Poland in 1939.

In wartime Hitler was the supreme warlord, personally directing the nature of the campaign and the movement of armies. Nothing illustrates his strength as a dictator better than his control of the war effort. His aims were so well-known to political subordinates such as Philipp Bouhler, head of his Chancellery office, or Martin Bormann, or to his generals that written orders were not required. All policies carried the authority of 'Führer-orders', often verbal orders or merely nods of the head. Speer recorded 2,500 such 'nods', each implementing a new directive or strategic initiative. It is also clear that Hitler's personal ideology was the driving force throughout the regime. His deep-seated anti-Semitism and obsession to destroy the Treaty of Versailles, destroy Russia and win living space determined the course of the regime. All other objectives were subordinated to the achievement of these obsessions that were sustained fanatically to the last days of the regime.

CONCLUSION

- There is no doubt that Hitler remained in control of key decisions throughout his dictatorship.
- In the first year in power Hitler had to make tactical alliances and compromises with important institutions of the state. However, these institutions never seriously threatened his supreme power.
- Despite the apparent chaos of the Nazi state, which meant that power was devolved and decisions delayed, this never prevented Hitler from pursuing his ideological ambitions.

SECTION 3

The Nazi economy

RECOVERY, 1933–6

Key points

- There is little doubt that the economic recovery Germany experienced between 1933 and 1936 was real. Its roots lay in the solving of three of the main structural problems of the German economy. These problems were the weakness of German capital, lack of domestic demand and over-exposure of the economy to the extremes of the world economic cycle. This was achieved by increased state interference and regulation.
- Such policy took place against the background of an improvement in world trade. Economic recovery was also helped by confidence in the economy produced by political change. The anti-labour legislation acted to create low labour costs.
- These factors explain the extent and nature of economic recovery. It should be argued that the ideology and methods of the Nazi regime limited such recovery. The priority of the state was to create an economic recovery and reduce unemployment. Given the experience of the German economy in the late 1920s and early 1930s, a priority was given to creating a form of 'economic nationalism' whereby the health of the German economy was not over-reliant on the international capitalist economy. From the start, Hitler, the Nazi leadership and their political allies were committed to a programme of rearmament.

Historical interpretation

There is little historical debate about the nature of the recovery of the German economy before 1936. In *The Nazi Economic Recovery* (1982), **Richard Overy** stresses the importance for the new regime of solving the problems of unemployment. He also stresses the continuity of institutions used by the state. According to Overy, the key factor in the economy's recovery was the extent to which the state was prepared to intervene and manage the economy.

How did government intervention shape the nature of the recovery?

Introduction. The government's actions were the most important factor in shaping the nature of the German economic recovery. This is because the government was prepared to intervene in the economy to kick-start it out of the recession it found itself in the early 1930s. The new ideological priorities of the regime dictated that the recovery was based on protection, regulation and a commitment to rearm.

Investment and the reduction of unemployment. The overriding consideration in Nazi economic planning was the creation of an autarkic (self-sufficient) economy. Such a policy reflected the wider aims of Nazism. However, it was not until the mid-1930s that the Nazis were sufficiently dominant to make this the overriding priority for economic planning. Whilst Schacht was charged with the task of building an economy *capable* of rearmament, it should be argued that the reduction of unemployment was the primary target for investment in the period 1933–6. The main method of reducing the numbers of unemployed was for the state to act to stimulate demand. This policy did not herald a change from that of previous regimes. However, what set the regime apart was the extent of direct state investment as the table below shows.

Year	1929	1933	1934	1935	1936	1937	1938
Total expenditure	12.4	9.4	12.8	13.9	15.8	19.3	29.3
Percentage of GNP	15.7	18.9	22.9	22.0	22.5	24.5	33.5

Government expenditure in Germany, 1929–38 (bn RM).

The reason for this was that the regime's credibility depended on reducing unemployment rapidly. It is not that the regime immediately launched itself into a rearmament programme from the start, more that it created an economic pattern that could be suited to such a policy later – i.e., state investment and controlled foreign trade.

Apart from the fact that the Nazis needed to tackle the unemployment problem, they were not in such a politically dominant position in 1934 as they were later in the decade. Therefore they had to balance their ideological demands on the economy with that of business and political security in particular.

Public investment. The level of direct investment in the economy between 1933 and 1936 was the main reason for the economy's recovery and shape. The growth of public investment is shown in the table below:

1932	1933	1934	1935	1936
2.2	2.5	4.6	6.4	8.1

Public investment in Germany, 1932–36 (bn RM).

Public investment went into a range of industries but, as the historian Richard Overy has pointed out, the main beneficiaries were the motor industry and construction. One of the more significant means by which much of this direct investment was funded was through the Mefo Bills. Issued by the government, these bills could either be used as currency or held as an investment. If the latter course of action was chosen, they would deliver four per cent interest a year before being exchangeable after five years. The important consequence of such funding was that it increased the amount available for public expenditure in industries (especially those connected with rearmament – see table below).

Public expenditure in Germany, 1932–6 (bn RM).

Date	1932	1933	1934	1935	1936
Construction	0.9	1.7	3.5	4.9	5.4
Rearmament	0.7	1.8	3.0	5.4	10.2
Transportation	0.8	1.3	1.8	2.1	2.4

The state also attempted to stimulate demand by promoting private investment. For Schacht, such a move was essential because the confidence of private investors was so low after the 1930s' depression. However, the state attempted to control private investment to bring it in line with centrally determined 'needs'. In 1934, a series of regulations and laws limited the amount of profit that could be taken out of businesses in dividends. Such regulation encouraged individuals to reinvest any profits into business.

Financial autarky. The Nazi economy was autarkic in nature from the start. In the 'New Plan' of 1934, Schacht introduced measures that regulated the relationship between the German and foreign economies. The movement of capital, trading in currency and protectionist tariffs formed the backbone of the new regime's economic policy. However, such a move was not intended simply to set Germany on the path to rearmament. It was a policy aimed at ensuring that the disaster of the late 1920s and early 1930s could not be repeated. The damage to Germany's trade of Schacht's bilateral trade treaties was immediate and long lasting, as seen in the table below. However, protecting the German economy in this way was highly popular. In 1934 the Nazi regime still needed to court popularity. Such 'economic nationalism' was universally welcomed. Even businesses that were affected by the fall in the volume of trade were to an extent placated by the promise of rich pickings from public works and the prospective growth in armaments contracts.

Exports and imports by volume, 1929–38 (1913=100).

Date	1929	1930	1931	1932	1933	1934	1935	1936	1937	1938
Exports	98.0	92.2	82.7	55.6	50.7	47.1	51.5	56.9	64.2	54.7
Imports	96.6	86.0	69.9	62.5	62.8	68.4	60.8	59.8	69.0	74.6

Consumer confidence. Initially, in 1933–4, the state attempted to boost demand in the economy by boosting consumer demand and confidence. This was done in a variety of ways. In 1934, the government offered marriage loans for newly-wed couples wishing to furnish their homes. However, it was not the aim of the state to boost the economy through wage inflation, in fact quite the opposite. It was the policy of Schacht and Hitler that demand should be driven through investment in capital industries, with the aim being to cut unemployment, so wages were kept low to achieve that aim. Indeed, many did not receive wages at all and the introduction of conscription through compulsory Labour Service in 1935 highlights the priority of the regime.

'GUNS OR BUTTER'? 1936–9

Historical interpretation

There is little debate that the years 1936–9 were marked by an economic policy centred on rearmament and autarky. In *The Nazi Dictatorship* (1985), **Ian Kershaw** explains that the move to prioritise rearmament at the expense of **consumer industries** marked a turning point in the decision-making structure. In particular it marks the strengthening of the Nazis and their allies at the expense of the more conservative such as Schacht.

KEY TERM

Consumer industries are those which make goods for the home and luxury items.

There has been a wide-ranging debate about the *extent* to which the German economy in the period 1936–9 was geared to war and rearmament. Post-war research based on United States strategic bombing surveys suggested that the economy was less prepared for war than had been previously thought. In particular, **Burton Klein** claimed in *Germany's Economic Preparations for War* (1959), that the planning in the period 1936–9 was not geared to an extensive war. Instead, Klein suggested that there was a balance in the economy between 'butter and guns', i.e., between consumer and armament/heavy industries. Indeed, such a balance was to cause the economy problems. By 1936–7, the strain was beginning to show with a shortage of skilled labour and foreign currency essential for the growing heavy industry. On top of this, full employment was creating inflationary pressures as a result of pressure on wages and prices. This led historians such as Klein and **Timothy Mason** (1975) to suggest that the way out of these pressures for the regime was the seizure of land such as the *Anschluss* with Austria in 1938 or short 'lightning' wars (blitzkrieg).

The main critic of this line of argument has been **Richard Overy**. In *The Nazi Economic Recovery* (1982) and *Göring: The Iron Man* (1984), Overy argues that between 1936 and 1939 the German economy restructured to prepare for war. That war took place in 1939, however, was not the result of a crisis in the economy, but because of foreign policy decisions. Overy stresses that consumer industries were not given preference between 1936 and 1939 and neither was there a balance between consumer and heavy industry. Similarly, he states that there was no deliberately small war economy in 1939, capable of sustaining only blitzkrieg. Overy stresses that economic and political policy was aimed at providing the means by which sustained total war could be fought. However, the declaration of war in 1939 was earlier than expected and the economy was not yet fully ready.

It should be argued that the years 1936–9 did indeed see a distinct prioritisation of heavy industry. This matched the ideological priorities of the regime. However, the damage this did to consumption should not be exaggerated. What is apparent in this period is a shift in the balance between the two, consumption and heavy industry, in the priorities of the state.

What was the significance of the Four Year Plan, 1936?

An increase in military expenditure. The introduction of the Four Year Plan marked a turning point in the Nazi regime's economic policy. With the appointment of Hermann Göring as Plenipotentiary in charge of the Plan, there was a change in emphasis in the management of the economy. Central to this change in emphasis was an increase in investment in military expenditure. In 1936, 9.4 per cent of Net Domestic Product was invested in armaments. By 1939 that figure had risen to 38.1 per cent. In his secret memorandum of 1936 to those who were to implement the plan, Hitler wrote: 'the economy, economic leaders and theories . . . all owe unqualified service in this struggle for the self-assertion of our nation'.

This statement of intended priorities was backed up by Göring who in December 1936 in a speech to industrialists said: 'The context to which we look forward calls for enormous efficiency. No end to rearmament is in sight. All that matters is victory or defeat'.

To this end, the more conservative economic leaders were sidelined such as Schacht, who was replaced as Minister of Economics by Walther Funk in 1937. However, the new administrative machinery created to administer the plan targeted specific industries rather than the economy as a whole. The body placed in overall charge, the General Four Year Plan Council headed by Göring, focused on the issues of self-sufficiency in essential raw materials of steel, oil and rubber. The result was significant growth in those areas as the table shows.

The centrepiece of this strategy was the huge *Reichswerke Hermann Göring* at Watenstadt. The plant was built to rectify the lack of native

Date	1936	1939
Iron ores	2,259	3,928
Gasoline	1,257	1,935
Synthetic rubber	1	22

Production of strategic raw materials, 1936 and 1939 (000 tons).

high grade iron ore by processing low grade ore. Göring's aim was to reduce reliance on foreign ore from 80 per cent of German consumption to 50 per cent.

Failures of the Four Year Plan. Despite this decisive shift in priorities, there was not a radical restructuring of the economy. Indeed, the period should be seen as a further step on the road to a war economy but with an understanding that autarky was by no means complete. There were significant failures to make Germany self-sufficient by 1939, e.g., on the eve of war Germany was only producing 18 per cent of the demanded amount of synthetic oil. In this sense the nature of economic change very much matched that of the regime. Whilst its intentions were crystal clear, the differing and competing agencies which made up the decision-makers of the regime created a situation whereby autarky was the primary goal, but other economic considerations still had to be taken into account.

Did consumption fall, 1936–9?

Levels of consumption maintained. Although consumption was not the driving force of the recovery between 1936 and 1939, its importance should not be dismissed. As the table below shows, by 1937 the production of consumer goods reached the levels of 1927 and continued to rise, although this rise was at a slower rate than the rate of growth in other sectors of the economy. What the change in priorities of the Four Year Plan created was a contradiction: an ideological commitment to squeeze consumerism but a political priority to maintain politically acceptable levels of consumption.

Date	1927	1929	1930	1931	1932	1933	1934	1935	1936	1937	1938
Capital goods	97	102	84	62	47	56	81	99	114	130	144
Consumer goods	103	97	91	82	74	80	93	91	98	103	108

Index of industrial production, 1927–38 (1928 = 100).

Food imported to maintain levels of consumption. In his memo of 1936 that heralded the Second Four Year Plan, Hitler wrote that: 'the most important task of our economic policy is to see to it that all Germans are incorporated into the economic process, and so the prerequisites for normal consumption are created'.

In the same memorandum, he continues to suggest that the demand for consumption articles of 'general use' could be met by an increase in production, which at least partly occurred as could be seen in the table. The problem for Germany was its inability to produce sufficient foodstuffs to feed itself. Therefore, agriculture was mobilised as part of the Second Four Year Plan. This mobilisation was partly introduced so as to create grain stockpiles for the outbreak of war, but also because it was necessary to satisfy demand. Before the war German agriculture could still only produce 55 per cent of fats consumed. Whilst there was heavy investment in industries which could produce synthetic raw materials, there was not sufficient capital to invest in new ways to make agriculture more efficient. However, the regime continued to import foodstuffs despite the fact that this used up both essential foreign exchange or trade credits. Indeed, one of the main reasons why the regime failed to reach its targets of self-sufficiency was because it was not able significantly to reduce the importation of foreign goods for consumption.

Dampening of consumer demand. The Nazi regime attempted to dampen down consumer demand. Indeed it is remarkable that in an era of full employment between 1936 and 1939, real wages remained static. This was achieved through the government's imposition of wage and price controls in 1936. However, such controls were not universal. As the economy neared a state of full employment in 1936, so companies looking for skilled labour introduced a range of benefits, such as better-paid overtime, to entice workers to take employment. From 1936 to 1939, consumption did not grow at the same rate as rearmament related industries. But neither was consumption completely squeezed.

WHAT WAS THE RELATIONSHIP BETWEEN HITLER AND BIG BUSINESS?

Historical interpretation

The debate about the extent to which German business colluded with Nazi economic policy, and helped formulate that policy, has raged for many years. In *The Nazi Dictatorship* (1985), **Ian Kershaw** argues that German business neither dictated economic policy nor was policy dictated to it. Instead, 'big business' was an important factor in the creation of policy. Kershaw insists that business was more influential before 1936 when its interests were fully served by the job creating policies of Schacht. However, it is wrong to argue that after 1936 the influence of business disappeared. The drive for autarky was supported by many sections of the business community and many of their needs were incorporated into Nazi policy.

The line taken by Kershaw was in response to **Tim Mason**'s argument explained in *The Primacy of Politics – Politics and Economics in Nazi Germany* (1972). Mason argues that after 1936 economic policy becomes subject to Nazi ideology. To Mason, the interests of big business became swamped by the drive for autarky. As the state dominates, so it manipulates the markets, damages trade and reduces standards of living. Therefore one sees 'the primacy of politics'. Such a view has been backed up by historians such as **P. Hayes**, *Industry and Ideology* (1989), who argues that even though companies such as IG-Farben (and individuals from these companies, such as Karl Krauch) participated in the creation of the Four Year Plan, their interests were secondary when the plan was implemented.

The view that political considerations very much dominated economic decision-making has been presented by a range of respected historians in the last 30 years. In *The German Dictatorship* (1973), **Karl Bracher** argues that political goals were of primary importance in determining economic policy. That view is shared by **Richard Overy** in *The Nazi Economic Recovery* (1982): ' . . . the Third Reich . . . set about reducing the autonomy of the economic elite and subordinating it to the interests of the Nazi state.' Such an argument has been refuted by Marxist historians who believe that the interests of capital dominated throughout the Nazi period.

Shared interests between business and the Nazi regime

Big business backed Hitler financially after 1929 and welcomed the Nazi seizure of power; the threat of a communist revolution disappeared. The trade unions were closed down and political stability and law and order was restored. Despite his anti-capitalist rhetoric, Hitler was keen to maintain a close relationship with the industrialists. They were one of the first groups he addressed after taking power and it was partly because of pressure from industrial barons like Krupps that his old supporters in the SA were purged in the Night of the Long Knives. Business chiefs became closely involved in political decisions. Krupp was appointed General Secretary of the Reich Association of German Industry, the giant chemical empire IG-Farben provided one director for the Four Year Plan and two-thirds of the Reich Office for Economic Expansion, and many firms gave directorships to important party officials.

How business benefited. Industrialists, particularly those engaged in construction, car manufacture and iron and steel, prospered during the public works programme after 1933 and the rearmament drive after 1936. The imposition of 'Courts of Honour', or having to eat soup in a workers' canteen, could be tolerated as profits quadrupled between 1933 and 1937. Big business was also the chief beneficiary of the Aryanisation of the economy and territorial expansion after 1939. Krupps, for example, was offered Dutch shipyards, Belgian metalworks, French machine tools, Yugoslav chromium, Greek nickel and Ukrainian iron and steel. Likewise the company happily exploited prisoner and slave workers – 70,000 by 1944. The building of the *Reichswerke Hermann Göring* is often given as an example of how, from 1936 to 1939, the interests of the state dominated those of industry, in this case the Ruhr iron and steel producers. However, the reality is more subtle. The Four Year Plan was implemented with the active support of important areas of the business community, IG-Farben (the leading chemicals company) taking an active role in drawing up the plan. Indeed, a member of the IG-Farben board, Karl Krauch, was an important member of the office of the Four Year Plan. It is probable that Krauch fulfilled his role with the drive for autarky as his paramount consideration. But his appointment and the continuing role of business in the formulation of Nazi economic policy qualifies the belief that after 1936 the influences on policy came only from the Nazi Party.

Limitations to the influence of business. Despite the benefits gained by big business, it would be wrong to argue that during the Nazi dictatorship Nazism was the expression of capitalism. Hitler's alliance with business was pragmatic rather than ideological. Industrialists were cultivated because they served the needs of the regime and growing tensions illustrate that it was the state that triumphed over ever-powerful economic interests. Some industrialists resented excessive state interference and feared the drive for self sufficiency and an expansionist foreign policy. The sacking of Schacht in 1936 marked the failure of business to retain some independence of policy and the Four Year Plan gave Göring wide powers of control over raw materials, investment and foreign currency. Business was set production targets, taxed more heavily and compelled to invest in state projects. Steel bosses contributed 130 million RM to the Hermann Göring steelworks, Krupp was forced to finance Buna (a synthetic rubber project) and coal magnates were forced to invest in schemes to extract petrol from lignite. If the wealth and status of big business was enhanced during the Nazi regime, it was a by-product, not an objective of policy.

WHAT WAS THE SIGNIFICANCE OF HJALMAR SCHACHT AND HERMANN GÖRING?

The nature of Nazi economic policy closely reflected the economic philosophy, ideology and political fortunes of these two individuals.

Hjalmar Schacht

Hjalmar Schacht was a career civil servant who was politically right wing. As head of the state bank (the Reichsbank) in 1923, and as a negotiator with the Allies over the terms of the Dawes and Young Plans, he shared the view of the far right to the extent that he joined the **Harzberg Front** in 1931. (This organisation was an alliance, set up to oppose the Brüning government, between the Nazi movement and nationalist DNVP, and sympathisers, such as bankers, generals and representatives from heavy industry.) Whilst not being a professed Nazi, Schacht shared many of Hitler's ambitions, in particular the creation of a strong German economy capable of full rearmament.

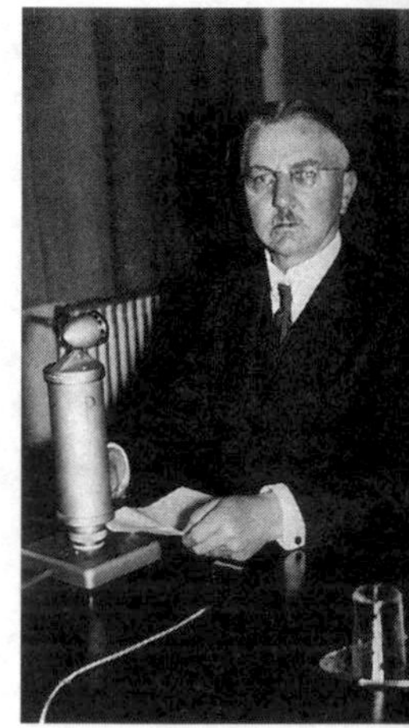

Hjalmar Schacht.

The role of Schacht. Yet Schacht was also a skilled financier. As President of the Reichsbank and Minister for Economics, the methods he used to achieve economic consolidation and a fall in unemployment were those proposed by nationalists before 1933. In essence, the government's role in the regulation of the economy was increased (the New Plan 1934). The introduction of Mefo Bills (see page 189) was a masterpiece of deficit financing long advocated by those who believed that the state could take a role in helping economies out of depression. The government also controlled the nature of foreign trade and set up a series of bilateral trade agreements that were to Germany's advantage.

Schacht opposes all-out rearmament. It was Schacht's responsibility to create a more dynamic economy that could satisfy the political need to reduce unemployment and the ideological impetus to rearm. Schacht was not opposed to rearmament after 1936 but he was suspicious of a policy of all-out autarky as proposed by the Four Year Plan. His suspicions were twofold. Firstly such a policy marked the end of his supremacy over economic matters. Secondly, Schacht believed that further rearmament could only be funded in the long run by improving German exports in order to earn the currency necessary to import cheap raw materials. To Schacht, the attempt to rearm by producing synthetic raw materials was uneconomic and therefore potentially damaging. His view was the view of many within the business community who were more traditional in their understanding of economics.

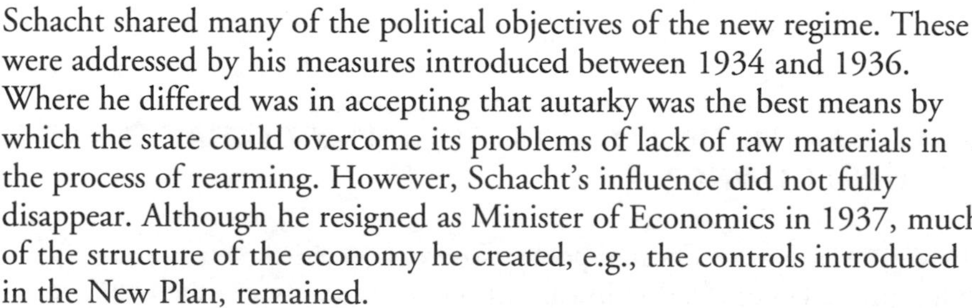

Schacht shared many of the political objectives of the new regime. These were addressed by his measures introduced between 1934 and 1936. Where he differed was in accepting that autarky was the best means by which the state could overcome its problems of lack of raw materials in the process of rearming. However, Schacht's influence did not fully disappear. Although he resigned as Minister of Economics in 1937, much of the structure of the economy he created, e.g., the controls introduced in the New Plan, remained.

Hermann Göring

The appointment of Göring as Commissioner of Raw Materials in April 1936 was an indication of the determination of the regime to overcome

Hermann Göring.

the problem of the supply of raw materials. As head of the Luftwaffe, Göring's priorities were to secure a German source of essential raw materials, most importantly fuel. He was also interested in increasing his own personal power. The Four Year Plan was designed by planners from IG-Farben who had also provided strong links with the Air Ministry. As part of the organisation of the plan, state secretaries were appointed from the Agriculture and Labour ministries who were directly responsible to Göring. In doing so, he increased his power base considerably. Such an increase in influence was possible because Göring's stated intentions of prioritising rearmament reflected the wishes of Hitler.

However, if it is accepted that Göring's aims were to increase the production of synthetic raw materials and, at the same time, increase his own personal power and wealth, then this also explains the nature of the Four Year Plan. It involved a considerable readjustment in the economy but Göring did not have the technical expertise necessary to drive through a policy of total autarky. His was the role of economic dictator, but in that there opened up the problems of an economy directed and planned by the state. Whilst Göring amassed a huge fortune from the *Reichswerke Hermann Göring*, there was not the complete readjustment to a war economy his rhetoric promised. In his famous 'Guns or Butter' speech in 1936, Göring promised the German people that if they had to make a choice between the two then it would have to be guns. However, Göring's understanding of economic matters was limited. He isolated those who challenged him, such as Schacht, and appointed those who were prepared to accept his decisions without questions, including Schacht's successor as Minister of Economics in 1938, Walther Funk.

Göring did not have an all-encompassing view of the economy. This helps to explain why the economic system in 1939 had not been fully transformed into a war economy. His aim was the creation of an autarkic economy, whatever the cost. It might well be argued that Göring's legacy was the creation of an economic system that was increasingly dominated by the state. However, he had political allies in industrial circles and that helps to explain why, by 1939, big business still had considerable autonomy. It was regulated by controls on prices and wages but the regime relied on business to implement the policy on rearmament.

CONCLUSION

The nature of the Nazi economic recovery between 1933 and 1939 reflected the interests and priorities of the new regime.

- From 1933 to 1936 this revolved around the reduction of unemployment whilst making the German economy financially self-sufficient.
- It was also of political importance that the economy was being geared towards rearmament. The following three years saw a change in priorities with rearmament and autarky being the stated priorities of the regime. However, by 1939 such a change was incomplete. This was partly due to the enormity of the task, and the inefficiency of central planning methods, but also to the fact that it was politically important not to undermine the general levels of consumption.

The nature of the German economic recovery very much matched the regime's political as well as ideological priorities. It also reflected the interests of a wider group who benefited from protectionism.

SECTION 4

Nazi society

INTRODUCTION

Hitler attempted to unite all Germans in a racially pure, classless people's community – *Volksgemeinschaft*. In this community the Nazis promised that there would be no political, religious, economic or social divisions. The status of a German would be determined by racial purity and ideological commitment to the state. Even relations between husband and wife and parents and children were to be less important than the demands of the state.

These revolutionary ideals were relentlessly put forward and enforced over twelve years by the Nazi regime. Therefore they were bound to leave some imprint on society, especially as they were accepted by so many Germans. However, no regime which failed to survive even a generation could create a 'social revolution' in the sense of a total transformation of society. Nazi ideals were in any case often contradictory and some had to be abandoned in the face of practical politics. Nonetheless, the dictatorship did accelerate a significant restructuring within society even before total war unleashed more destructive forces.

KEY POINTS

- The Nazis were not the agents of any one particular class and aimed to implement policies that reduced the importance of class distinctions.
- Hitler did succeed in integrating the majority of Germans into a national community.
- Nazi policies did result in some mobility within social groups, but did not fundamentally alter the existing class structure of society.
- There was no social revolution in peacetime but war did initiate significant social changes.
- After some initial benefits the status of farmers continued to decline. The Nazis failed to reverse the long-term decline in the rural community.
- The status of women in society was not significantly altered by Nazi propaganda or policies.
- Young people were most easily attracted by Nazism and became the most active supporters of the regime.

HISTORICAL INTERPRETATIONS: WAS THERE A SOCIAL REVOLUTION DURING THE THIRD REICH?

Most historians now reject the old-fashioned Marxist interpretation represented by **Franz Neuman** in *Behemoth: The Structure and Practice of National Socialism* (1942) that Nazism aimed to reinforce existing class divisions, but the impact of Nazi policies remains a subject of debate.

David Schoenbaum in *Hitler's Social Revolution: Class and Status in Nazi Germany 1933–1939* (1966) has claimed that the Nazis exerted a powerful modernising force that stimulated a revolutionary shift in social values and attitudes. **Ralf Dahrendorf** in *Democracy and Social Structure in Germany* (1961) argues that the destruction of social elites in wartime helped pave the way for the modernisation of post-war German society. A social revolution was achieved by projecting an image of a society devoid of the traditional ties of class and status. This interpretation is still questioned by other historians, such as **Ian Kershaw** in *The Nazi Dictatorship* (1995), who claims that Nazism did not come remotely near producing a social revolution.

HOW DID THE NAZI DICTATORSHIP AFFECT RELATIONS BETWEEN SOCIAL CLASSES?

The working class

The destruction of union power. The Nazis failed to dislodge working-class allegiances to the Communist and Social Democratic parties in the elections of 1932. Some white-collar workers did vote Nazi, but the unskilled and semi-skilled blue-collar workers tended to be strongly unionised and remained staunchly loyal to the parties of the Left. For all Nazi promises about quality of life for all classes, the first victims of the dictatorship were the leaders of working-class power. The Communist Party was banned in February 1933. Social Democratic leaders were arrested after their opposition to the Enabling Act in March and working-class leaders filled the concentration camps in the early years of the regime.

Trade unions were abolished on 2 May 1933 and workers were regimented in the German Labour Front (DAF) led by Robert Ley and by Nazi Factory Cell organisations. Any hopes of a genuine 'social revolution' appeared to be destroyed by the purge of the radical SA in June 1934. Instead Hitler appeared to be cultivating the support of bankers, generals and conservatives.

Employment and living standards. It would be wrong, however, to assume that Hitler's interest in destroying the existing class system was a political gimmick. Hitler's alliance with business and conservative interests was politically useful for a time and was abandoned by 1936. Many Nazi policies were introduced with the benefit of the working classes in mind. The most immediate and valuable benefit was a job, which almost all Germans enjoyed by 1936. Training schemes for the unskilled and apprenticeships for working-class school leavers were significantly expanded. Most workers were earning 20 per cent more by 1939 in real terms compared to 1933, and though non-skilled workers saw little or no such increase most accepted this in return for job security and improved social benefits.

KEY TERM

Paternalism is when a group or individuals look after other individuals.

Propaganda and paternalism. Nazi **paternalism**, directed by organisations such as Strength through Joy and the Beauty of Labour, raised morale and distracted workers from the monotony of their work and the increasing regimentation of their lives. Workers were able to appreciate offices and factories which were better heated, illuminated and decorated and in their leisure time they were offered evening classes, musical recitals and concerts, art exhibitions, theatre trips, sporting events and package holidays.

Courts of Honour were set up to resolve disputes between worker and employer fairly and bosses were encouraged to show solidarity with their workers by eating soup in the same canteen. In an effort to encourage friendliness and camaraderie, neighbours were urged to look after each other during times of hardship and the Winter Help programme offered food and support to the old and poor during the winter months. The promotion of cheap housing and the availability of mass-produced consumer goods, including a 'people's radio' and a 'people's car' (*Volkswagen*) also demonstrated the regime's attempt to embrace all classes in the growing prosperity of the nation. Hitler was very proud of his lowly social origins and saw himself as a man of the people who sat next to his chauffeur, ate simple meals and addressed workers with the intimate plural form, *Ihr*.

Nazi paternalism did enjoy a wide degree of popularity. By 1938, 180,000 had been on a cruise and 10 million, or one in three of the workforce, had enjoyed a state-financed holiday. Even SPD reports conceded that 'Strength through Joy is very popular, recognising the yearning of the little men . . . to take part in the pleasures of top people. It is a clever appeal to the petty bourgeois inclinations of the unpolitical workers'. Speer certainly took the policy seriously and believed that paternalism was beginning to break down class divisions.

Working class unrest and discontent. It is difficult to gauge the response and mood of the working classes given the nature of the dictatorial regime. Some workers had always been ideologically hostile and remained implacably, but impotently opposed. Others were more pragmatic but became disillusioned as their wages stagnated, regimentation increased and working hours lengthened. Industrial accidents, illness and absenteeism doubled between 1936 and 1939. Moreover there is evidence of dissent and opposition from the workers.

There were strikes in 1936 in Russelheim and Berlin and a Report of the Defence Industry Inspectorate from Nuremberg on 15 June 1936 found insubordination, sabotage and go-slows. The lack of more overt opposition is hardly surprising and does not suggest any real enthusiasm for the regime. The working classes had been demoralised by the impact of mass unemployment after 1929 and were quickly emasculated by the abolition of their trade unions and arrest of their leaders. An SPD report of 1936 claimed that the abolition of collective bargaining had 'atomised' the workforce and destroyed worker solidarity. Workers felt increasingly isolated and vulnerable, cowed by spies, informers and constant political interference. Another SPD report of 1938 claimed that 'everyone is afraid of saying a word too many and landing oneself in a spot'. Many workers became fatalistic about their plight, bored by regimentation and numbed by the relentless propaganda. They grumbled quietly or were silently apathetic.

At the same time some workers, especially skilled workers, or those with little union tradition were enthusiasts or became converted to the regime. SPD reports often complained about the compliance of the workers and their desertion of the class struggle. In exasperation one such report of 1935 claimed that the positive response of the working class to the regime was 'the real mystery in Germany'. This allegiance was naturally bolstered by the restoration of national prestige in the 1930s and by patriotism generated by war, but it was also the product of a growing identification.

The breaking of class divisions. It is true that the Nazi leadership itself was recruited from the ranks of the lower middle class, and Nazi organisations such as the Hitler Youth and Youth Labour Service were genuinely classless. A spirit of equality was even encouraged within the armed forces and the SS. Even in peacetime, Christabel Bielenberg (an opponent of the regime) was impressed that 'social divisions were melting', and an American diplomat at the Berlin Embassy, George Kennen, thought that Hitler was 'stamping out the last vestiges of particularism and class differences'.

Hitler claimed in 1939 to have broken with a world of prejudices, 'we have broken down classes' he proclaimed 'to make way for the German people as a whole'. Leading Nazis such as Göbbels, Himmler and Bormann also believed in this campaign. Leaving aside the claims of the regime, it is true that the Nazis went some way towards ending the traditional sense of alienation between the German worker and the state. Society before 1914 had been highly stratified and workers had been repressed and excluded. The Weimar Republic had partly rehabilitated the working class, but political influence remained with the conservative elites of business, army, civil service and judiciary. The subordination of these elites by the Nazis enhanced both the morale and the political influence of the working class. Status was no longer confined to social class but to ability, racial purity and ideological commitment.

Class continuity. Nonetheless, though there was some upward social mobility for the workers, the social structure was not fundamentally altered. The traditional elites were often merged with new elites and non-party elites such as business and the civil service. The army continued to recruit from the same social groups as before. Education also continued to be dominated by the middle classes. Grammar school boys may have burned their caps, but they still preferred their social equals as their friends.

The 'Mittelstand'

Introduction. The German middle classes, particularly the lower middle class or *Mittelstand* of shopkeepers, clerks, trades people and skilled craft workers, were Hitler's most enthusiastic supporters during his rise to power. Of all social groups it was the *Mittelstand* with which Hitler most readily identified: he shared their fears, hopes and prejudices. Their cause also found powerful philosophical support from Nazi thinkers such as Feder, Wagener, Darré and Rosenberg. The *Mittelstand* welcomed the restoration of political stability, the imposition of wage controls and the punishment of what they considered to be anti-social elements such as vagrants, the work-shy and homosexuals. They also won some temporary protection from competition from department stores and were offered low interest loans and a generous share of confiscated Jewish businesses. Despite such relief, the economic position of the *Mittelstand* was by no means secure. Department stores continued to provide strong competition after 1934 and many shopkeepers were squeezed between the Reich Food Estate that fixed agricultural prices and the price freeze in shops. Traders who survived tended to be old and were forced to work longer hours for diminishing returns amidst increasingly burdensome bureaucratic control. Rearmament and war also tended to undermine small businesses and accelerated the concentration of monopoly capitalism.

The social elite

Shared interests. Most aristocrats thought that Hitler was a danger to their class. This was a view shared by Hindenburg. A minority, however, driven by sentimentality for Imperial Germany, and fearing the communists, were dazzled by Hitler and joined his cause. The support of the social elite, symbolised by the status of the naive Papen as Vice-Chancellor in Hitler's first cabinet, undoubtedly smoothed the establishment of the Nazi regime. The marriage of the 'old and new' Germany was symbolically demonstrated at the Commemoration Day celebration at Potsdam in March 1933. Many from the old elite formed the new political elite in the SS, perhaps a fifth of the officer class being of aristocratic blood.

Attack on the social elite. Hitler had nothing but contempt for the German social elite. He believed that the upper classes were patrons of Jewish decadent art, and he thought that their lifestyles of dinner parties, gambling, theatre, concerts and political intrigue was degenerate and un-German. Within months of coming to power the Nazis banned hunting with dogs, Hitler believing that fox-hunters were feminine and their culture too much like the English. Protection of wild animals took second place to Hitler's fanatical class war, and there is no doubt that the anti-hunt campaign would have gone further had it not been for the intervention of Göring who, as Reich Master of the Hunt, was not prepared to sacrifice shooting and fishing. The campaign against the pleasures of the idle rich was intensified in wartime when Martin Bormann made attempts to close down theatres, casinos and restaurants. There is no doubt that Hitler was serious in his attempt to break the monopoly of the old social elite in the army, civil service and high politics. The Conservative and Nationalist parties were banned in July 1934 and the promotion of able professionals was encouraged in both the army and bureaucracy.

By 1936 the percentage of aristocratic generals had declined from 61 to 25. Whilst the great Prussian landowners remained rich, and indeed were the chief beneficiaries of the annexation of western Poland in 1939, many landowners did feel that their traditional status was threatened by radical *Gauleiters* and administrators from the Food Estate, the head of which was a humble pig breeder. Some party activists demanded the carve-up of the great estates. Aristocrats also resented their obligation to invite the small fry of rural society to their hunt balls and the loss of many of their traditional social functions to the party. The old elite remained Hitler's staunchest critics and his most active and daring opponents. He successfully depicted the Stauffenberg Bomb Plot of 1944 as a last-ditch attempt by the old aristocracy to topple him and the purge following the failure of the plot did much to break their power.

Rural Germany

Introduction. For the rural population the regime preached a traditionalist anti-urban philosophy of 'Blood and Soil' which glorified the peasant as the staunch defender of true German values – honesty, decency, deference, hard work, family bliss, national pride and racial purity.

Emergency relief was offered in 1933, protecting farmers with increased tariffs and reducing or deferring their debts. The Reich Entailed Farm Law (September 1933) classified about 600,000 medium-sized holdings (of about 30 acres) as hereditary, to be bequeathed intact to the eldest son. Owners were honoured with the title of *Bauern*, 'farmer peasant'. Agriculture was regulated by the Reich Food Estate, a huge corporate organisation led by Walther Darré from June 1933. This employed 20,000 full-time officials and fixed agricultural prices and wages, set production quotas, dictated crop rotation and allocated scarce resources.

Ideology and policy. Nazi thinkers such as Walther Darré and Gottfried Feder demanded a rural revolution that would reverse the relentless urbanisation of German society by the creation of a romantic 'back-to-land' movement. Hitler was attracted by such a notion, glorifying the German peasant as honest, hard-working, uncorrupted and racially pure, and enthusiastically embraced an ideology of 'Blood and Soil'. More realistically, he needed a viable and efficient agricultural industry to supply cheap food for factory workers, to release valuable foreign exchange for rearmament and to provide 'nutritional freedom' to ensure self-sufficiency in time of war. The bond between the peasants and the regime should not be underestimated. The Nazis rescued thousands of farmers from bankruptcy in 1933 and defended more than half a million middling farmers by declaring their farms hereditary and indivisible. Many farmers were exempt from insurance payments. Mortgages were reduced and the burden of taxation was lifted by £60 million between 1934 and 1938. By 1937 agricultural wages had recovered to their levels of 1928 and farmers could exploit generous family allowances, improvement grants and credit for house purchase.

Limitations of policy. Welcome though such benefits undoubtedly were to a depressed and vulnerable peasantry, there is little evidence of any real revolution of the land. The idealistic plans of Feder and Darré were abandoned as economic reality and practical politics dictated. Rapid and sustained economic growth fuelled by consumer industries, the drive for rearmament after 1936 and the demands of wartime production accelerated industrialisation and urban growth. Conditions on the land remained grim and rising wages of industrial workers drew many young Germans from their *Haimat* (homeland). The much-vaunted racial purity of the German peasantry was tarnished by the employment of 3 million foreign workers on the land by 1944.

DID THE NAZIS CREATE A SOCIAL REVOLUTION?

Social continuity. The Nazi policies did not create a social revolution. The year 1933 did not mark a decisive break in social status and attitudes. Class divisions in Germany as elsewhere were narrowed by the trench solidarity of the First World War and continued to decline during the more progressive Weimar Republic. It would be wrong to underestimate the seriousness of Hitler's commitment to a *Volksgemeinschaft*, or to neglect important shifts within the social system, but the point to note is values, habits, allegiances, lifestyles and relationships were too deeply entrenched to be dislodged by Nazi ideology and social engineering.

Consensus and dislocation. The Nazi regime could not abolish the class system in Germany, nor did it attempt any real redistribution of wealth. Class prejudice and social distinctions survived the Nazi seizure of power. Nonetheless the dictatorship did create some social dislocation. By destroying the power base of the traditional elites and fostering a meritocratic ethos (where promotion came by merit alone) the Nazis did accelerate the upward social mobility of the lower middle class and the ambitious workers. It is also important to see Nazi society in its contemporary context. In Russia one class – the *Kulaks* – were almost eliminated. In France the social classes were not on speaking terms, whilst in Spain they were at war with each other. Compared with such bitter divisions, the Nazis achieved a remarkable social consensus. Total war accelerated this dislocation. Conscription, relocation of workers and the importation of foreign labour destroyed patterns of employment. The patriotic spirit generated by war and the shared fears and deprivations did foster a greater sense of social unity. As bombs fell indiscriminately on Nazi and non-Nazi, morale was sustained by a collective solidarity as all Germans gritted their teeth and revelled in sticking it out together – '*ausharren*'. The physical disintegration of Germany by 1945 helped to pave the way for a more modern, classless, pluralist society. By 1945, 4 million Germans were dead, 10 million were refugees, 15 per cent of housing was destroyed and industrial production had collapsed. This indeed was a social revolution brought about as the result of the failure of Nazism.

NAZISM AND WOMEN

Introduction

For women the regime preached the virtues of *Kinder, Küche, Kirche* (Children, Kitchen, Church), exploiting romantic ideals of domestic bliss. Women were banned from professional employment in 1933, offered interest-free loans in return for not seeking employment, and restricted from university education. Efforts were made to increase the population. Mothers won tax concessions and were awarded medals to celebrate their fertility: eight children warranted a Gold medal, six a Silver and four a Bronze.

Abortion was banned and attempts were made to breed perfect Aryan specimens by selection through the *Lebensborn* (Spring of Life) programme in 1935. State propaganda condemned all threats to the romantic ideal of rustic female innocence: make-up and lipstick were denounced and smoking and the wearing of slacks strongly discouraged. Such ideas were championed by state organisations such as the National Socialist Womanhood and German Women's Enterprise.

What was the impact of Nazism on German women?

The return to traditional values. It is difficult to detect any transformation in the status of women in the Third Reich. There is no doubt that the Nazi dictatorship did succeed in mobilising the allegiance of most women. Nazi ideology on women was fundamentally conservative: women were providers of healthy little Aryans, defenders of the faith and the mistresses of a domestic idyll. This romantic vision promoted by the propagandist mantra of *Kinder, Küche, Kirche* attracted sympathy from women whose so-called liberation from domestic routine during the 1920s had failed to fulfil expectations. Many women were easily seduced by Nazi rhetoric that glorified their exalted status as wives and mothers. Marriages increased by 130,000 per annum, births by over half a million per annum between 1933 and 1939. Women were barred from professional employment and a sixth had left all employment by 1937. Nazi women's organisations were enthusiastically supported.

Limitations of the regime's policy on women. Such success, however, represented not so much a social revolution as an attempt to return to traditional values. The direct impact of Nazi policies was limited. Earlier marriages and a rising birth rate were related more to increasing prosperity not to social policy. With the achievement of full employment by 1936, women returned to the workplace, increasing from 11.6 million to 14.6 million between 1933 and 1939. War further undermined Nazi social ideology. Even though Bormann and Sauckel frustrated Speer's efforts to recruit more women to factory work, about one million were mobilised by 1944. Mobilisation of men, the relocation of workers and the increasing use of foreign workers encouraged infidelity and promiscuity. By 1945, one in six women in Berlin had resorted to prostitution and one in three girls suffered from venereal diseases. War produced a sex imbalance between men and women of 1 to 3. Far from subordinating the role of women, the regime had by 1945 destroyed forever the 'cult of the German man' and had paved the way for the total liberation of women in society.

YOUNG PEOPLE

Historical interpretation

The traditional interpretation is that most young people were enthusiastically mobilised by Hitler, though this has been challenged by **Gerhard Weinberg** (1970) who claims that the Nazis were only temporarily successful in integrating young Germans.

Introduction

The indoctrination of young people was considered paramount. All youth groups were Nazified in June 1933 and membership of the Hitler Youth movement became compulsory in December 1936. Non-Nazi teachers were sacked, subjects, especially history and biology, were rewritten and Jewish children were denigrated by fellow classmates. Special schools were established to propagate Nazi ideology to the future elite: National Political Education Institutes, Adolf Hitler schools, 'order castles' (*Ordensburgen*), and a Supreme School at Frankfurt in 1941.

What was the impact of Nazism on young people?

The extent of indoctrination. The Nazis needed the allegiance of young people in order to achieve their aim of building a thousand-year Reich and aimed to educate all children 'physically, mentally and morally in the spirit of National Socialism'. The dream, however, was only partly achieved. There is no doubt that the regime did mesmerise a generation of young Germans. The humiliation of the Versailles Treaty and the weakness of the Weimar Republic was blamed on the flawed and submissive generation. The strength, vigour and dynamism of Nazism made a powerful appeal to a bored and demoralised youth. Thousands of young people were beguiled by the excitement of hiking, camping, competitive sports, marching in smart uniforms or simply by a yearning to belong. By 1939 7.5 million young Germans were active participants of the Hitler Youth. Education submitted passively to Nazification. Teachers were heavily over-represented in the Nazi Party and schools purged the dissident minority.

Discontent and rejection. Youth enthusiasm for the regime did decline by 1939 as young people became disaffected by growing regimentation, petty restrictions and ineffective and ageing youth leaders. The introduction of curfews and the banning of smoking and drinking after 1940 provoked further alienation at a time when young people could be mobilised to fight. Rival youth gangs revolted against the regime. Working-class youths formed 'pirate' bands whilst disillusioned middle-class adolescents aped American trends by chewing gum and playing jazz in the 'swing movement'. Nonetheless despite evidence of growing alienation, the affinity of young people with the dictatorship was sustained. Parents were often helpless in dissuading their children from their fervour and young people remained Hitler's staunchest supporters. It was appropriate that it was to these that Hitler made his last public appearance in April 1945 and that it was the young who fought most fanatically for him in the streets of Berlin during the last days of conflict. If there was a social transformation during the Nazi dictatorship then it can be detected most easily in the ideas and attitudes of young Germans.

NAZI SOCIETY – CONCLUSION

- Social relationships in Germany were disrupted by the impact of the Nazi dictatorship. The landed aristocracy were undermined, social deference destroyed and religious allegiances weakened.
- Germany emerged from its defeat in the First World War as a more equal, open and pluralistic society. Some of this change was the result of long-term economic modernisation, such as urbanisation and the move towards large-scale production, which were both later accelerated by the demands of total war. Military defeat also dislodged the traditional supremacy of the old aristocracy (*Junkers*) represented in the political establishment and the army.
- The specific impact of Nazi ideology is more difficult to detect but it can be concluded that the emphasis on merit and achievement did weaken the established social hierarchy. In this sense the dictatorship accelerated rather than caused social change

SECTION 5

The Holocaust

THE FINAL SOLUTION – WHY?

Key points

- There is no convincing evidence to suggest that Germans in 1933 supported any extremist or violent anti-Semitic policy. Neither is it possible to suggest that the Germans as a nation were guilty of the extermination policy.
- The anti-Semitic policies adopted by the Nazis between 1933 and 1939 were not part of a systematic preparation for the so-called Final Solution. There is no evidence to suggest a long-term programme to exterminate all European Jews. The Final Solution was adopted after a decision made by Hitler in the autumn of 1941 and was implemented in response to the collapse of existing policies.

Historical interpretation

The magnitude of this question, the sensitivity of any conclusions, and the deliberate policy of deception deployed by the Nazis mean that the origins of the 'Final Solution' will continue to provoke controversy. **Lucy Dawidowicz**, *The War against the Jews*, **Gerald Fleming**, *Hitler and the Final Solution* and **Daniel Goldhagen** in *Hitler's Willing Executioners* argue that the extermination of all Jews had always been Hitler's objective. Hitler systematically conditioned public opinion to accept mass extermination and used war as a cover to implement his ideological programme. This **intentionalist** interpretation is rejected by historians such as **Martin Broszat** in the *The Hitler State* (1981), **Hans Mommsen**, *National Socialism and Hitlerism* and **Ian Kershaw**, *The Nazi Dictatorship*, who argue that the evolution of the Final Solution was an improvised response to the crisis arising by 1941.

In *Hitler's Willing Executioners* (1996), **Daniel Goldhagen** argues that popular opinion in Germany was already sympathetic to a policy of Jewish extermination before the Nazis came to power. **Dawidowicz** in *The War against the Jews* (1975) and **Katz** in *The Holocaust in Historical Context* (1994) have also interpreted the Final Solution as the inevitable outcome of long-term German hatred of Jews.

This interpretation is rejected by most other historians known as **structuralists**, notably by **Norman Finkelstein** and **Ruth Birn**, in *A Nation on Trial* (1998), who claim that most Germans were not strongly anti-Semitic and that any popular anti-Semitism was no different from that found in other countries at the same time. **Peter Pulzer** also argues in *The Rise of Political Anti-Semitism in Germany and Austria* (1992) that anti-Semitism drew little strength from the working class. **Richard Evans** in *In Hitler's Shadow* (1989) and **Ian Kershaw** in *Popular Opinion and Political Dissent in the Third Reich* both argue that anti-Semitism was not an electoral issue in the Weimar Republic.

Goldhagen claims in *Hitler's Willing Executioners* (1996) that Germans enthusiastically welcomed the persecution of Jews by the Nazi regime in the period 1933–9. This interpretation is rejected by **D. Bankier**, *The Germans and the Final Solution* and **Kershaw** in *Popular Opinion and Dissent in the Third Reich*. Both argue that there were few popular assaults on Jews and that Germans overwhelmingly condemned Nazi anti-Semitic atrocities.

HOW STRONG WAS ANTI-SEMITISM IN GERMANY IN 1933?

Deep rooted anti-Semitism in Germany. There is no evidence to suggest that popular opinion in Germany in 1933 supported a radical or violent campaign against Jews. It is true that many Germans did share the anti-Semitism deeply ingrained in Central and East European culture. Jews had, for centuries, been the victim of persecution by governments and their non-Jewish neighbours. Popular myth depicted them as Christ-killers, greedy moneylenders, disloyal, parasitic wanderers who brought disease, took jobs and enriched themselves at the expense of others.

Nineteenth century. Anti-Semitism increased during the second half of the nineteenth century in Germany, as elsewhere in Europe, as Jews came to dominate business, the professions and the arts. Anti-Semitism was also fuelled in Germany by the strength of nationalism following unification in 1871 and encouraged by the repressive nature of German politics at the time. There were outbreaks of anti-Semitic violence in Berlin and Pomerania in 1881 when shops were ransacked and synagogues burned down. Adolf Stocker founded the radical anti-Jewish Christian Social Workers' Party in 1878 and organised a petition signed by a quarter of a million in 1881 which identified the Jews as a race, demanded the prohibition of further Jewish immigration and their exclusion from certain professions.

Anti-Semitism also found influential academic support. Von Treitschke and De Lagarde won considerable respect in academic circles for their claims that the Jews formed a 'nation within a nation'. Writers such as Ernst Haeckel and Houston Stewart Chamberlain sought to prove scientifically that the superiority of the Germanic races would be undermined if diluted by intermarriage with Jews. Just as such nineteenth century racist theories influenced Nazi philosophy, it is also possible to detect clear similarities between Nazi proposals and the ideas of earlier anti-Semites. A student conference held in 1896 claimed that the Jewish citizens of the Reich should not be regarded as Germans.

Scapegoats for failure. Such anti-Semitism could easily be exploited by nationalist speakers after the First World War. Small nationalist and racist parties proliferated after the war, the most infamous being the German Workers' Party formed by Anton Drexler and joined by Hitler in 1919. The Jews became the scapegoats for Germany's defeat, the humiliation of the Versailles Treaty and the political and economic chaos of the early years of the Weimar Republic. The murder of a Jew, Walter Rathenau the Foreign Minister, in 1922 is an illustration of the racist extremism of a minority of Germans. Anti-Semitism was then revived during the mass unemployment after 1929, when Jews were blamed for speculation and profiteering.

Limits to German anti-Semitism. The depth and widespread acceptance of such anti-Semitism should not, however, be exaggerated. Certainly there was no general acceptance of any plan of extermination. The academic racists of the nineteenth century do not reflect the opinions of the majority of Germans. In any case it should be remembered that policies of resettlement, in Palestine, were also put forward by Zionist organisations. Nor was German anti-Semitism unique. There was no equivalent in Germany of the riots that followed the Dreyfus case in France, nor was anti-Semitism as violent or deep-rooted as it was in Russia or Austria.

Anti-Semitic violence in Germany before 1933 was sporadic, localised and usually manipulated by ambitious rabble-rousers. It was directed against the stereotypical Jewish moneylender rather than against the Jew as an alien. Anti-Semitic parties lost power as prosperity returned and even at their peak could only muster 21 deputies in the Reichstag. By contrast, the most popular party in Germany by 1914 was the Social Democrats that opposed Jewish discrimination. Similarly, as the Weimar Republic recovered after 1923, anti-Semitic parties, including the Nazis, lost support and governments were dominated by a moderate coalition of Social Democrats, Liberals and the Centre.

Mass unemployment following the Wall Street Crash in 1929 transformed the electoral success of the Nazis. In the elections of 1932 anti-Semitism was not an important issue. Hitler recognised the apathy of Germans on the subject and hardly discussed it in his election campaign. Millions of Germans voted for Hitler, not to persecute Jews, but to get a job, save their farm, crush the communists or because of their exasperation with the ineffectiveness and corruption of other parties.

WAS ANTI-SEMITIC POLICY 1933–9 INTENDED AS A PREPARATION TO THE FINAL SOLUTION?

Ideological background. The nature of Nazi anti-Semitism after 1933 does not suggest any systematic or predetermined approach. This is not to underestimate the ideological drive against the Jews. For Nazis such as Julius Streicher and Alfred Rosenberg, anti-Semitism was the core of their political creed and the attack on the Jews was an ideological crusade to safeguard Aryan purity. Hitler was impressed by Rosenberg's 'scientifically-based doctrinaire' anti-Semitism and his apparent remoteness from policy during this period should not be interpreted as apathy. Hitler continued to foster a strongly anti-Semitic approach and encouraged subordinates to advocate solutions designed to marginalise Jews.

Early restraints to anti-Semitism. The Nazis deliberately concealed their real objectives in order to avoid offending the foreign press as well as moderate German public opinion. Clearly Hitler had good reason to adopt a moderate approach to the Jewish Question in the early years of his dictatorship. He was sensitive to popular apathy on the subject and feared that a repressive policy would threaten his fragile alliance with the conservatives and undermine the economic recovery. He was impressed by a report from Hjalmar Schacht in August 1935 that warned of 'serious damage to the German economy produced by the exaggeration and excesses of anti-Semitic propaganda' and argued that 'the drift into lawlessness among other things is putting the economic basis of rearmament at risk'. For Hitler and other leading Nazis, however, their approach was less dogmatic.

A similar deception was played after 1935 when the anti-Semitic campaign was relaxed so as not to offend foreign opinion during the 1936 Berlin Olympics. This convinced many Jews that the worst excesses were now over and even enticed some Jews back from exile. The Nazis also recognised that it was important to condition public opinion by a campaign to first marginalise, then dehumanise the Jews. There was a relentless propaganda war after 1933 conducted through posters, textbooks, radio and films that pilloried the Jew as alien, subversive and sub-human.

The nature of early anti-Semitic action. Nonetheless, despite the need for caution and indoctrination, it does appear that the regime had no clear long-term objective to deal with the Jews. It seems that policy evolved haphazardly. Although anti-Semitism was now official state policy, the momentum for attacks on Jews was much as it was before 1933 – short-term economic crisis and political opportunism. The boycott of Jewish shops in April 1933 and the dismissal of Jewish professionals were for the most part a response to the economic crisis after 1929. Middle-class Germans in particular were jealous of Jewish dominance in business and the professions and believed that the Jews had prospered during the 1920s and had survived the worst ravages of the depression. For the regime the boycott was a reward to their SA street gangsters and a useful means of perpetuating the climate of crisis and struggle in which the Nazi movement flourished. Similarly, the Nuremberg Laws were devised in 1935 to rally party morale and to please the SA which, even after their purge a year earlier, remained a large, restless and ruthless faction within the movement. Nazi radicals were disappointed by the moderation of the regime and were uneasy with the alliance with conservatives such as Schacht and Blomberg. Activists were already attacking neighbours who had been seen with Jews before Göbbels and Streicher demanded legislation.

The significance of 'Kristallnacht'. The first example of systematic violence against Jews came during the events of *Kristallnacht* (Crystal Night) in November 1938. Despite efforts to advertise the agitation as a 'spontaneous outburst of popular anti-Semitism', this was a carefully planned attack by the regime which led to the arrest and imprisonment in concentration camps of 20,000 Jews. Albert Speer certainly believed that an important point had been reached. It would, however, be simple to argue that this was another stage in the inevitable elimination of Jews. The agitation should be examined within the context of internal Nazi politics at the time. By 1938 there was growing pressure for a more radical campaign against the Jews. Excitement following the occupation of the Rhineland and the Olympics in 1936 had evaporated and party sources reported a sense of boredom and apathy among the German working class, who by now took employment for granted.

The move towards violence. Hitler's break with conservatives such as Schacht in 1937 and his purge of dissidents in the army such as Blomberg and Fritsch permitted a more radical approach to the Jews. More importantly, the cruel persecution of Jews in Austria after the *Anschluss* of March 1938 set a more violent tone of repression which some Nazis were keen to adopt. The catalyst for the violence was Göbbels who demanded that the SA have their final fling. This suited Göbbels' personal ambitions admirably: he was recognised to be the leader of the radical wing of the party and was keen to rehabilitate himself at this time when his relationship with Lida Baarova had caused a rift with Hitler.

The context of war. The outbreak of war in 1939 intensified the persecution of Jews. War destroyed any hope of an agreement with Britain that might have moderated Nazi anti-Semitism and might have allowed the plan to resettle Jews in Palestine. Moreover, the unassimilated Orthodox Jews of Poland more clearly reflected the racial stereotyping of Nazi propaganda. War corroded moral sensitivities and legitimised the dehumanisation and wholesale killing, including civilian deaths.

HOW SIGNIFICANT WAS THE ROLE OF LEADING NAZIS IN THE FINAL SOLUTION?

Hermann Göring. Göring was more of a pragmatist on the Jewish Question but could see the political advantage of participation in the formulation of policy. He accelerated the Aryanisation of the economy after 1937 and championed the emigration programme in 1940. More importantly, as his career declined it was Göring who commissioned **Reinhard Heydrich** on 31st July 1941 with the task of devising a Final Solution of the Jewish Question. Göring was, however, a rather marginal character by 1941. He did not have a central role in creating or implementing the extermination policy.

Joseph Göbbels. Göbbels' staunch anti-Semitism led to his having access to Hitler. His relentless Jew-baiting stemmed partly from his own deep-rooted sense of inferiority and from his aim of creating a common enemy to feed popular resentment and to mobilise the masses. He considered himself the champion of the radical wing of the party and as such took the initiative in organising the book burning in 1933. In November 1938, after losing favour following his affair with Lida Baarova, he sought to recover his position by directing the *Kristallnacht* programme. Göbbels became one of the chief architects of the Final Solution. He warned that war would lead to the extermination of the race and personally supervised the deportation of Jews from Berlin in 1942, proposing that they should be regarded as 'unconditionally exterminable'.

Heinrich Himmler. Himmler played a central role in the evolution of the Final Solution. He was from the outset obsessed by the dream of creating a master race of Aryans by the selection of the racially 'pure' and the elimination of the 'impure'. Since 1934 his SS had organised the concentration camps and he alone of all the Nazi leaders visited an extermination camp – Auschwitz – in July 1942. Himmler's SS *Einsatzgruppen* systematically murdered Jewish civilians in Russia from June 1941. He was given control of the policy to devise a Final Solution on 31 July 1941. Himmler came nearest in officially proclaiming the extermination policy in his speech in Poznan on 6 October 1943. Recognising that even some of the hardened SS were troubled by the killing of civilians, and fearing that every German had his own 'decent Jew', he urged his men to sacrifice themselves to achieve their 'Page of Glory'. Important though Himmler's role clearly was, it is unlikely that he could have devised the Final Solution. He was a functionary, a brilliant and ruthless functionary, but he was not a thinker or creator and lacked imagination and independence. His brother concluded 'Heini was such a worm. He'd never do anything as big as that all on his own'.

Reinhard Heydrich. If anyone, other than Hitler, could have devised the Final Solution then it would have been Heydrich. Certainly he had the knowledge, power, ambition, ruthlessness and fanatical racism to do it. He also had energy, independence and imagination. An extremist solution raised no moral scruples for Heydrich, but offered unlimited scope for ultimate power for a man who expected to succeed his Führer. His record as a killer had been established in Prague and it was natural that he, though subordinate to Himmler, should be given the commission on 31 July 1941 to devise a Final Solution. Referring to the commission, Heydrich conceded that the policy suggested would amount to total elimination, claiming that 'unfit' Jews would die 'through natural selection' whilst the rest would be 'dealt with accordingly'. Heydrich left no room for doubt in what he meant by this, adding that 'the lesson of history' demanded that nothing be left to resurrect the Jewish race. The policy having been determined, Heydrich organised and chaired a conference in Wannsee in January 1942 in order to implement the programme.

WHAT WAS HITLER'S ROLE IN THE FINAL SOLUTION?

In 1941 the Nazis implemented a programme to exterminate all European Jews by gassing in specially constructed extermination camps – the so-called 'Final Solution of the Jewish problem'. Disagreement among historians continues about the precise timing and nature of the decisions that led to this policy. There can be no doubt that Hitler was the author of the Final Solution. He fostered the climate of amorality and destructiveness in which policy was developed. He appointed subordinates such as Himmler and Heydrich who keenly championed a policy of extermination. Whatever the structural chaos of his regime by 1941, it is inconceivable that a decision to round up and exterminate all Jews could have been taken without his direct authorisation.

It is, however, difficult to accept that Hitler had always planned the Final Solution. There is no evidence to suggest any long-term commitment to such a solution, nor is it possible to time the decision to exterminate all Jews until the autumn of 1941 when existing policies were failing. It would certainly be a mistake to dismiss Hitler's earlier writings and speeches as the empty rhetoric of a crank. He did set out to achieve many of his dreams and the ambiguity and obscurity of some of his writings should not in themselves marginalise the significance of their content. Nevertheless, the evidence suggests that, however important his anti-Semitic prejudice, Hitler publicly announced upon taking power until the eve of war that his ultimate goal was not the annihilation but the forced emigration of the Jews.

Immediate evidence. This was not merely a further radical evolution of existing policy, but a decisive change of policy. The lack of any conclusive documentary evidence linking Hitler with the Final Solution is not surprising. Hitler never wrote orders, preferring instead verbal 'Führer Orders' or merely a nod of the head or a wave of the hand. Moreover, after the outcry about the euthanasia policy (when mentally and physically handicapped Germans were gassed) in 1940, Hitler insisted that the extermination programme should not be organised from the Chancellery. Recently discovered evidence from KGB archives nonetheless do document a secret meeting on 18 December 1941 with Himmler at which Hitler authorised the extermination of Jews as partisans. As Russian Jews were already being shot this could only mean the authorisation for the extermination of all European Jews.

Despite the secrecy that shrouded the policy, anecdotal evidence also suggests that Hitler did authorise the Final Solution. Transferred from the euthanasia programme, both Wirth and Victor Brack claimed that they were acting upon, respectively, a 'special commission for the Führer' and a 'Führer-order'. Moreover, Hitler authorised the SS *Einsatzgruppen* in June 1941 to eliminate Russian Jews. Himmler reassured a troubled commander that their orders 'came from Hitler as Supreme Führer of the German Government and that they had the force of law'.

Heydrich. Further evidence to back this up concerns Heydrich's commission. By the time of his commission in July, Heydrich could have been in little doubt what the 'Final Solution' was to be. Certainly the mechanics of extermination still had to be resolved and possibly, as has been suggested, the fate of women and children was not yet made clear, but the extermination of European male Jews was a foregone conclusion. Himmler told Hoess, the commandment of Auschwitz in July 1942, that the Führer 'had ordered the extermination during the war of all the Jews we can reach'. Likewise, Heydrich assured Admiral Canaris that the 'murders were due exclusively to the personal orders of the Führer Adolf Hitler'.

WHY DID HITLER AUTHORISE THE FINAL SOLUTION?

A product of his culture. 'Intentionalist' historians such as **Fleming** and **Goldhagen** argue that Hitler's authorisation of the Final Solution was the triumph of his long-term ideological obsession to destroy all Jews. Many other explanations have been offered for Hitler's passionate hatred of Jews: his isolation as a boy, his physical deformity, sexual impotence, the death of his mother whilst under the care of a Jewish doctor, his failure as an artist in Vienna or his education under Carl Lüger, the anti-Semitic Mayor of Vienna. However, a more straightforward reason is more likely. Hitler simply inherited the anti-Semitism of his generation and cultural background and allowed this to fester. His prejudice against the Jews became an obsession following Germany's defeat in 1918. He boasted that his anti-Semitism was part of his 'granite firm foundation' and as early as September 1919 argued that the Jewish problem should be resolved 'scientifically'. *Mein Kampf* clearly recorded his obsessions with race, Aryanism, and 'racial cleansing'. In one passage Hitler advocated the gassing of 12,000 or 15,000 Jews as a means of winning the First World War. In his infamous speech to the Reichstag on 30 January 1939 Hitler predicted that war would result in the 'annihilation of the Jewish race in Europe'. It is also argued that the consistent savageness of his language and the ruthlessness with which the extermination programme was conducted both suggest that it was part of his ideological obsession.

WHEN DID HITLER DECIDE TO ADOPT THE FINAL SOLUTION?

Historical interpretation. Whilst rejecting the unorthodox claim by **David Irving** in *Hitler's War* that Hitler was unaware of the Final Solution until 1943, both **Hans Mommsen** (1971) and **Martin Broszat** (1981) suggest that, given the evolution of uncontrolled killing by local authorities, no decision from Hitler was required. Most historians reject this though. The precise timing of the Final Solution continues to be a source of debate. This is more than an academic issue because to be able to discover when Hitler chose to order the extermination of the Jews will also help us understand why. A decision before autumn 1941 would suggest that the Final Solution had always been intended: a decision in autumn 1941 supports the interpretation that extermination was more likely an improvisation.

Eberhard Jäckel (1969) argues that Hitler made the key decisions as early as the summer of 1940. **Helmut Krausnick** (1968) believes March 1941, whilst **A. Hillgruber** (1977) argues that May 1941 is more convincing, claiming to have located a verbal order from Hitler to Himmler to prepare the Einsatzgruppen for extermination of Russian Jews. **Ian Kershaw** (1985) suggests that a decision in mid-September is more likely given that Nazi policy was not clear, whilst **Christopher Browning** (1985) and **Martin Broszat** claim that no policy had been clarified until October 1941.

WHY DID THE FINAL SOLUTION TAKE PLACE WHEN IT DID?

The decision to exterminate all Jews was not taken until the summer or early autumn of 1941. It is true that mass deportations and the exploitation of slave labour in 1940 resulted in a large number of deaths and certainly the use of *Einsatzgruppen* in Russia in June 1941 marked a new phase of killing, but as yet the fate of all European Jews remained unclear.

July to December 1941: the decision is made. Hermann Göring's commission to Heydrich on 31 July 1941 did not specify physical destruction or those Jews to be included. It is also unclear whether the SS *Einsatzgruppen* followed a single order: Group A rounded up and killed all Jewish men, women and children, whilst Groups B, C and D eliminated only Jewish men. Moreover, Hitler was still only considering deportation of Jews in Berlin and continued to discuss alternative solutions such as resettlement in Madagascar or Siberia. Further evidence of confusion comes from prolonged disputes between Himmler and the Governor of Litzmennstadt about the absorption in the latter's region of another 20,000 Jews. Given such confusion it seems that options were still being considered and that the decision to undertake a Final Solution was resolved as late as December. On 23 October the Gestapo chief, Müller, published Himmler's order that no Jew could now emigrate from the Reich.

By October Hitler had finally rejected the idea of a Jewish State and on 21 November demanded an 'aggressive policy' to rid Berlin of Jews. In late November invitations were issued for the Wannsee Conference, originally planned for December and work began on the conversion of Auschwitz. Lohse, the Commissioner for Ostland who had ordered the gassing of Jews in October, concluded that by November 'the Jewish Question has probably been clarified by verbal discussions'. However, confusion persisted into November, as 5,000 German Jews were shot in Lithuania, while in Lodz the Germans were worrying about the sanitary conditions in the ghetto. It is likely, therefore, that Hitler's meeting with Himmler in December was critical in resolving any further doubt. The ruthless enforcement of the Final Solution from January 1942, and the huge logistic effort required to sustain it as Germany began to lose the war, suggests that by then a decisive clarification of policy had been made.

The importance of the invasion of the Soviet Union. It was the invasion of the Soviet Union in June 1941 that determined the fate of all Jews. Far from being a stage on the route to the Holocaust, the invasion of Russia was an important reason for its implementation. Nazi propaganda relentlessly insisted that war with Russia was a 'racial war', but this focus was intended to convince an increasingly anxious public of the justification for the invasion. It should be remembered that Hitler's driving ambitions throughout his career were the destruction of communism and the conquest of *Lebensraum* (living space) in the East. The destruction of the Jews was a consequence of this policy. As in Poland two years before, the conquest of Russia brought contact with Orthodox Jews condemned as sub-human by racist extremists within the SS. It should also be remembered that the tradition of pogrom (a state organised attack on a group in society) was strong in German-occupied Russia and the wholesale killing of Jews was welcomed by a significant proportion of the Slav population.

Moreover, the land captured by German troops between June and November trapped about four million Jews, thereby rendering existing policies of transportation to ghettos impractical. Existing ghettos were already full and commandants were demanding alternative solutions from higher authorities. The failure to knock out Russia by blitzkrieg in the early autumn ruled out the most favoured solution of resettlement beyond the Urals. After two years of war there was such an established practice of arbitrary violence that the local commanders were already adopting their own solutions of mass shootings and even gassing by carbon monoxide vans.

WHAT ROLE DID ORDINARY GERMANS PLAY IN THE HOLOCAUST?

Historical interpretation. The traditional interpretation presented by historians such as **Hans Mommsen** (1971) is that most Germans were unaware of the Final Solution. This view has been challenged by **D. Bankier** in his 'German public awareness of the Final Solution', in Cesarini's *The Final Solution* and by **J. Hiden** in *Republican and Fascist Germany*. Most historians continue to reject the claims of **Daniel Goldhagen**, in *Hitler's Willing Executioners*, that Germans were willing participants in the mass killings.

How guilty were ordinary Germans? There is no evidence that most Germans supported the Final Solution. Certainly a small minority must have been directly involved in the extermination. Some claimed to have been brainwashed by Nazi propaganda, others were sadists or psychopaths, whilst some protested that they were just obeying orders. It is clear that many SS officers saw themselves as a privileged elite championing a noble mission on behalf of their race. Most were untroubled by their work in the extermination process.

The silence of the great majority of Germans does not suggest complicity. It is clear that public opinion during the 1930s remained hostile to radical and violent attacks on Jews. Most Germans tried to break even the one-day boycott of shops in April 1933 and most condemned the indiscriminate and arbitrary violence of Nazi extremists against individual Jews. The *Kristallnacht* onslaught was condemned by most Germans, even at the risk to their own liberty. Whilst opinion did support the Nuremberg Laws of 1935, it was because it was thought such official legislation would contain a more illegal persecution. Even in wartime there was hostility to the decree in September 1941 forcing Jews to wear the yellow Star of David, although few Germans bothered to concern themselves with the disappearance of their Jewish neighbours after 1940 and most chose to ignore rumours after 1942 that Jews were being exterminated.

No doubt some Germans had been impressed by Nazi propaganda against the Jews and as bombing increased and the prospect of defeat increased some may have welcomed the destruction of the Jews as another national enemy. It would be a mistake to attribute such inertia as silent approval. Ignorance was a popular excuse after 1945. The Holocaust was indeed 'Hitler's Terrible Secret'. Decisions were held in the strictest secrecy. The language of extermination was deliberately sanitised and extermination camps were constructed outside Germany and run mainly by non Germans. Moreover, war always fosters wild rumours and stories of extermination could easily be blamed on foreigners and communists. Films fooled the Red Cross that Jews were being happily resettled and it should be remembered that neither refugees from Germany nor BBC contacts in Central Europe made any accusations of genocide until 1944. Jews themselves were often deceived by Nazi propaganda, sometimes cooperating with state agencies in their transportation. It is therefore not surprising that the German people so wedded to the notions of legality and loyalty to their state should find the concept of extermination inconceivable. Nonetheless it cannot be maintained that an entire nation was ignorant.

It must be remembered that the Germans were a particularly inquisitive and politically conscious people. The scale of the extermination programme, involving thousands of police, clerks and train drivers could not easily be concealed. Moreover, soldiers from the Eastern Front reported atrocities to their families and friends and it is clear that some church leaders did voice concern about such crimes. Apathy and fear, however, ensured that Germans remained acquiescent. A survey of Nazi

Party members by Michael Müller Claudius undertaken after the war revealed that 5 per cent approved of the murder of the Jews, whilst 69 per cent were indifferent. By 1941, eight years of incessant propaganda, regimentation, spying and intimidation had bred a sense of helplessness among German people. Opposition in wartime was seen as unpatriotic or treasonable and contact with anyone outside the close circle was already difficult in such a cowed and atomised society. It wasn't so much that Germans did not hear stories about genocide, but that most chose not to believe them.

CONCLUSION

- Despite the continuing debate on the origins of the Holocaust, it can be concluded that Hitler's role in the extermination of the Jews was decisive. He encouraged their persecution and the extremists in the Nazi movement. This is not to say, however, that he had always envisaged the elimination of the Jews. The evidence suggests that Hitler had no clear programme to deal with the 'Jewish problem' until late 1941.
- Hitler's authorisation of the Holocaust was determined by the pressure of other leading Nazis, party officials and SS officers. Certainly he was aware of the policy of extermination and only he had the authority to reverse it. Rather he accepted it as his mission and offered it in 1945 as a grotesque monument to his personal dictatorship.

SECTION 6

Opposition to the Nazis

KEY POINTS

- Hitler's opponents were drawn from a wide range of social, religious and political groups. They were motivated by a combination of personal, religious and ethical principles.
- Only the army had the means to seriously oppose Hitler and confront the SS.
- There were serious weaknesses in the opposition to Nazism. It was weakened by the speed and ruthless nature of Hitler's consolidation of power. It failed to realise the real nature of the dictatorship and that it could only be destroyed by Hitler's removal. The opposition groups could only operate underground. Hitler's opponents lacked unity of purpose, leadership and organisation. Most critically, they lacked the support of the majority of Germans.

HISTORICAL INTERPRETATION

Historians are divided about three aspects of opposition: the scale of active opposition, the credit for the resistance to the Nazis, and the motivation for opposition.

What was the scale of opposition? **John Wheeler-Bennett** and **Lewis Namier** writing in **Geoffrey Plum**'s *Sowjetsystem und Demokratischen Gesellschaft* (1992) argue that only a small number of Germans actively sought to resist Hitler. The opposite view is offered in its most extreme form by **A. Hillgruber** in *Auswartiges Amt-Informationsdienst für die Auslandersvertretungen* (1973). He claimed that Germany was in effect an occupied country in which all Germans more or less actively resisted the Nazis. The most recent study of this question by **Joachim Fest**, *Plotting Hitler's Death* (1996), takes a more balanced view. Fest suggests that whilst the resistance was socially broadly based and persistent, the rebels found little support from the German people.

Who resisted the Nazis? Earlier works such as *The German Opposition to Hitler* (1948) by **Hans Rothfels** and *The German Resistance* (1958) by **Gerhard Ritter** exaggerated the role of conservative groups whilst neglecting the importance of communist and socialist opponents. That neglect was rectified by **Hans Mommsen** in the essay 'Social views and constitutional plans of the resistance' in **W. Schmitthener** and **H. Bucheim**'s *The German Resistance to Hitler* (1970). Mommsen's concentration on the opposition from the left has been backed up by the work of **J.A. Hillgruber** who claims that only the communist resistance consistently fought the Nazis. A compromise interpretation is presented by **Fest** and by **Martyn Housden** in his *Resistance and Conformity in the Third Reich* (1997). Housden stresses the importance of both sections.

What was the motivation for opposition to the Nazis? **J. Wheeler-Bennett** and **L. Namier** argue that the Bomb Plot of July 1944 was an attempt by militarists to save the army and by the old elites to preserve their social status. This view is supported by **Hans Mommsen** (in Schmitthener and Bucheim) who claims that the conspirators had little interest in parliamentary democracies. Instead they looked back to the authoritarian Germany of pre-1914 rather than the pluralist, democratic Federal Republic of Germany which was to be created in the Western Sector after 1945. Therefore opposition to the Nazis developed from the desire to maintain authoritarian government. For many in the army, German domination of Europe could only be assured with the removal of Hitler and the creation of an anti-Bolshevik alliance. This view was proposed by **W. Schmitthener** and **H. Bucheim** in *The German Resistance to Hitler* (1970).

This interpretation is rejected by **G. Ritter** who claims that the rebels embraced the ideas of liberal democracy and envisaged the concept of a united states of Europe. **J. Fest** and **M. Housden** adopt a similar approach, claiming that resistance was motivated not by short-term political reasons but by a principled moral and ethical opposition to the dictatorship.

HOW SIGNIFICANT WAS THE COMMUNIST OPPOSITION?

Communist strength. In theory the communists should have been Hitler's fiercest opponents. He had promised to destroy Bolshevism and there was little doubt as to the seriousness of his threats. In 1933 the KPD (the German Communist Party) was well-organised and popular with a membership of 30,000. It had consistently won a large share of the popular vote in elections up to 1933. In the presidential election of 1932, the KPD leader Ernst Thälmann won 5 million votes and in the Reichstag elections of November 1932 they won 100 seats and 17 per cent of the vote. Important urban areas including Berlin, Halle, Frankfurt an Main, Stuttgart and Dusseldorf were captured by the KPD in these elections. Unlike the Social Democrats, who were constrained by their commitment to legality, the KPD had been founded in 1919 with a revolutionary ideology. Therefore it had no problems about using subversion and violence to achieve its objectives.

Ineffective opposition – Nazi ruthlessness. Despite this, communist resistance to the Nazi regime was ineffective. This was in part due to the speed and ruthless nature of the Nazi takeover. Communists were the first and most persecuted victims of the Nazi regime. Communist leaders and activists were beaten and about 100,000 arrested following the Emergency Decree of 28 February. Against the might of the Gestapo and its network of informers, communist resistance was easily broken. There are numerous examples of small revolutionary groups who were crushed, especially after the invasion of the Soviet Union in 1941. In February 1942, the group led by Bappo Römer and Robert Uhrig in Berlin was destroyed, in March revolutionary socialists in Bavaria were arrested and the 'Red Orchestra' was broken up in August. The level of persecution of the communists helps explain why the extent of opposition was limited. By 1945, over half of German communists had been imprisoned or arrested and around 25,000 had been executed. These figures include most of the pre-war leadership, including Thälmann who was shot in Buchenwald concentration camp in August 1944.

Communist weakness. It should also be remembered that although the German communists enjoyed significant popular support before 1933, they did not have the important advantages held by the Russian communists in 1917. They had no leader of the status of Lenin or Trotsky, they did not have control of a network of organisations such as the soviets and, most importantly, there was no Red Guard. Moreover, their popularity generated a powerful coalition against them. Most Germans were terrified by the prospect of a communist revolution and welcomed the Nazi repression of the KPD.

Communist miscalculation. The ineffectiveness of communist resistance was due also to their own miscalculation. Both before and after the Nazi takeover of power in 1933, they fought a bitter ideological battle against the socialist SPD. In 1928, the Soviet communist leader Stalin had called on all communists to concentrate their anger against socialists. In 1932, the KPD went as far as allying with the Nazis to defeat a socialist inspired strike in Berlin. All of this robbed Germany of any mass broad-left coalition capable of mobilising working class and trade union support against the Nazi regime.

Soviet intervention. What weakened the communist opposition so significantly was the fact that the KPD took its orders from communist Moscow that insisted on a passive policy towards the Nazi regime. In the 1930s, Germany became the Soviet Union's most important trading partner and Stalin wished to see this continue. He strongly believed that

Nazism would inevitably collapse leading to the triumph of communism in Germany. In the meantime he suggested that any communists adopt a wait-and-see attitude towards the Nazi regime. The communist opposition was further undermined by the waves of purges of Communist Party members inspired by Stalin's purges in the Soviet Union. The improvement in Germany's economic situation in the 1930s, and the fall in unemployment in particular, left the communists isolated and with a dwindling support. Perhaps the most crushing blow to communist opposition was the signing of the Nazi–Soviet Pact in 1939. This further confused and deflated communist opponents of the regime. By the time the Germans invaded the Soviet Union in June 1941, communist opposition had been isolated and crushed by the effective Nazi terror machine.

HOW EFFECTIVE WAS SOCIALIST OPPOSITION?

Introduction. The collapse of socialist opposition to the Nazi regime is, in some ways, surprising. Following the introduction of the universal franchise in 1871 and rapid industrialisation, the socialist SPD won mass support. In 1912 it became the largest party in the Reichstag. This level of popularity remained throughout the years of the Weimar Republic. Therefore, the political party best placed to oppose the Nazis was the SPD. Allied to their political strength, the Social Democrats could rely on the support of most of Germany's large and well-organised trade unions.

Socialist weaknesses. However, socialist resistance and opposition to Hitler was as ineffective as that of the communists. This was in part due to their fall in support *before* 1933. The depression in Germany had tempted many skilled workers into the Nazi movement whilst unemployment crippled the trade unions and robbed them of their traditional weapon, the effective general strike. This was important because mass action to prevent the Nazis coming to power was not a realistic course of action. Unlike members of the conservative opposition, the Social Democrats had few contacts with the establishment and so they were more easily marginalised. Within weeks of Hitler's appointment, the leaders of the socialist movement, including Otto Wels, went into exile or were sent to concentration camps. The move against leading socialist politicians was triggered by their opposition to the Enabling Act in March 1933. The main institutions of the socialist movement were banned in 1933, trade unions in May and the SPD in June. Illegal, leaderless and still constrained by their commitment to the rule of law (they would not act to break the law), the Social Democrats were poorly equipped to resist the Nazi regime. The lack of unity with the communists similarly weakened the communist opposition. Some socialist groups such as 'Red Faction', 'Socialist Front' and 'New

Beginning' did begin to forge some links with communist groups. However, despite the desperate state of the opposition to the regime, such links were frowned upon by the SPD leadership in exile.

The SPD leadership in exile wrote reports on the state of German society based on evidence sent from inside Germany. For the socialist leadership such evidence often made demoralising reading. Many workers accepted and even embraced the new regime that brought work, a growing sense of national pride and some social benefits. By 1938, a growing cynicism about the regime emerges from such reports but by then resistance to the regime inside Germany had become futile and dangerous. Socialist leaders inside and outside Germany recognised that open defiance of the regime was hopeless and they confined themselves to publishing reports, keeping their membership intact and preparing for post-war politics.

WHY DID CONSERVATIVE OPPOSITION FAIL?

Conservatives compromised. The conservatives were in a stronger position to resist Hitler, at least in the early years of the Nazi regime. Their strength came through their contacts in the army, bureaucracy and with President Hindenburg until his death in 1934. Despite such potential strength and a greater knowledge of the regime's excesses, conservative opposition was minimal. Hitler moved quickly to wipe out dissident conservatives such as ex-Chancellor von Schleicher during his purge of June 1934. As with the socialists, conservative opposition was weakened by its commitment to legal methods. Conservatives were also very much compromised by their collaboration with Hitler. The electoral pact of 1930 between Hitler and the nationalist leader Alfred Hugenberg had given the Nazis respectability. It was conservatives such as Papen and Werner von Blomberg who had lobbied for the Nazis to be included in the government in 1933 and who had served in Hitler's first cabinet. Locked into a coalition government with the Nazis, the conservatives were too blinded and compromised to mount an effective political challenge.

Conservative sympathy for the regime. It is also clear that many conservatives were sympathetic to Hitler or were converted to his cause after 1933. Many doubts were removed by Hitler's glorification of the old social and political order at the Commemoration Day at Potsdam in March 1933 and by his elimination of the radical factions of the SA in June 1934. Conservatives welcomed the suppression of the communists and the return of a more authoritarian form of government. As with all potential internal opposition, they were contented with the restoration of business confidence and the improvement in economic outlook. Although some conservatives questioned the boldness of Hitler's foreign policy, few questioned his policies of rearmament, conscription and the restoration of German domination in Central Europe. Although Papen questioned the nature of the regime in his Marberg speech in 1934, this was an isolated incident. There was no organised conservative opposition.

Isolated resistance. Those conservatives who did resist after 1934, did so in isolation or in small groups such as the 'Wednesday Club' or the 'Golf Circle'. Both were discussion groups of like-minded conservatives who met to maintain their own morale. They were hardly a threat to the totalitarian regime. The most important group, the Kreisau Circle, was joined by influential conservatives including the Prussian Minister of Finance, Johannes Popitz. Led by Peter Yorck von Wartenberg and Helmuth von Moltke, it posed a far more significant threat to the regime as it included in its membership disillusioned generals. However, the Kreisau Circle suffered from the same problems that made all opposition groups ineffective. It was weakened by uncertainty, internal divisions about the nature of a post-Nazi Germany (should it be authoritarian or democratic?), the reluctance to use force against Hitler and mistrust of the Allies. They feared that despite the good intentions of some, too many of the conservative opposition shared the Nazi aim of a German-dominated Europe.

WHAT WAS THE SIGNIFICANCE OF THE CHRISTIAN CHURCHES?

Inadequate opposition. Both Protestant and Catholic churches succumbed easily to the Nazi dictatorship. This was surprising given the apparent strength of both churches. In a survey in 1932, some 90 per cent of Germans professed themselves to be Christian. Both churches were very well established and organised. The Catholic Church in particular had the potential to stand independent of the regime. It was internationally based and ran a flourishing network of schools, clubs and youth groups. Unlike political groups, the churches could not be abolished or incorporated into the regime. Despite this, the churches as institutions failed to offer serious opposition to Hitler. The main reason for the relative insignificance of church opposition was that it was an uneven battle. The churches used the weapons of pamphlets, sermons and papal encyclicals (letters) to occasionally criticise the regime. These were not enough against an officially atheist and dictatorial regime. The regime dealt brutally with its opponents in the churches. The Catholic minister Erich Klausener was murdered in August 1934.

Pastor Niemöller and the German Confessional Church. Pastor Niemöller and many fellow pastors were sent to concentration camps as hundreds of priests were intimidated, arrested and executed. Niemöller created the

Pastors' Emergency League in 1934 to defend the Lutheran Church against the anti-Christian attitude of the new Nazi regime. The same year he drew up the Six Principles at the Bremen Synod that affirmed the determination to resist the advance of any Nazi-tainted Christianity. Initially Niemöller won the support of some 7,000 pastors in a new German Confessional Church. However, the nature of this movement and its subsequent difficulties are an excellent example of the nature and problems of the opposition to the Nazis as a whole. Much opposition was based on a single issue, in this case a defence of Lutheran principles. It was also quickly crushed as individuals were identified and then persecuted by the Gestapo. Niemöller spent the war in various concentration camps, but survived the regime. Others, such as Dietrich Bonhöffer and Alfred Delp, were executed for their part in the Bomb Plot of June 1944.

Naive leadership. Religious opposition also failed because the leadership of the churches was naive in believing that it could reach an understanding with the Nazi regime. The Protestant churches had always closely identified with the state since its creation in 1871. Many Protestants welcomed the downfall of the Weimar Republic which they saw as a 'Catholic Republic' because of the influence of the Centre Party in many coalition governments. The Commemoration Ceremony at Potsdam in 1933, which calmed the conservative elite, also acted to appease the churches by presenting the new regime as Christian in outlook. The Catholic leadership were easily fooled. They were impressed by the Lateran treaties signed between the Vatican and Mussolini in Italy in 1929.

The dispute over education. With the Catholic Papen as Vice-Chancellor, the Catholic church believed that it could retain control of its schools and youth groups. In July 1933 the Church signed a Concordat (an agreement) with the Nazi state. By the agreement, priests were not allowed to involve themselves with politics whilst all new bishops had to be agreed by the state. In return, Catholic schools and societies were permitted to exist. However, the Church was naive to believe that the Nazis would permit it to educate Germany's children. In the coming years, the government did much to discredit the Church and undermine its education system. Leading churchmen, such as Cardinal von Faulhaber, protested against such policies. In 1937, Pope Pius XI issued an encyclical *Mit Brenneder Sorge* (*With Deep Anxiety*). In it he attacked the persecution of Catholics and the inhumanity of Nazism. Neither protest had any effect.

Church sympathy and collaboration. However, one must not blame the naivety of the Church or the repression of the state for being the only reasons why church opposition to the Nazis was generally ineffective.

There were significant sections of all churches that found themselves sympathetic to many aspects of Nazi ideology. To many churchmen, the Weimar Republic had been morally corrupt. Others shared the anti-Semitism of the Nazi regime and, in particular, its anti-communism. There were churchmen such a Cardinal von Faulhaber who collaborated with the regime to the end despite some reservations about its excesses.

WHY DID OPPOSITION TO THE NAZIS IN THE ARMY FAIL?

Only the army possessed the means to overthrow Hitler. Its failure to do so was because Hitler enjoyed the confidence of the great majority of its officers and generals for much of his dictatorship. When some generals did lose confidence after 1942, Hitler's position was almost unassailable.

The disappearance of early tensions between army and regime. The army dissidents were in small and isolated groups. From the beginning of the regime there were some tensions between the army and the Nazi regime. Some aristocratic generals despised Hitler as a dangerous and uncouth upstart (remember Hitler had served in the First World War as a corporal). Many generals feared the revolutionary and violent storm troopers of the SA. Later army leaders felt threatened by the SS and some generals believed that Hitler's recklessness would ignite a war before Germany was fully prepared. On the whole, however, the army remained loyal. With the apparent patronage of President Hindenburg and the appointment of General Blomberg as Minister of War, most generals believed that they could safely restrain Hitler.

Military success and support for the regime. Most of the generals supported Hitler's programme of rearmament from the early 1930s and the reintroduction of conscription in March 1935. Even more important to many within the army was the restoration of German borders after the humiliation of Versailles. The success of operations in the Rhineland in 1936 and Austria in 1938 convinced all but the most sceptical of generals of the value of the Nazi regime. Whilst Germany was militarily successful, opposition from the army was minimal. In 1938 a plot by General Ludwig Beck to overthrow Hitler in opposition to the plans to invade Czechoslovakia came to nothing. It collapsed partly as a result of Chamberlain's appeasement at Munich, but also because of the lack of support from other generals. The army as a whole was dazzled by the military successes of the period 1939–41. Germany's supremacy in Europe ended any meaningful talk of overthrowing the regime amongst the upper echelons of the army. It is this fact more than any other that reveals the nature of much of the army's opposition to Hitler. Whilst many leading generals found Hitler and the Nazis distasteful, they only plotted seriously when the war began to go against Germany. Critical to growing opposition was the defeat at Stalingrad in January 1943. What unnerved many generals was Hitler's increasing isolation and unwillingness to take advice. Another factor that boosted opposition amongst some army officers to the regime was first-hand experience of the atrocities committed in the name of the regime against Slavs and Jews on the Eastern and other fronts.

Failure of plots, 1942–4. A series of plots to overthrow Hitler hatched between 1942 and 1944 ended in failure. This was due to the strength of Hitler's security and bad luck. An example of the latter was the failure of Operation Flash in March 1943. The attempt to kill Hitler failed because the bomb placed on the Führer's plane by Major General Henning von Tresckow failed to explode. The most famous plot, that of July 1944, failed because of a catalogue of bad luck. The wooden building in which the bomb exploded diffused the impact of the explosion. During the briefing the bomb was moved away from Hitler and he was partly shielded from the impact of the bomb by the leg of an oak table. Human error also played a part in the failure of the plot. Conspirators in Berlin fatally delayed action and communications between Rastenburg and Berlin were not cut. The failure of the bomb plot showed the logistical difficulties of overthrowing the regime. This could only be done by assassinating Hitler. The problem, however, was that after 1941, Hitler was either in his bunker in Berlin or his headquarters in Rastenburg and therefore inaccessible to all but his most trusted followers and protected by SS guards, the Gestapo and an army of anonymous informers.

Support for the regime amongst the generals. An even more fundamental reason for the failure of military opposition was that so few generals were prepared to actively resist the regime. Despite growing knowledge of atrocities, including the elimination of the Jews from 1942, and despite the defeat at Stalingrad in early 1943, the overwhelming majority of generals and officers remained either passive or enthusiastic supporters of Hitler. Those who became critical often failed to resist. From August 1934, every officer had to take an oath of allegiance to the Führer, a fact that should not be dismissed in explaining the lack of opposition. The 'stab in the back' theory of supposed disloyalty by politicians at the end of the First World War was a powerful myth which haunted all ranks of the army.

Ideological support for the regime. The point remains that the leading members of the army were as loyal to the regime as they were ideologically committed to it. It is not convincing to suggest that the army was a professional non-ideological body. It had been politically active in Germany before 1914. Its leaders plotted against Weimar governments, it had enthusiastically helped purge the SA and accepted the murders of Generals Schleicher and Bredow, and the army leaders had volunteered to swear the oath of allegiance to the Führer in 1934. In 1938, dissident Generals Blomberg and Fritsch were purged and younger, more politically 'pure' officers were promoted. The army as an institution was compromised by its association with the Nazis. Numerous letters from soldiers on the Eastern Front reveal the extent to which the army willingly played an active part in the ideological war against Slavs and Jews. Indeed, it was with some justification that Hitler was able to present the Bomb Plot of 1944 as the work of a clique of aristocratic officers. In all only 22 out of 2,000 generals were executed for their part in the conspiracy. Army resistance was therefore heroic, but belated. It was confined to a few individuals. Its leadership was too naive and isolated to pose a sustained threat to the regime.

CONCLUSION

- Opposition to the Nazis existed but it was generally ineffective. The opposition was divided, lacked leadership and was ruthlessly suppressed.
- Those who were in a position to form effective opposition to the Nazis failed to act decisively until late in the war.

SECTION 7

Expansion and aggression: German foreign policy, 1933–45

KEY POINTS

- Hitler had definite foreign policy objectives. These were the destruction of communism and the Versailles settlement, the establishment of *Lebensraum* in the East and Aryan racial domination. These objectives were to be achieved through diplomacy and aggression.
- The precise timing of the programme was not defined.
- Hitler was able to achieve many of his objectives by 1941 by the skilful exploitation of events.

HISTORICAL INTERPRETATION

A.J.P. Taylor's *The Origins of the Second World War* (1961) controversially challenged the existing consensus that Hitler followed a clearly devised programme of foreign policy. Taylor argued that Hitler had no specific objectives but instead had vague ideas and grand daydreams. According to Taylor, Hitler's spectacular success in foreign policy up to 1941 was not the result of careful planning but of skilful improvisation. His particular skill was to exploit unforeseen events and to take advantage of the mistakes of his opponents, factors that clearly apply to the events of 1936–8. Therefore, the implication of this argument is that by appeasing Hitler, Britain and France were responsible for causing the outbreak of war in 1939.

Whilst no other historian accepts this argument in full, many agree that Hitler's foreign policy was pragmatic, i.e., he responded to events. **Alan Bullock**, in *Hitler: A Study in Tyranny* (1952), argued that Hitler skilfully took advantage of the opportunities he had. He repeats this argument in *Hitler and Stalin, Parallel Lives* (1991). Bullock argues that Hitler had limited scope for manoeuvre in the early part of his dictatorship in particular. His long-term aims, such as *Lebensraum* (living space), should not be seen as the main driving force of foreign policy decision-making, but rather general themes that guided policy in a looser sense. To Bullock they were a 'magnetic pole' to which Hitler would return throughout his career. An example Bullock gives is the signing of the Non-Aggression Treaty with Poland in 1934. It gave the regime flexibility in relations with Poland for the future; it could either be used as an ally against the Soviet Union or destroyed as part of the process of the conquest of the East.

To most historians, Hitler's foreign policy should be seen much more in terms of the following of clearly defined objectives, e.g., *Lebensraum*, global domination, the reversal of Versailles, the destruction of communism and a racial war. **Norman Rich** in *Hitler's War Aims* (1973–4), **Eberhard Jäckel** in *Hitler in History* (1984) and **A. Hillgruber** (1973) argue that Hitler methodically set out to achieve his defined objectives. There has been disagreement about the extent of Hitler's ambitions. According to **Fritz Fischer**, *Germany's Aims in the First World War* (1967), Hitler was simply maintaining the traditional strategy of *Weltpolitik*, the establishment of continental supremacy. **Hugh Trevor-Roper** in *Hitler's War Aims* (1960) argues that Hitler's main objective was the conquest of living space, *Lebensraum*, in European Russia. **Norman Rich** has argued that Hitler's main aim was the establishment of Aryan racial supremacy. **Hillgruber** has gone further by claiming that Hitler followed a set plan. This plan aimed first to establish domination of Europe, then *Lebensraum*, to be followed by the conquest of an African Empire and finally global domination.

To other historians, Hitler's foreign policy can be seen as an attempt to solve economic problems and distract from social tensions. **Martin Broszat** in *Social Motivation and Führer – Bindung des Nationalsocialismus* (1970) argues that foreign policy was essentially a response to political pressures. He believes that it was used and exploited in the 1930s to bolster popularity for the regime. Resentment of the humiliation at Versailles and the loss of traditional German lands ran deep. Therefore actions taken to reverse this humiliation, e.g., the reintroduction of conscription in 1935 or entry into the Rhineland in 1936, were almost universally popular. Broszat has argued that Hitler did not have any blueprint for war. He is supported by historicians such as **Richard Overy** (1982) who has argued that much foreign policy was undertaken with the aim of providing Germany with the raw materials it so desperately lacked but needed to win any future war. Therefore *Anschluss*, the invasion of the Sudetenland (brown coal, synthetic fuel) or Poland (agricultural resources, labour, coal) should be seen as an attempt to mobilise resources in Eastern Europe.

Much of the historical debate has been over the extent to which there was a blueprint, a concrete plan for Nazi foreign policy. For many historians such as **Ian Kershaw**, *The Nazi Dictatorship* (1982), or **Richard Overy**, *Why the Allies Won* (1995), the idea of a foreign policy based on a blueprint is far too simplistic. Kershaw argues that Nazi foreign policy was the result of numerous differing factors including strategic, diplomatic, political and economic considerations. However, both historians stress that despite the lack of a plan, the nature of German foreign policy cannot be divorced from the personality and ambitions of Hitler.

THE CHALLENGE TO VERSAILLES, 1933–7: A REACTION TO EVENTS OR THE RESULT OF IDEOLOGY?

Background. The destruction of the Treaty of Versailles was Hitler's first objective. The treaty was already being undermined at the time of Hitler's coming to power. The reduction of reparations in 1924 and 1929 and their cancellation in 1932 showed the growing realisation amongst the Allies that this part of the settlement was unacceptable. The Great Depression of the 1930s and growing unemployment weakened the determination of Britain and France to uphold the Treaty of Versailles. The Japanese invasion of Manchuria in 1931 focused world attention away from Germany and raised serious fears as to the security of its empire in the Far East. The United States was committed to isolation and was deeply hostile to the Soviet Union. This was the context to German foreign policy in the early and mid 1930s. To the Allies, a more positive attitude towards Germany seemed not only sensible but the only possible strategy. This played very much into Hitler's hands. It made possible his gradual destruction of the Versailles settlement.

The opportunity to destroy Versailles. By introducing rearmament and conscription in 1935, Hitler was exploiting a favourable diplomatic climate. Essentially the Allies turned a blind eye, despite both policies breaking the terms of Versailles. Similarly, the reoccupation of the Rhineland in 1936 was undertaken at a time of greatest advantage to Hitler. The German army was still weak and under-armed. It could not have resisted any military action from the French in particular. However, the Saar plebiscite and Anglo-German Naval Agreement of 1935 had appeared to demonstrate Germany's commitment to peaceful diplomacy. There was also a sense in both Britain and France that Germany was seizing what was rightfully its own. More importantly, Italy's invasion of Abyssinia diverted attention away from Germany. It also showed how weak the League of Nations was and it destroyed the anti-German alliance of Britain, France and Italy represented by the Stresa Front. The opportunity to destroy the Versailles settlement was presented to Hitler. A politician as ruthless as he did not let such an opportunity pass.

The ideological importance of the destruction of Versailles. Hitler's destruction of the Versailles settlement was, however, much more than a response to events. It was at the root of his ideology. It also was of primary importance politically. Hitler had come to power vowing to destroy Versailles. It was the trauma of 1918 and the humiliation of the post-war settlement that had propelled Hitler into politics. It also provided him with the drive to continue until his goals had been achieved. Point 2 of the first Nazi Party programme in 1920 demanded the tearing up of the Versailles treaties. Hitler was obsessed with Versailles. In *Mein Kampf* and in many of his speeches in the 1920s its destruction is a key theme. However, this obsession should be placed into a context. It was one Hitler shared with the great majority of Germans, including moderates and respectable politicians, such as Gustav Stresemann, who was Foreign Minister between 1924 and 1929. It was Hitler's opposition to Versailles that gave him political respectability as a member of the alliance of right-wing parties against the Young Plan in 1929 and as a member of the Harzberg Front in 1931. Such opposition to Versailles also brought Hitler support from conservatives and the army at crucial moments in the 1930s. The destruction of Versailles was therefore the fulfilment of a dream. Hitler was given the opportunity to undermine the settlement, but also had the personal drive and ability to translate the hopes of many Germans into reality.

WHAT WAS THE SIGNIFICANCE OF THE 'ANSCHLUSS' WITH AUSTRIA?

Failure in 1934. Hitler's absorption of Austria was also predetermined. Austria was the country of Hitler's birth and upbringing. To him it was an integral part of a Greater Germany. But, it is unlikely that Hitler ever planned the precise timing of a union between Germany and the country of his birth. In 1934, the Austrian Chancellor Dollfuss was murdered by Austrian Nazis. However, the whole affair had been badly planned and undertaken without direction from Berlin. Any chance Hitler might have had to take advantage of the situation and invade Austria was made impossible by the actions of Italy. Fearing a German presence close to the Austro-Hungarian border, Mussolini moved troops to the Brenner Pass. Hitler recognised that Germany was too weak militarily and isolated politically to exploit the crisis in Austria in 1934.

1938, the opportunity presents itself. The crisis of 1938 arose from the intense pressure placed on the Austrian Chancellor Dr Kurt Schuschnigg by Nazis from inside and outside Austria. His position was not helped by the forming of the Rome–Berlin Axis in 1936. Schuschnigg was determined to protect Austrian independence to the extent that in 1938 he ordered a plebiscite (vote) to be held on this issue. Such a move threw Austria into chaos and offered an infuriated Hitler the opportunity to intervene. In March 1938, the German government gave Austria an ultimatum. Either it postpone the plebiscite and Schuschnigg resign or it faced invasion. However, it was external circumstances that made such a move possible. The successful Japanese invasion of China in 1937 showed how boldness and aggression could be rewarded. France was paralysed by bitter political divisions and Britain under Neville Chamberlain was committed to a policy of appeasement to Germany. Union with Austria was forbidden by the Treaty of Versailles, but that was ignored. Most importantly for Hitler, he was able to invade Austria because Austria could no longer rely on Italian support. On 12 March 1938, German troops crossed the border into Austria.

The importance to Hitler of 'Anschluss'. The timing of *Anschluss* with Austria was dictated by events. The determination to achieve this was central to Hitler's desire to see German domination of Central Europe. As already shown, *Anschluss* was also part of the determined attempt to destroy the hated Treaty of Versailles. Such an action was at the very heart of Nazi Party policy. Point 1 of the party's 25 Points demanded 'the union of all Germans in a Greater Germany on the basis of the right of national self-determination'. Hitler had always regarded the German state of 1871 (which excluded Austria) as incomplete. On a personal level it made Hitler a foreigner in Germany. It also identified Germany too narrowly as dominated by Prussia and as essentially Protestant. In *Mein Kampf* Hitler condemned the border policy of the 'bourgeois world'. For Hitler, the Germany of 1871 was only half-born as *Volk* or blood was the sole means of determining the German nation. Therefore, a united Germany and Austria was high up on his political agenda.

THE CONQUEST OF CZECHOSLOVAKIA: OPPORTUNISM OR PLANNED?

The situation in 1938. As with Austria, the crisis in Czechoslovakia in 1938 which Hitler was able to exploit so successfully was not of his own making. Encouraged by the *Anschluss*, Nazis in the Sudetenland led by Conrad Henlein agitated for a similar union with the German Reich. Despite the strength of the Czech frontier defences and the Czech army, and its alliances with France and Russia, Hitler was able to exploit the vulnerability of the Czech state. His principal enemies, Britain, France and the Soviet Union, were bitterly divided. Britain and France both feared the spread of communism and the Soviet leader Stalin was convinced that Britain and France had some kind of agreement with Nazi Germany. The Soviet Union had been seriously weakened by the purges of the 1930s. It was also in a difficult geographical position to help the Czechs given the hostility of Poland to the Soviets. To both British and French governments, the Czech question seemed a remote one. On top of that, German claims to the Sudetenland could be justified on the grounds of national self-determination. Both governments has resisted intervention on behalf of a legitimate government in the Spanish Civil War in 1936 and were still committed to appeasement.

Hitler's determination to destroy Versailles. Despite such circumstances, it is wrong to assume that Hitler's role in the Czech crisis was limited. Even if the immediate crisis, the agitation of the Sudeten Germans, was not of his making it is clear that his policy of expansion was the key to Czechoslovakia's fate. Hitler had always been committed to destroying the Czech state. It was a product of Versailles and, to Hitler, an unnatural state that placed Germans in a disadvantaged minority. To Hitler these 3.5 million Germans rightfully belonged in part of a Greater German state. The political and economic domination of Central Europe had been a key feature of German foreign policy since before 1914. The importance of Czechoslovakia to the German economy should not be overlooked. In 1938, the twin policy of autarky and rearmament was firmly in place. Czechoslovakia was a rich source of essential raw materials including coal and home to engineering companies, in particular the important Skoda.

The importance of 'Lebensraum'. The most important reason for the destruction of the Czechoslovak state in 1938 was that it was part of Hitler's planned eastward expansion. As *Lebensraum* to the East was a mainstay of Hitler's ideology, so the conquest of Czechoslovakia was important strategically to this plan. Czechoslovakia was not destroyed because of the opportunism of Henlein, the weakness of its Prime Minister Beneš, the naivety of the French or British, but because of the ruthless and calculated expansionism of Hitler.

WHAT IS THE SIGNIFICANCE OF THE CONQUEST OF POLAND, 1939–41?

Hitler's determination to destroy Poland. Hitler had always intended to destroy the Polish state. The reasons for this are clear. To Hitler, the Slav peoples were sub-humans whose only fit purpose was to serve the interests of the Germanic Aryan race. At the Hossbach Conference in 1937 Hitler stated his aim of eastward expansion with *Lebensraum* for Germans. The domination of Eastern Europe had been traditional German policy before 1914. It was the objective of most Germans to recover West Prussia and Posen that had been taken from Germany at Versailles. The loss of these lands and the formation of the Polish Corridor isolated East Prussia. It is clear that this was one of the most despised terms of the Versailles settlement. Hitler made clear throughout the 1920s and 1930s that recovery of these lands was a national priority.

Tension arises. In 1934, however, Hitler signed a Non-Aggression Pact with Poland. This action seems to contradict all which has been stated above. However, this pact should be seen as an attempt by Hitler to deceive his opponents and buy time. In the early years of the Nazi regime it was important for Hitler to secure Germany diplomatically. As the 1930s progressed, circumstances allowed Hitler to achieve his goal. The policy of appeasement followed by Britain and France, added to the short-sightedness of Stalin in agreeing to a pact with Germany in August 1939, left Poland isolated and vulnerable. In March 1939, the German government demanded from Poland the right to build a railway across the Polish Corridor and the return of the port of Danzig to Germany. It was in response to these demands that Britain and France offered a mutual aid pact to Poland. The invasion of Poland in 1939 was by Nazi and Soviet forces. The division of the country into two zones of influence delayed complete German domination. However, near complete victory in the West and the apparent weakness of Russia allowed Hitler to complete his conquest of Poland in June 1941.

DID HITLER PLAN FOR WAR IN THE WEST?

Desire to avoid war with Britain. Hitler believed that all his expansionist ideas could be achieved without war against Britain. His foreign policy aims focused around an empire in the East, a racial war and the destruction of communism. None of these directly threatened British interests. Although Hitler believed Britain and France to be in decline, he also felt that the former in particular was not an automatic enemy. It was Hitler's belief that Britain had never fully supported the Versailles settlement and he took heart from the sympathy expressed in some sections of British public life in the 1930s that the settlement needed revision in Germany's favour. Hitler understood that Britain's strategic, commercial and ideological interests lay in protecting its Empire and not in continental European affairs. Hitler also realised that the violent anti-communism of the British Foreign Office could also act in his favour. In 1936, Anglo-French relations hit a low point following only half-hearted criticism by the French of Mussolini's invasion of Abyssinia. It was Hitler's hope that the mutual suspicion between Britain and France which had dominated nineteenth-century diplomacy would return.

The signing of the 1935 Anglo-German Naval Pact appeared to justify Hitler's instincts. Britain's deep-seated hostility towards the Soviet Union seemed to suggest the possibility of a full-scale alliance between Britain and Germany. Indeed, Hitler continued to suggest this as a possibility to his ambassador in London, Ribbentrop. Such an alliance would be built around the concept of German domination of continental Europe whilst Britain kept its Empire. Hitler believed that Britain's Empire gave it a false sense of security and the Empire's inevitable collapse would expose its vulnerability.

Desire for war with France. On the other hand, Hitler expected a war against the French. Hitler had no admiration for the French and there was no sense of mutual admiration or any historical ties to moderate a sense of hatred. For Hitler, the defeat of France was essential to reverse the humiliation of 1918. He also saw the French as being primarily responsible for the Treaty of Versailles. Hitler recognised that France was unlikely to remain neutral whilst Germany established itself as the dominant power in Europe. Indeed, in 1935 France hurried into an alliance with the Soviet Union on news of German rearmament. Successive news of German expansion in the East led to the hastening of French rearmament and fortification of the border. Hitler's determination to challenge France was encouraged by France following a policy of appeasement. He was also encouraged by French economic difficulties, e.g., in 1936 and 1938 the franc was devalued. France was also torn apart by bitter political divisions which were heightened by the election of a radical Popular Front government in 1936 led by Léon Blum. However, the determination to challenge France was clearly part of a wider long-term strategy to dominate continental Europe. That could not be achieved without the destruction of France. In *Mein Kampf* the ex-corporal who had suffered endless misery on the Western Front fighting the French promised 'one last decisive battle' to destroy French power once and for all.

The invasion and defeat of France had an obvious military logic. The First World War had seen Germany suffer from fighting a simultaneous war on Eastern and Western fronts. If Hitler's most fundamental foreign policy objective was the destruction of communism in the Soviet Union, then it was vital that France was removed as a military threat first. The military tactic of blitzkrieg was used with frightening efficiency against France in 1940. Having experienced the stalemate of trench warfare in 1914–18, Hitler was a keen supporter of blitzkrieg. It was a perfect tactic for Nazis in that it did not need a total mobilisation of the economy. The tactics associated with blitzkrieg emerged as a critique of the bloodbath of 1914–18. They were to be used to reverse the humiliation of that bloodbath.

OPERATION BARBAROSSA, 1941: PROGRAMME OR OPPORTUNISM?

Hitler's confidence that the Soviet Union could be defeated. On 22 June 1941, Germany and its allies unleashed a force of some three million men against the Soviet Union. Events in part presented this time as a good opportunity for the invasion of the Soviet Union. In particular, the Red Army was still recovering from the brutal purges of the late 1930s which had removed so many of its experienced commanders including the most senior officer Marshal Tukhachevsky. The spectacular success of blitzkrieg against Poland in 1939 and against the West in 1940 left the Soviet Union isolated. Hitler compared these triumphs to the difficulties the Red Army had in crushing the Finns in 1940. His conclusion was that the Soviet Union could be easily conquered.

Despite the fact that the events of 1939–41 created a favourable context for Hitler to invade, the invasion of the Soviet Union has its roots in Hitler's deeply-held prejudices. Historically, Germany had feared an invasion from the east. This was a deep-rooted anxiety based partly on the lack of natural frontiers. The attempted communist revolution of 1919, the continual 'Red Threat' simply heightened Hitler's fear of communism. For Hitler, the defeat of the Soviet Union and the destruction of Bolshevism would represent the ultimate triumph of his career. It went hand-in-hand with the concept of *Lebensraum* and the concept of a racial war. To Hitler, Bolshevism was a Jewish creation to be destroyed in tandem with the destruction of the Jewish race. The success of Operation Barbarossa would represent the ultimate triumph of Nazism as an ideology. There are few problems for the historian in finding evidence to back up this theory. It is the theme that runs through both Hitler's speeches and his written work.

CONCLUSION

- There is little doubt that German foreign policy in the period in question was shaped by events. The attitude of other countries and circumstance gave Hitler the opportunity to destroy the Versailles settlement and to attempt to dominate Europe.
- This opportunity should be seen in the context of German foreign policy. Its driving force, its shape and direction came from the ideology and ambition of Hitler.

A2 ASSESSMENT – WEIMAR AND NAZI GERMANY

Sources assignments

Example 1 in the style of Edexcel. Hitler and the Nazi state 1933–39.

Reading. For help in answering the questions you should read Chapter 10 (pages 87–96) and Section 2 (pages 187–198).

Study Sources A to F and then read the following questions.

Source A

There was no more of a Code Hitler to rival the Code Napoleon than a Hitler Constitution. Hitler preferred to ignore or subvert the legal system rather than nazify it. Nor did he show any interest in reorganising the state administration to produce a clearer division of responsibilities. When he wanted something to be done to which he attached great importance, he created special agencies outside the framework of the government, e.g., Göring's organisation for the Four Year Plan which cut across at least four ministries.

Relations between party and state remained equally ill defined. The party was disappointed in its hopes of taking over the state . . . but the civil service had to accept Hitler's and other leaders' constant interference with due process . . .

Hitler's was 'revolution by instalments', the character of which only became clear as the different stages succeeded each other, a warning which particularly applies to the earlier period when Hitler was at pains to conceal his real thoughts and motives . . .

Hitler personally withdrew from the day to day business of government after he succeeded von Hindenberg. His resisted attempts to comprehensively reform the state's administration. This left more powerful Nazi leaders free not only to build up rival empires but to feud with each other and with the established ministries in a continuing fight to take over parts of each other's territory . . .

This state of affairs extended to the policy making and legislative functions of government as well as the administration . . . Henceforth decrees and laws alike were issued on the authority of the Chancellor.

Hitler detested discussion and never took a formal vote in the cabinet . . . Hitler's authority was unquestioned and, whenever he chose to intervene, was decisive . . . Göring, Göbbels and Himmler had direct access to the Führer and could secure his agreement to decrees without consultation or co-ordination with other ministers.

Adapted from Alan Bullock, *Hitler and Stalin: Parallel Lives* (1992).

Source B

In various ways my work offers a corrective to the oversimplified picture of a monolithic system and of a well oiled super state, which derived from the concept of totalitarianism. What presented itself as the new government of National Socialists Germany in 1933–34, after the seizure of power was completed was, in effect, a form of power sharing between the new Nazi mass movement and the old conservative forces in state and society . . . Until about 1936–7 the relationship between state and party was full of conflict. Hitler practised no leadership but, from time to time jolted the government or party into action, supported one or other initiative of Party functionaries or departmental heads and thwarted others, ignored them or left them to carry on without a decision . . .

The characteristic conflict between forces in the Third Reich cannot solely be understood merely in terms of a policy of 'divide and rule', deliberately instituted by Hitler to make himself indispensable. On the contrary, it was the result of Hitler's absolutism and was not conducive to the long-term survival of the regime . . . We can only explain why the Hitler regime fell prey to a policy of irrational destruction after years of astonishingly impressive success, against the background of ever changing structural circumstance.

Adapted from Martin Broszat, *The Hitler State* (1983).

Source C

The whole structure of government has been accurately called 'authoritarian anarchy'. the popular picture of the Third Reich as a monolithic unity with all parts of the well-oiled machinery responsive to the Führer's will has long been discredited by historians. A more exact parallel would be with feudal society, where vassals great and small struggled endlessly with each other and with their overlords to establish themselves as the King's Chief Adviser. The administrative structure of Nazi Germany formed a complex picture of party and state agencies will ill-defined and over-lapping jurisdictions, sometimes complementing each other, more often mutually antagonistic, all striving to obtain a monopoly of power in their own domain . . . A practice which permitted men such as Himmler and Göring to build up immensely powerful bases by combining government and party office was not, of course, without its dangers. Quite illogically, Hitler believed that the strong, once they had survived the battle, would serve him loyally . . . Some degree of administrative anarchy was probably inevitable in the Third Reich whatever kind of man Hitler had been.

Adapted from William Carr,
Hitler: A Study in Personality and Politics (1978).

Source D

We live in a state where areas of authority have been unclearly divided . . . the consequence is a complete lack of direction in German domestic policy . . . from this developed most of the quarrels between the real leaders and the ruling authorities.

Adapted from the diaries of Joseph Göbbels written in March 1943.

Source E .

- At the Head of the Reich stands the leader of the NSDAP as leader of the German Reich for life . . .
- The Führer and the Reich Chancellor is the constituent delegate of the German people, who without regard for formal pre-conditions decides the outward form of the Reich, its structure and general policy.
- The Führer is the supreme judge of the nation.

Adapted from a speech by Hans Frank made in 1938.
Frank was head of the Academy of German Law
and Nazi Association of Lawyers

Questions

1 Study Sources A, B and E. Please refer to all three sources in your answer. Using your own knowledge and the evidence of these three sources explain what you consider were the main powers Hitler used in government in the period 1933–9.

How you should answer this question. This question is asking you to do the following:

- Make a judgement about Hitler's powers in Germany, what were the main ones he exercised?
- Back up your judgement with evidence from your own knowledge and all three sources.
- Make links between your own knowledge and the sources.
- You might show that you understand that there are different interpretations to the one you have presented. You should comment on those interpretations.

Plan. After studying the question you should read through the sources and identify Hitler's 'main powers' suggested in each. This will help you to identify your main points of argument in your plan.

Style. Below is an example of the style of writing you might chose to use in answering this type of question. You should note that the extract attempts to follow the advice given above in the '*How to answer this question*' section.

Without doubt one of the most important of Hitler's 'main powers' is that he exerted a dominant influence over policy-making throughout his dictatorship. His methods were unconventional, as Source A points out 'he never took a formal vote in cabinet'. Similarly one could point to the fact that Hitler hated meetings and rarely wrote orders. Source B goes as far as to suggest that he 'practised no direct and systematic leadership'. However his powers stem from the fact that dictators do not need to act in the same way as leaders of democratic governments. It is clear that on issues of personal interest Hitler's decisions were decisive. Even though Source E is presented as the theory of Nazi rule, it was accepted that in decision making Hitler was indeed the 'supreme judge of the nation'. The sterilisation programme of 1933, the final draft of the Nuremberg Laws of 1935 and the adoption of the children's euthanasia programme of 1937 were results of Hitler's personal authorisation. Moreover Hitler took the key decisions in 1941 which authorised the extermination of Jews.

Linked to this power of decision making was the equally important power Hitler had over his subordinates. This was partly generated by giving them what Source A describes as the freedom 'to build up rival empires'. It might be argued that this limited Hitler's power but ultimately he was able to demand absolute subservience from his subordinates. This was primarily because his subordinates were totally committed to his ideology; secondly because of the emphasis placed upon loyalty. Insubordinate colleagues such as Rohm and Strasser were ruthlessly eliminated in 1934 whilst ultra-loyalists such as Bormann and Himmler rose from obscurity as Gauleiters to figures of national prominence. Thirdly Hitler ruled by the 'Führer Principle' – his will was law and the source of all executive authority. The Nazis promoted Hitler as the embodiment of the state that was the living organism of the German people. This is shown in Source E whereby Hitler is pronounced 'the constituent delegate of the Third Reich'. This domination of the state can be demonstrated in two respects – his close direction of questions of personal interest and by the central role of his ideology during the regime.

2 How far do you agree with the claim in Source C that it is inaccurate to interpret the 'Third Reich as a monolithic unity with all parts of the well-oiled machine responsive to the Führer's will'.
Use all five sources and your own knowledge to answer this question.

How to answer this question. This question focuses on the idea of the making and supporting of a historical interpretation. Your task is to make and support a judgement about the validity of this interpretation. To answer this question successfully you must try to do the following:

- Show that you can draw on your understanding of a range of historical interpretations. This does not mean that you simply write out what different historians have said. Historiographical 'own knowledge' is not in itself a requirement for the highest level. However if you integrate an awareness of the debate into your argument then that information will be rewarded as will be all other 'own knowledge'.

- You need to show that you can link your own knowledge and the information from all of the sources.

Plan. Before you start writing you need to draw up a plan with your main points of argument. It is important that these points directly answer the question.

- Whilst 'monolithic unity' is not an accurate description, there is no doubt that Hitler remained in control of key decisions throughout his dictatorship.
- In the first year in power Hitler had to make tactical alliances and comprises with important institutions of the state. However, these institutions did not seriously threaten his supreme power.
- It is inaccurate to describe the workings of the state being like a 'well-oiled machine'. However despite the apparent chaos of the Nazi state which meant that power was devolved and decisions delayed Hitler was not prevented from pursuing his ideological ambitions.

Style. Below is an example of the style of writing you might adopt. The answer attempts to argue in response to the question, develop an interpretation, select from the source and recall knowledge.

It is clear that the Nazi state was not a well ordered monolithic structure neither was it a 'well-oiled machine'. Instead it was more of a collection of competing bureaucracies and power blocs over which Hitler presided. Such was described by Broszat in Source B who sees Hitler's absolutism as the cause of what Carr in Source 3 describes as 'administrative anarchy'. The 'lack of direction' in domestic affairs which Göbbels complains about in Source D was a clear consequence. However one must be careful not to exaggerate. The Nazi state was not 'monolithic' because the complexity of Hitler's system of government encouraged initiatives from competing levels of authority: regional Nazi officials, high-ranking bureaucrats, and from the Nazi elite.

By devolving power, Hitler's style of dictatorship did create the potential for rivals to challenge his authority, but after 1934 no other Nazi was able to seriously threaten Hitler's exercise of supreme power. It is correct to argue that the leading Nazis were not directly responsive to Hitler's will. Göbbels, Himmler, etc., had considerable autonomy in decision making, an example being the order for Kristallnacht being given by the former in 1938. This was the type of 'attendant danger' described by Carr in Source C. However such initiatives were however only successful if they won Hitler's active support.

Example 2 in the style of AQA. The Holocaust 1938–45.

Reading. For help in answering this assignment you should read Chapter 13 (pages 127–134) and Section 5 (pages 210–222) in this book.

Read the following sources and then answer the questions.

Source A

Hitler and his lieutenants cloaked their most criminal activities in euphemistic language, [and] tried . . . to keep their murderous plans secret . . . Hitler was reluctant to commit himself to paper . . . and preferred to give his instructions orally.

Adapted from *The Holocaust in History* by M. Marrus writing in 1988.

Source B

. . . death camps . . . were built at the end of 1941 . . . Four thousand inmates including Jewish women were forced to build Auschwitz, which was made up of forty camps including Burkina. One third died during the building. the death camps were surrounded by many smaller camps, where conditions varied. Some were labour camps (such as Auschwitz III where slave labour worked for I.G. Farben) and some were smaller killing centres.

Adapted from *From Prejudice to Genocide* by C. Supple (1993).

Source C

We were taken to a train station under SS guard, with the Gestapo standing on all sides. Our route passed through the streets of Prague . . . some of the women wept openly when they saw how cruelly the Nazis treated us . . .

Adapted from an account of a Jewish eye-witness and quoted in *From Prejudice to Genocide* by C. Supple (1993).

Source D

Everything was 'go' for the Polish invasion . . . Göring as Plenipotentiary for the Four Year Plan called a meeting . . . to discuss manpower problems that war would impose on Germany. Funk [minister in charge of the economy] was given the responsibility of deciding what kind of work could be assigned to war prisoners and inmates of . . . concentration camps. Himmler promised that greater use would be made of the concentration camps during war-time, and Göring talked of employing foreign workers in Germany. The most extensive and inhumane network of forced and slave labour began to be organised.

Adapted from *The War Against the Jews* by Lucy Davidowicz (1975).

Questions

1 Use your own knowledge and Source A to answer this question.
How accurate is the interpretation put forward by Marrus in Source A that the planning of the Final Solution was secret?

How to answer this question. The question asks you to refer to the source as a stimulus. The main part of your answer is to come from your own knowledge. In your answer you must show that you understand the issue of secrecy surrounding the Final Solution and that you write a clear analytical answer which is well supported with evidence.

Plan. Your answer to this question should revolve around the issue of secrecy. You need to comment on the wide range of the regime's policy concerning the Jews. Before you write you should identify your lines of argument. Here are some examples:

- The planning of the detail of the Final Solution was kept hidden from the public.
- However the regime's attitude towards the Jews was not secret. This can be seen in its propaganda, *Mein Kampf* and government's foreign, social and economic policy.

Structure.

Introduction. Write out the main points of analysis from your plan.

Paragraph 1. Secrecy of planning. You should argue that the regime was secret in its planning of the detail of the Final Solution, e.g., the Wansee Conference and Hitler's role. You should refer to Source A and how the regime used 'euphemistic language' to hide its activities.

Paragraph 2. The persecution of Jews. In your argument you should explain that the Jews were persecuted openly and with increasing ferocity. This was apparent in the regime's social and economic policy.

Paragraph 3. Propaganda. Whilst the planning of the Final Solution may have been kept secret, the anti-Semitic messages issued by the regime's propaganda were clear.

Conclusion. You should briefly go over the points of argument you have made.

In your answer you will gain marks for accurately crediting historians.

2 Use your own knowledge and Source C to answer this question. How reliable is Source C as evidence of the treatment of Jews who were deported during the war?

How to answer this question. This question is testing your understanding of reliability. When answering questions about the reliability of evidence you should not concentrate on the content of the source. Instead you should ask the following questions of the evidence.

- What was the purpose of the author in producing the evidence?
- What was the author's situation?

3 Use your own knowledge and Sources B and D to answer the question. How valid is the view that Nazi ideology was the most important factor in the development of the Holocaust?

How to answer this question. This question asks you to show that you know why the Holocaust took place. You must ensure that you refer to the sources in question and use your own knowledge. The debate between intentionalist and functionalist historians which is relevant to this question is explained on pages 210–211 in this book.

Plan. To reach the highest level you need sustain an argument throughout the answer. Therefore it is essential that you clarify in your plan what your line of argument is going to be. Here are some examples of points to follow:

- The evidence of Sources B and D do not prove the validity of the statement despite the arguments put forward by intentionalist historians.
- There is no evidence to prove that Nazi ideology included a long-term decision to destroy the Jews of Europe despite Hitler's public utterances. However Nazi ideology encouraged persecution.
- The development of the Holocaust was primarily due to the decision of Hitler made in autumn 1941 and implemented in response to the collapse of existing policies.

Style. To answer such a question you need to bring together the sources and your own knowledge. Here is an example of a judgement being made in direct response to the question.

It was the invasion of the Soviet Union in June 1941 that determined the fate of all Jews. Far from being a stage on the route to the Holocaust, the invasion of Russia was an important reason for its development. It should be remembered that Hitler's driving ambitions throughout his career was the destruction of communism and the conquest of lebensraum (living space) in the East. The development of the Holocaust was a consequence of this policy. The land captured by German troops between June and November 1941 trapped about 4 million Jews thereby rendering existing policies of transportation to ghettos impractical. Existing ghettos were already full and commandants were demanding alternative solutions from higher authorities. The economic considerations suggested in Source D of an 'extensive and inhumane network of forced and slave labour' were, by 1941 only part of the Nazi solution. The failure to knock out Russia by Blitzkrieg in the early Autumn ruled out the most favoured solution of resettlement beyond the Urals. It is in this context that the policy of mass murder was developed and camps such as Auschwitz were hastily expanded as suggested by Source B 'death camps . . . were built at the end of 1941'.

Essay questions

Section A in the style of AQA.

Introduction. To be awarded top marks in essays of the type in Section A, you will be expected to do the following:

- **Analyse throughout the essay.** This can be done by making sure that you plan a line or argument before you start writing. At the start of each paragraph you must make the next point of your argument, explain it and then use evidence to back your point up (see next point). There is a clear difference between narrative (telling the story) and analysis (putting forward a reasoned argument in response to a question).

A tip for how to ensure that you are analysing. You need to start each paragraph with words which will lead onto analysis. These might include:

The most important reason.........
Another key point is that...........
One should argue that...............
Essentially............

If you use the following words at the start of a paragraph you are more likely to fall into a narrative style of writing:

In (followed by a date)........
This was followed by ....

- **Back up your argument by using well selected evidence.** The evidence you select must be accurate and relevant to the point you are trying to make.

- **Make a clear and consistent attempt to reach a judgement.** In your essay you must argue throughout. You must reflect on the evidence you have given and make points which answer the question directly.
- **Show evidence of independent thought.** You do not have to be original. Independent thought means that you have reflected on what you have read in this an other books and that you can explain the ideas that you have picked up in your own words.
- **Language skills.** It is essential that you write in paragraphs, that you are grammatically accurate. There are two tips to ensure this takes place:

Always read your work through after you have finished and correct any errors.

Get into the habit of structuring your essays in such a way that a new point of your argument means a new paragraph.

1 How far did Germany undergo a 'social revolution' between 1933 and 1945?

Reading. Before answering this question you should read Chapter 12 (pages 107–126) and Section 4 (pages 199–209).

How to answer this question. The question demands that you consider a range of social and cultural issues. In particular you need to focus on the idea of a social revolution and explain how successfully the Nazis changed German society through propaganda and indoctrination.

You will need to show that the pace of change varied depending on the social issue.

Content. The question of whether or not Germany underwent a social revolution is addressed in Section 4 pages 199–209. Anti-Semitism in Germany is discussed on pages 210–211. In addressing the question you should focus on the following areas:

- education, youth movements, women, class, anti-Semitism, religion and Nazi culture

Plan. The essay is a large one and will cover many different aspects of society. The essay needs to maintain a clear focus throughout. Below are some points of argument you might use.

- The extent of the social revolution affected by the Nazis was minimal. This was particularly the case during peacetime. They did succeed in integrating the majority of Germans into a national community but failed to alter the status of women or remove class distinctions.

- The most convincing areas in which the Nazis did create change was in the treatment and perceptions of the country's Jewish community. One can also argue that the Nazis successfully transformed the attitudes of many of Germany's youth.
- A real social transformation took place in defeat in 1945.

Style. Below is an example of a paragraph you might write in this essay. The focus of the paragraph is on women. As you will see it attempts to analyse throughout, contains well selected evidence and makes clear judgements.

The Nazi policies did not create a social revolution. The year 1933 did not mark a decisive break in social status and attitudes. Class divisions in Germany as elsewhere were narrowed by the trench solidarity of the First World War and continued to decline during the more progressive Weimar Republic. It would be wrong to underestimate the seriousness of Hitler's commitment to a Volksgemeinschaft or to neglect important shifts within the social system but the point to note is values, habits, allegiances, lifestyles and relationships were too deeply entrenched to be dislodged by Nazi ideology and social engineering. The social structure was not fundamentally altered. The traditional elites were often merged with new elites and non-party elites such as business, and the Civil Service. The Army continued to recruit from the same social groups as before.

2 The central thrust of Nazi economic policy between 1933 and 1939 was to prepare Germany for war rather than to improve the standard of living.

Reading. Before answering this question you should read Chapter 11 (pages 97–106) and Section 3 (pages 187–198) in this book.

How to answer this question. The question asks you to make a judgement about the main thrust of Nazi economic policy in the years of the Four Year Plan.

Plan. Your lines of argument should allow you to answer the question fully. Here are a couple of suggestions you can write down in your plan.

- Rearmament an preparation for war was the main priority of the Four Year Plan. However by 1939 change was incomplete. This was due to the inefficiency of central planning methods.
- However one should not underestimate the political importance for the regime of maintaining levels of consumption and the standard of living.

Content: In your essay it is expected that you will select from the following areas:

- Government spending priorities, levels of rearmament, the impact of Göring and Hitler on policy, Anschluss and the invasion of Czechoslovakia, consumption and standards of living.

3 To what extent do you agree with the assertion that Hitler was a weak dictator? Use all the sources and your own knowledge to answer this question.

How to answer this question. The question wants you to explain and weigh up the different interpretations of Hitler as a dictator. Although the question suggests that Hitler was a 'weak dictator' you do not have to agree with this interpretation. Instead you are expected to analyse the issue by using the sources and your own knowledge. When using the sources you should directly refer and quote from them. In your answer you are expected to make clear what your interpretation is.

Plan. A detailed plan is crucial for this question.

You need to marshall your key points of argument before you start. Here are two examples of points which can be made in response to the question.

- Disagree with the statement to a considerable extent because Hitler remained in control of key decisions in the economic, social and political spheres throughout his dictatorship.
- Despite chaos of the Nazi state, Hitler was not prevented from pursuing his ideological ambitions.

Content. There is a discussion of this question in Section 2 on pages 175–186. You should use the content in this Section to answer the question.

Style. To be awarded the highest mark possible you are expected to give a direct response to the question. Below is an example of the style of writing you should use.

The claim that Hitler was a 'weak dictator' ignores Hitler's central role in the decision making process of the Nazi state. His importance is stressed by Bullock in Source A where he comments on Hitler's authority being 'unquestioned' and that when he made decisions his influence 'was decisive'. It is clear that on issues of personal interest, Hitler's role was decisive e.g. the adoption of the child euthanasia programme of 1938–9. Although his subordinates built up considerable power, in Source C Carr talks of Himmler and Goring building up' immensely powerful bases', this does not mean that Hitler was a weak dictator. Most importantly, he was able to demand subservience from his subordinates. Himmler was able to wield considerable power as head of the SS. However, this was only possible because of his loyalty to what Frank called in Source E 'the supreme judge of the nation'. Those whose loyalty was suspect such as Röhm were ruthlessly eliminated.

Section B in the style of Edexcel.

Introduction. To be awarded top marks in essays of the type in Section B, you will be expected to do the following:

- **Analyse throughout the answer.** Do not lapse into descriptive narrative. Throughout you need to make clear judgements on the issues in the question.
- **Apply knowledge.** Use clear and accurate examples.
- **Write in a clear style.** The structure of your work must be clear. You must use paragraphs and your grammar and syntax must be accurate.
- **Historiographical interpretations.** Candidates who show an awareness of different historical interpretations have a better chance of being marked at a higher level.

Reading. To answer questions on foreign policy you should read Chapter 15 (pages 141–152) and Section 7 (pages 233–243) in this book.

1 How accurate is the view that 'Hitler's single aim in foreign policy was Lebensraum'?

How to answer this question. You need to judge the accuracy of the view given.
Plan. This is a relatively straightforward question. Here are examples of the types of arguments you might follow.

- It is inaccurate to state that Hitler's foreign policy aims were based solely on *Lebensraum*. His foreign policy objectives were more complex.
- As well as the establishment of *Lebensraum* in the east and Aryan racial domination Hitler aimed for the destruction of communism and the Versailles settlement. These objectives were to be achieved through diplomacy and aggression.

2 'Hitler's foreign policy successes between 1936 and 1939 rested on his remarkable tactical skills and ability to exploit his opponents' weaknesses'.

How to answer this question. You need to balance up the importance of the factors given in the question, Hitler's 'tactical skills' and the exploitation of 'his opponents' weaknesses' with other factors.
Plan. You should aim to place the different episodes of foreign policy in this period: the Rhineland, Czechoslovakia, *Anschluss*, Munich, the Nazi-Soviet Pact, Poland into the context of an argument. These are two examples the main points:

- Hitler's tactical skills and the exploitation of the weakness of his opponents are fundamental in explaining German success in this period. However here is little doubt that German foreign policy success in the period in question was shaped by events. The attitude of other countries and circumstance gave Hitler the opportunity to destroy the Versailles settlement and to attempt to dominate Europe.

This opportunity should be seen as the context to German foreign policy. Its driving force, its shape and direction came from the ideology and ambition of Hitler.

BIBLIOGRAPHY

The books have been listed in distinct sections. However there should be no reason why books suggested for AS students could not also be used at A2 and vice versa.

AS Section – Weimar and Nazi Germany

J. F. Corkery and R. C. J. Stone, *Weimar Germany and the Third Reich*, Heinemann (1980)

E. J. Feuchtwanger, *Germany 1916–41*, Sempringham (1997)

C. Fischer, *The Rise of the Nazis,* Manchester University Press (1995)

R. Geary, *Hitler and Nazism,* Routledge (1993)

J. Hiden, *The Weimar Republic,* Longman (1974)

J. Hiden, *Republican and Fascist Germany*, Longman (1996)

A. de Jong, *The Weimar Chronicle,* Paddington Press (1978)

I. Kershaw, *The Hitler Myth: Image and Reality in the Third Reich*, OUP (1989)

G. Layton, *Germany: Third Reich 1933–45,* Hodder and Stoughton (1992)

S. J. Lee, *Hitler and Nazi German,* Routledge (1998)

R. Lenman, *The Nazi Seizure of Power*, Warwick History Videos no. 12

L. Rees, *The Nazis: A Warning from History,* BBC Books (1997)

W. Simpson, *Hitler and Germany*, Cambridge University Press (1991)

Although it would be a difficult text for many AS students we would also recommend

E. Kolb, *The Weimar Republic*, Routledge (1988)

A2 Section – Weimar and Nazi Germany

M. Bloch, *Rippentrop*, Bantam Press (1994)

K. D. Bracher, *The German Dictatorship*, Weidenfeld and Nicholson (1971)

M. Brozsat, *The Hitler State*, London (1991)

A. Bullock, *Hitler: A Study in Tyranny*, Penguin (1952)
A. Bullock, *Hitler and Stalin: Parallel Lives*, Harper Collins (1991)
M. Burleigh (ed.), *Confronting the Nazi Past*, Collins and Brown (1996)
W. Carr, *Hitler: A Study in Personality and Politics*, London (1978)
R. J. Evans, *Re-thinking of German History: Nineteenth Century Germany and the Origins of the Third Reich*, London (1987)
R. J. Evans, *In Hitler's Shadow: West German Historians and the Attempt to Escape from the Nazi Past*, London (1989)
J. Fest, *The Face of the Third Reich*, Penguin (1970)
J. Fest, *Plotting Hitler's Death*, Weidenfeld and Nicholson (1994)
G. Fleming, *Hitler and the Final Solution*, London (1985)
A. Gill, *An Honourable Defeat*, Mandarin (1994)
R. Grunberger, *A Social History of the Third Reich*, Penguin (1971)
J. Hiden and J. Farquharson, *Explaining Hitler's Germany: Historians and the Third Reich*, London (1983)
H. Höhne, *The Order of the Death's Head: The Story of Hitler's SS*, London (1969)
I. Kershaw, *The Nazi Dictatorship: Problems and Perspectives of Interpretation*. London (1985)
I. Kershaw, *Hitler*, Longman (1991)
I. Kershaw, *Hitler vol. 1 Hubris*, Penguin (1998)
M. Kitchen, *Nazi Germany at War,* Longman (1995)
H. W. Koch (ed.), *Aspects of the Third Reich*, London (1985)
C. Koonz, *Mothers in the Fatherland*, Methuen (1988)
H. Krausnick, H. Buchheim, M. Broszat and H. A. Jacobsen, *Anatomy of the SS State,* London (1968)
R. Overy, *The Nazi Economic Recovery*, London (1982)
R. Overy, *Göring: The 'Iron Man'*, London (1984)
R. Overy, *The Origins of the Second World War*, Longman (1987)
D. Schoenbaum, *Hitler's Social Revolution: Class and Status in Nazi Germany*, London (1966)
G. Sereny, *Albert Speer. His Battle with Truth*, Picador (1995)

J. P. Stern, *Hitler: The Führer and the People*, London (1975)
A. J. P Taylor, *The Origins of the Second World War*, Penguin, (1961)
J. Toland, *Adolf Hitler*, New York (1976)
D. Welch, *The Third Reich: Politics and Propaganda*, Routledge (1993)

Source books

J. Noakes and G. Pridham, *Nazism 1919–45, Volumes 1–4*, University of Exeter Press
H. Trevor-Roper, *Hitler's Table Talk*, OUP (1953)
H. Trevor-Roper (ed.), *The Göbbels Diaries; The Last Days*, Pan (1979)

Personal Accounts

C. Bielenberg, The Past is Myself, Corgi (1970)
B. Engelmann, Hitler's Germany. Schocken Books (1986)
J. Steinhoff, P. Pechel, D. Showalter, *Voices from the Third Reich*, Grafton Books (1991)

Websites

There are many websites which deal with the subject of Nazis and the Holocaust in particular. However many these websites have to be treated with extreme caution.

INDEX